Netscape Navigator Survival Guide

Reload pages and refresh the screen

Go to previous pages you've visited

Mark your favorite Web pages

Configure Navigator

Go to some helpful Netscape sites

E-mail, news, and your address book

Open, save, and print Web pages

Copy and paste text

URL (address) of current document

Get help

Toolbar (for shortcuts)

Links

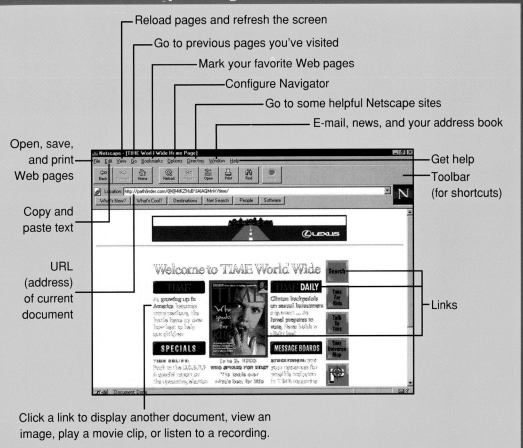

Click a link to display another document, view an image, play a movie clip, or listen to a recording.

Netscape Navigator by Button

Back — Go back one page	**Open** — Open a page
Forward — Go forward one page	**Print** — Print the current page
Home — Display the first page	**Find** — Find some text in the document
Reload — Reload the current page	**Stop** — Stop loading this page
Images — Display the images on the page	

que®

cut here

Top 15 Web Sites (My Favorites, Anyway)

To go to any of these sites, drag over the entry in the URL text box, type the site's URL, and press **Enter**.

Top 5% Web Sites	**http://www.pointcom.com/**
Yahoo's List of Internet Sites	**http://www.yahoo.com/Entertainment/**
World Wide Arts Resources	**http://wwar.com/index.html**
Peeping Tom Home Page	**http://www.ts.umu.se/~spaceman/camera.html**
Dunn & Bradstreet (Business) Information Services	**http://www.dbisna.com/**
Microsoft Corporation	**http://www.microsoft.com/**
Stroud's Consummate Winsock Applications List	**http://www.stroud.com**
America's Job Bank	**http://www.ajb.dni.us/**
The Internet Movie Database	**http://us.imdb.com/welcome.html**
MSARP Virtual Slide Show	**http://www.ucalgary.ca/UofC/faculties/ SS/ARKY/show/showintro.html**
Adam Curry's The Vibe	**http://metaverse.com/vibe/index.html**
The Palace	**http://www.thepalace.com/**
The Branch Mall	**http://branch.com/**
Nando X Sports Server	**http://www.nando.net/SportServer/**
Epicurious Travel	**http://travel.epicurious.com/travel/a_home page/ home.html**

Netscape Navigator TurboTips

➤ Open the **Options** menu and select **Auto Load Images** to turn it off. (You can load images on a page by clicking the **Images** button in the toolbar.)

➤ **Ctrl+D** to mark a page with a bookmark. Bookmarks appear at the bottom of the Bookmarks menu.

➤ **Ctrl+H** to display a list of pages you've visited.

➤ **Right-click** a link to display a shortcut menu.

➤ **Right-click** a link, and click **Internet Shortcut** to place an icon for the link

The COMPLETE IDIOT'S GUIDE TO

Netscape 3

by Joe Kraynak

A Division of Macmillan Publishing
201 W. 103rd Street, Indianapolis, IN 46290 USA

To Marc Andreessen, Netscape founder, for demonstrating how easy it is to work your way through college.

©1995 Que® Corporation

International Standard Book Number: 0-7897-0958-9
Library of Congress Catalog Card Number: 96-69598

98 97   8   7   6   5   4

Interpretation of the printing code: the rightmost number of the first series of numbers is the year of the book's printing; the rightmost number of the second series of numbers is the number of the book's printing. For example, a printing code of 96-1 shows that the first printing of the book occurred in 1996.

Screen reproductions in this book were created by means of the program Collage Complete from Inner Media, Inc., Hollis, NH.

Printed in the United States of America

President
Roland Elgey

Vice-President and Publisher
Marie Butler-Knight

Editorial Services Director
Elizabeth Keaffaber

Publishing Director
Lynn E. Zingraf

Managing Editor
Michael Cunningham

Development Editor
Melanie Palaisa

Technical Editor
C. Herbert Feltner

Production Editor
Mark Enochs

Director of Marketing
Lynn E. Zingraf

Cover Designers
Dan Armstrong, Barbara Kordesh

Designer
Kim Scott

Illustrations
Judd Winick

Technical Specialist
Nadeem Muhammed

Production Team
Jason Carr
Michelle Lee
Darlena Murray
Kelly Warner

Indexer
John Hulse

Contents at a Glance

Contents

Introduction:
Picture This

You have some boring job using the Internet to do market analysis for a peanut company. As your eyes glaze over, you decide to take a break, and wander the Web. You zoom over to your favorite search page to check out the latest flicks.

You punch in MOVIES, and call up a list of 50 movie sites. You whack the TARANTINO button, and see a complete list of his movies. You pick PULP FICTION and copy a clip from the movie to play later. You copy the script. You copy a picture of Tarantino, the man himself. Then, as quickly as you hit the site, you're gone. Backed out and on your way to nab some still shots of the alien autopsies from your favorite UFO site. You grab a few shots to use as Windows backgrounds, and you're outta there.

A couple hours later, your hard drive is packed full of sound clips, movie clips, scripts, pictures, and comics... just some stuff to keep you busy during the slow periods. You decide that you'd better do some work before noon; your boss wants you to come up with a savvy marketing strategy for a new product line. You don't even know what a marketing strategy is, so you click on BUSINESS and then on DUNN & BRADSTREET. Lucky guess—Dunn & Bradstreet offers a quick primer on developing a marketing strategy. You pull some sales figures and marketing numbers off another site and type up your report.

By three o'clock, you've e-mailed your marketing plan to the boss. You still have two hours to check out the movie clips and graphics you nabbed earlier. You lean back with your second bag of microwave popcorn and start playing.

You Want It

This Flash Gordon/multimedia stuff isn't science fiction anymore. It's real. It's now. And it's here for anyone who has a computer, a modem, and a World Wide Web browser, such as Netscape Navigator.

With these few items and a bit of persistence, you can travel the world, accessing documents, video and sound clips, graphics, stock data, jokes, virtual worlds, games, and any other information and media that are stored on computers connected to the Internet.

But You'd Have to Be a Genius!

Nah! You don't have to be a genius to wander the World Wide Web or use Netscape Navigator. You don't have to know how the Internet works, or even how the text, pretty pictures, sounds, and movie clips travel from computers all around the world to your computer. You have more important things to learn, like:

> ➤ Where to get the latest version of Netscape Navigator.

> ➤ How to install, run, and configure Netscape Navigator (or Navigator, for short).

> ➤ How to use Navigator to bounce around the World Wide Web.

> ➤ How to make a list of your favorite Web documents.

> ➤ How to get pictures and video clips... and look at them.

> ➤ How to get files from other computers.

> ➤ How to use Navigator to harness the power of other Internet features.

In this book, you'll be up and running with Navigator in two—count'em, two—chapters. In the remaining chapters, you'll learn how to use Navigator to fly around in the Web and plunder its resources. You'll be surprised at how little you *need to know* in order to use Navigator... and how much you *can know* to cruise the Web like a master.

And You Are...?

In writing this book, I came up with a few generalizations about you. First, I figure you have some computer savvy. You know how to work with directories (folders), save and open files, and run programs. You've managed to set up your modem and establish an Internet connection (or you've suckered a friend into doing it for you). You may not sleep with your computer, but you feel pretty comfortable with it.

However, I could be wrong. If your knowledge of computers and modems is limited to what you've seen on *Good Morning America*, maybe you should start with a more general computer book first. I suggest *The Complete Idiot's Guide to PCs* (for general computer knowledge), *The Complete Idiot's Guide to Modems & Online Services* (to brush up on modem basics), and *The Complete Idiot's Guide to the Internet* (if you're not wired to the Internet yet).

How We Do Things in This Part of the Country

There are several conventions in this book to make the book easier to use. Here's a list:

➤ Any text you type or items you select appear **bold**. For example, you click the **Start** button or type **Help!**.

➤ If you have to press two or more keys to enter a command, the keys are separated with plus signs. For example, you might press Ctrl+C to copy a selected item. To enter the command, hold down the first key while pressing the second one.

➤ Finally, any text you might see on your screen is shown in a funny-looking type like this: OK. For example, you might see a Login: prompt asking you to type your username.

If you want to understand more about the Internet, the World Wide Web, Navigator, and the commands you're told to enter, you'll find some background information in boxes. I put this sideline information in boxes so you can skip the gory details. But, just in case you're interested, look for the following icons:

By the Way... These boxes contain notes, tips, warnings, and other information about the Web, the Internet, and Navigator. Some of these boxes contain only snide comments and quips.

Technical Twaddle These boxes contain high-tech fluff that I promised not to inflict on you, but I would feel guilty if I didn't include it. You can skip this background fodder (technical twaddle) unless you're truly interested.

Common Trademark Courtesy

As a courtesy to all the computer and program manufacturers who have complicated our lives, we have decided to list their trademarks or service marks here (so you'll know who's responsible). In addition, if we suspected a term of being a trademark or service mark (you just can't trust anyone these days), we capitalized it. We at Que cannot attest to the accuracy of this information, so don't expect any of this information to hold up in court.

We'd Like to Hear from You!

As part of our continuing effort to produce books of the highest possible quality, Que would like to hear your comments. To stay competitive, we *really* want you, as a computer book reader and user, to let us know what you like or dislike most about this book or other Que products.

You can mail comments, ideas, or suggestions for improving future editions to the address below, or send us a fax at (317) 581-4663. For the on-line inclined, Macmillan Computer Publishing has a forum on CompuServe (type **GO QUEBOOKS** at any prompt) through which our staff and authors are available for questions and comments. The address of our Internet site is **http://www.mcp.com** (World Wide Web).

In addition to exploring our forum, please feel free to contact me personally to discuss your opinions of this book: on CompuServe, I'm at 73353,2061, and on the Internet, I'm **mpalaisa@que.mcp.com**.

Thanks in advance—your comments will help us to continue publishing the best books available on computer topics in today's market.

Melanie Palaisa
Product Development Specialist
Que Corporation
201 W. 103rd Street
Indianapolis, IN 46290
USA

Part 1
Getting Wired with Netscape Navigator

The vast expanse of electronic data we call the World Wide Web is flowing through networks, cables, and satellites as we speak. You need to find some way to tap into this electronic flow and start pumping the resources into your computer.

Before you can start pumping, you need to get wired to the Internet and fire up Navigator. In this part, I show you just what to do. I tell you where to get the latest version of Navigator, how to install it, how to customize it to suit your tastes, and how to use some basic navigational tools to meander the Web. I'll even take you on a quick tour of the Web, giving you a little practice at the controls.

Chapter 1

The Top Ten Things You Need To Know

You've heard the hype, the promises of a global media network offering you a bottomless sea of information you can access with the simple click of a button. You have dreams of tapping into libraries around the world, of digging up dirt on the politicians you most despise, of hearing the latest recordings even before they reach the ears of your local deejay, or of playing games and exploring virtual worlds.

Now, you just want to connect and poke around a bit... to see for yourself if this Web thing lives up to its reputation. Well, here's your guide. The following list of ten things to keep in mind as you tour the World Wide Web and Netscape Navigator (Navigator, for short). It tells you what you'll need to connect, what to expect when you get there, and how to get out when you've had enough. Don't expect a whole lot of details; this list is just a teaser to make you want to read the rest of the book.

1. Think of the World Wide Web as a Huge Multimedia Encyclopedia

If your computer has a CD-ROM drive, chances are that it came with an encyclopedia on CD (or you bought one of these multimedia encyclopedias). Maybe you have Grolier's or Compton's Encyclopedia, or Microsoft Encarta. If you don't have one of these encyclopedias on CD, here's a picture that's fairly representative of what one looks like.

If you don't have an Encyclopedia on CD, here's what one looks like.

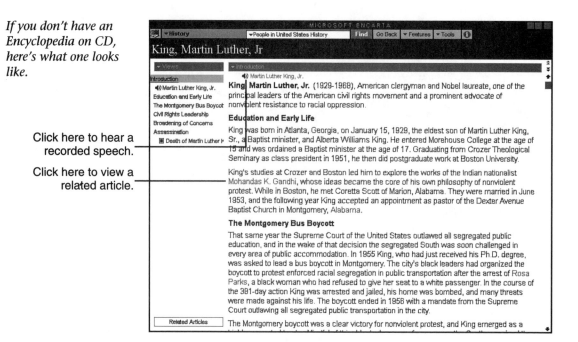

Click here to hear a recorded speech.

Click here to view a related article.

As the screen shows, these encyclopedias display articles about various topics. Each article usually contains highlighted text that you can click on to view an article about another *related topic*. For example, this article about Martin Luther King Jr. contains the highlighted text, "Mohandas K. Gandhi." You can display an article about Martin Luther King's role model simply by clicking on "Mohandas K. Gandhi." Notice that the article also contains an icon that you can click on to view a picture of Martin Luther King, and hear a portion of one of his most famous speeches.

Because these encyclopedias contain text, sounds, video clips, and pictures, they are commonly referred to as *hypermedia documents*. The "hyper" indicates that two or more articles are commonly linked (with icons or highlighted text), and "media" refers to the fact that the articles use different types of media (text, sounds, and video) to convey information.

The World Wide Web works in much the same way. You might pull up a general business page that contains highlighted text for "Starting Your Own Business" or "Stock Quotes." You simply click on the highlighted text or on an icon or button to display the specific information, play a video or audio clip, or take a look at a picture.

The only difference is that the pages you call up on the World Wide Web are not contained on a single CD. They are stored on computers all over the world. As you click on highlighted text (called *links*) and on icons, you might be traveling from Chicago to Milan to Tokyo!

2. Navigator Is Your Window to the World Wide Web

Although these hypermedia Web documents are there and ready for anyone to tap into, you can't just connect to a Web document and start reading it. You need a program that can convert the document (a collection of text and incomprehensible codes) into something your computer can understand and show on your screen.

This is where Navigator comes in. Navigator can read and interpret the codes that tell your computer how to display text, and indicate where other information (such as video clips and other Web documents) are located. Navigator displays the Web documents for you and handles the behind-the-scenes navigational tasks that make it possible for you to wander from one Web document to another.

Check This Out...

Web Documents and Pages

I commonly use the terms "Web document" and "Web page" interchangeably, because on the Web, a page is not necessarily a page. You might connect to a Web page that's 10 printed pages long, which is essentially a document. Other Web documents may consist of a series of single-page Web pages that are connected with icons or highlighted text.

3. Is Your Computer Powerful Enough?

I know, the salesperson at your local computer store said that your computer can handle all your needs well into the 21st century. But that was before the big multimedia push of '94, and long before Windows 95 changed its name from Chicago. Now, you're sitting on the beach with your puny 386SX, and your former friends are kicking sand in your face.

The point is that the Web is a multimedia document, and "multimedia" generally translates into "you need to upgrade your computer." Is your computer powerful enough to handle the Web? Here's what you need:

➤ An IBM PC or compatible with a 386 processor and 4MB of RAM or better (preferably better). If you're running Navigator from Windows 95, you'd better have a 486 processor with 8MB of RAM.

➤ Microsoft Windows (Windows 95 or Windows 3.1). This book includes instructions on setting up and using Netscape Navigator for Windows 95 and Windows 3.1.

➤ A Super VGA (SVGA) monitor that is capable of displaying at least 256 colors. Anything less, and the pictures and video clips you try to play will look blobby.

➤ A 16-bit sound card, if you want to hear the sounds and voices of the Web. Some Web pages consist almost entirely of sound recordings, and you'll want to play them.

➤ A direct Internet connection (if you're fortunate enough to be on a network at your place of business). A direct connection is a cable that connects your network directly to the Internet.
or
A 14,400 (or higher) bps modem and an Internet service provider that offers SLIP (Serial Line Internet Protocol) or PPP (Point to Point Protocol) accounts.

4. Rolling Through the Web

Navigator has a couple of high-tech navigation tools. Forget about them for now. All you need to know is that to display linked data, you click on an icon or a highlighted term, and wait for Navigator to make the necessary connections and "play" the data. If you get a message that Navigator can't make the connection, you've reached a dead end. Click **OK**, and then try a different term or icon.

In the upper left corner of the Navigator toolbar are two buttons you can click to move forward or back. With the links and these two buttons, you can move around the Web with sufficient ease (for now, anyway).

Moving around the Web with Navigator.

Click here to view the previous screen.

Click here to view the next screen.

Click a highlighted term or icon to "play" its data.

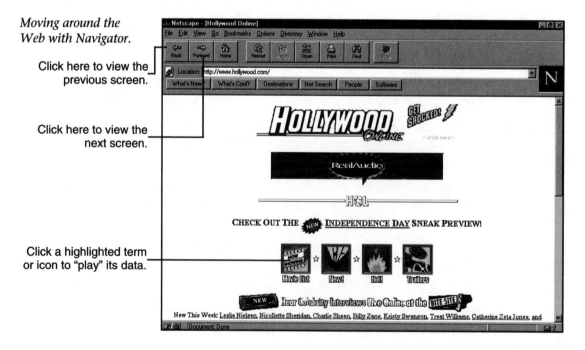

5. Going Places with URLs

URL stands for *Uniform Resource Locator*. URLs function as Web page addresses. Behind every link is a URL that tells Navigator where the linked file is located on the Web. As you click on link after link, you may not even notice that Navigator is using URLs to locate Web pages and files on the Web. Everything happens behind the scenes.

However, if you know the URL of a particular page (you've heard about the URL on TV, in a magazine, or from a friend or colleague), you can type the URL in the Location text box near the top of the Navigator window to pull up the associated page.

6. Returning to Your Favorite Haunts

In your wanderings, you'll no doubt stumble across some pages that intrigue you. You may want to return to the site later to pick up where you left off, but the URL is way too complicated to remember.

To help you revisit these favorite places, Navigator lets you tag them with *bookmarks*. When you come to a page you think you might want to revisit, simply open the **Bookmarks** menu, and click on **Add Bookmark**. The name of the page is added to the bottom of the **Bookmarks** menu. See Chapter 5, "Revisiting Your Favorite Pages," for details on how to add, delete, and edit bookmarks.

7. Playing Photos, Sounds, and Video Clips

Nobody hits the Web wanting only text. Every other Web page you bounce into will offer a picture, recording, or movie clip. The only trouble is that Navigator can't handle *all* these multimedia links by itself. Although Navigator can play most sounds and display most images, there are many file types that Navigator can't play. To play these files, Navigator needs help; it needs other programs that can play the sounds, video clips, interactive applications, and multimedia files stored on the Web.

These programs, called *helper applications*, are available as freeware or shareware (programs you can try for free and pay for if you decide to keep them). You can usually copy these applications from an online service or other Internet server. (Chapter 6 tells you all you need to know.) Once you have your helper applications in place, you can play Web clips simply by clicking them.

8. Extending Navigator's Capabilities

In addition to helper applications, Navigator uses programs called *plug-ins* that extend Navigator's capabilities. Unlike helper applications, which reside outside of Navigator and

7

are called upon to play specific file types, plug-ins actually upgrade Navigator and become an integral part of the browser.

To install a plug-in, you download it and run it. The installation utility adds the plug-in's power to Navigator, so when Navigator encounters a specific file type, it plays the file just as it "plays" a Web page. For more information on where to obtain plug-ins and how to install and use them, see Chapter 7, "Beefing Up Navigator with Plug-Ins."

9. Customizing Navigator

You can use Navigator right out of the "box," without changing its look or the way it behaves. However, once you've mastered the navigational tools, you might want to customize Navigator to provide more room for displaying Web pages or to increase the speed at which it loads pages.

All the options you need to customize Navigator are on the **Options** menu. From this menu, you can turn off the toolbar, the Location text box, and the directory buttons to create more room for displaying Web pages. You can also turn off Auto Load Images, so Navigator will display Web pages more quickly, *sans* pictures.

The Options menu contains several other, more complicated settings, which you can learn more about in Chapter 10, "Customizing Navigator To Make It Your Own."

10. Real-Time Chatting

Netscape Corporation offers other products that help you tap into other resources on the Internet. Netscape Chat, covered in Chapter 12, allows you to send messages back and forth to other people on the Internet, just as if you were talking on the phone using your keyboard.

CoolTalk is a new product from Netscape Corporation, which allows you to place telephone calls over the Internet. Currently, you can place calls only to other CoolTalk users, and these users must have some idea of when you're going to call (so they can be connected to the Internet when their "phone rings"). You can't simply call your grandma's phone. For details, see Chapter 17, "Free Long-Distance with CoolTalk."

Chapter 2

Downloading, Installing, and Connecting

By the End of This Chapter, You'll Be Able To...

➤ Grab the latest version of Navigator off the Internet... FOR FREE!

➤ Put Navigator on your hard drive

➤ Fire up Navigator for the first time

➤ Take a day trip on the Web

Navigator is the most popular and powerful Web browser around. With its support for the latest Web technology and its superior navigational tools, it commands 85% of the Web browser market. And it keeps getting better. But before you can tap into the power of Navigator, you have to snatch a copy of it and get it up and running. But where do you get Navigator, and, more importantly, how do you install it on your computer?

In this chapter, you'll learn where Navigator hangs out, which version you should use, and where to score the latest, greatest version. I'll even show you how to install it... and run it. By the end of this chapter, you'll be Web bound!

Where Can You Find Navigator?

Navigator is the Gideon Bible of Web browsers. You can find it everywhere—at your local computer store, on the inside back covers of some Netscape Navigator books, and even on the Internet. I expect that you'll soon be able to pick up a copy at the airport by making a small donation to a robed man with a shaved head.

But seriously, where can you get a copy of Navigator, and which version should you get? Here's a list to help you decide:

➤ **Commercial version (a.k.a. Netscape Navigator Personal Edition).** You can pick up Navigator wherever fine software is sold, for about $50 bucks. This gives you a licensed version, just in case the software police ever raid your home office. Netscape Navigator Gold (which includes a program for creating your own Web pages) is about $20 bucks more. Navigator Gold is almost identical to the standard version of Navigator, but it contains a couple extra options for editing Web pages. See Chapter 20, "Forging Your Own Hyperdocuments," to take a peek at Navigator Gold.

➤ **Latest Shareware version.** Netscape Communications Corporation has an Internet site that offers the latest version of Navigator (as of the writing of this book, version 3.0). You can connect to this site and download Navigator as explained later in this chapter. If you're a student, educational institution, beta tester, or are otherwise impoverished, you can use this version for free. Otherwise, you have to send a check to Navigator and register the program.

➤ **The 16-bit version.** If you have Windows 3.1, this is the version you want. It is designed to work under a 16-bit operating system, which is what Windows 3.1 is all about. If you have Windows 95, make sure you get the 32-bit version.

➤ **A book version.** Several books that compete with this book (MY book) include a version of Navigator. To appeal to the lowest common denominator, the 16-bit version of Navigator is usually the version you get. You can use this version of Navigator to download the 32-bit version from Netscape's Internet site, so if you have the 16-bit version, don't trash it yet.

Snatching Navigator Off the Internet

If you bought the latest version of Navigator or grabbed it off your computer at work, you can skip this part. However, if you don't have Navigator, or if you have an old version (pre-3.0), then you should use your Internet connection to download (copy) the file to your computer.

When you download a file from the Internet, you use something called *FTP* (*File Transfer Protocol*). This FTP thing is just a file transfer standard that ensures the sending and receiving computers are speaking the same language.

As with most Internet procedures, you can FTP in a number of ways. The easiest way is to use your current Web browser (a different Web browser, such as Mosaic, or an older version of Navigator). The next simplest way to FTP is to use an FTP program, such as WS_FTP, which you should have obtained from your Internet service provider. The following sections explain how to grab a copy of Navigator using either of these methods.

FTPing with Your Web Browser

You'll learn all about using Navigator to FTP in Chapter 11, but you have to get Navigator before you can use Navigator to get Navigator. (Sorry, I studied metaphysics in college.) However, if you have a Web browser (Mosaic, Internet Explorer, an old version of Navigator), you can use the browser to quickly download the latest version of Navigator. Here's what you do:

Don't Be Choosy If your service provider gives you a copy of a Web browser (any Web browser), take it. You can use just about any Web browser to FTP from the Internet, and it's a whole lot easier than using Windows Terminal or some other archaic method.

1. Do whatever you have to do to establish your Internet connection. (For example, if you have a modem, you have to run your TCP/IP program to dial into your service provider's computer.)

2. Look for a URL or Location text box or command. Most Web browsers display such a text box at the top of the Window, but others might require you to select the URL or Location command (usually from the File menu).

3. Drag over any text that might be in the URL or Location text box, type **http:// home.netscape.com** and press **Enter**. After a moment, you should be connected to Netscape Corporation's home page.

4. Click on the trail of links until you arrive at the Download Netscape Navigator Software page. Scroll down the page to display a form asking you to pick the product you want and the operating system you use.

5. From the drop-down lists, select the version of Netscape Navigator you want, the operating system you use (for example, Windows 95 or Macintosh), the language (for example, U.S. English), and your geographical location (for example, North America).

Netscape's Home Page contains a link for downloading the latest release of Netscape Navigator.

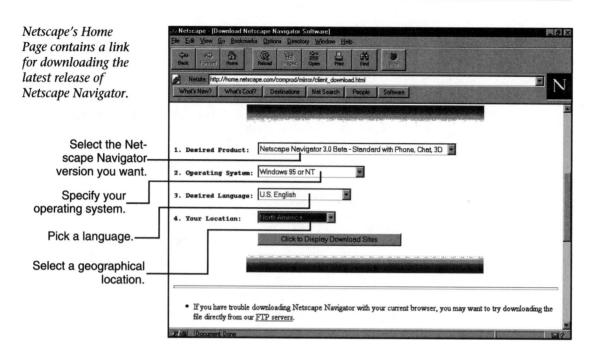

Select the Net-scape Navigator version you want.

Specify your operating system.

Pick a language.

Select a geographical location.

6. Click on the **Click to Display Download Sites** button. Scroll down the page for a list of download sites.

7. Click on the link for the download site nearest you. For example, if you live in the Midwest, you might click on the **Download** link for Washington University in St. Louis. What happens next depends on which Web browser you're using.

8. Take the required steps to download the file using your Web browser:

   With an old version of Navigator, you simply click the link, and then follow the dialog boxes to nab the file.

   With Mosaic, hold down the **Shift** key while clicking on the link, and then follow the dialog boxes to complete the task.

   With Internet Explorer, right-click on the link, and select **Save Target As**. Use the dialog boxes to save the file.

9. Wait until the file transfer is complete.

10. Close your Web browser, and then disconnect from your service provider by using your TCP/IP program.

Nabbing Navigator with an FTP Program

Poke around in your program groups to see if you have a Windows FTP program (your service provider may have slipped you an FTP program). One of the more popular Windows FTP programs is called *Ws_ftp*. If you have it, your job is going to be a lot easier. In fact, transferring files with a Windows FTP program is almost as easy as copying and moving files using the Windows Explorer or File Manager. Here's what you do:

1. Make a directory or folder on your hard disk called TEMP, if you don't already have one. (You'll store your files temporarily in this directory or folder.)

2. Run your FTP program. (You may have to run your TCP/IP program to connect to your service provider before you can run the FTP program.)

3. Enter the **Connect** command, and type **ftp2.netscape.com** in the **Host Name** text box. (This is the address of the remote FTP site where you'll get your files.)

   Netscape Corporation has several FTP servers you can try if the first one you try is busy. If you have trouble connecting to ftp2.netscape.com, try reconnecting at **ftp3.netscape.com**, **ftp4.netscape.com**, or another ftp number up to 20.

4. Type **anonymous** in the **User ID** text box.

5. In the **Password** text box, type your e-mail address. For example, you might type **jsmith@iway.com**.

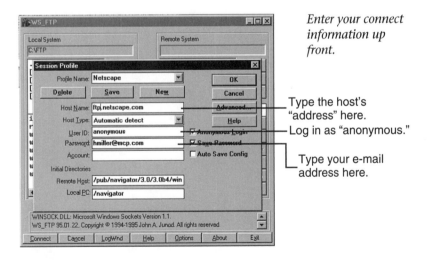

Enter your connect information up front.

Type the host's "address" here.

Log in as "anonymous."

Type your e-mail address here.

6. Click the **OK** or **Connect** button. If all goes right, the FTP program connects you to the remote server.

7. Select **Binary** as the Transfer option.

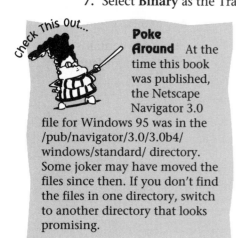

Poke Around At the time this book was published, the Netscape Navigator 3.0 file for Windows 95 was in the /pub/navigator/3.0/3.0b4/ windows/standard/ directory. Some joker may have moved the files since then. If you don't find the files in one directory, switch to another directory that looks promising.

8. Use the **Remote System** list to find the file you need: **n3230.exe** (for Windows 95), **n1630.exe** (for Windows 3.1), or **Netscape3.04Installer.hqx** for the Mac. (Netscape Corporation is constantly updating Navigator, so the file names you see might differ slightly.)

If you have Windows 95, make sure you get the file that has "32" in its name (meaning it is the 32-bit version). If you're still using Windows 3.1, make sure you get the file with "16" in its name.

The "30" represents the version number (version 3.0).

9. Use the Local System to change to the TEMP directory on your hard disk.

10. Click the name of the Netscape Navigator file (for example, **N3230.exe**) to high light it.

11. Click the arrow button to copy the files from the host computer to your PC.

Copy from one panel to the other.

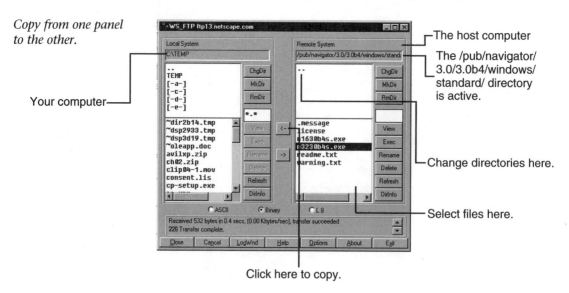

Your computer

The host computer

The /pub/navigator/ 3.0/3.0b4/windows/ standard/ directory is active.

Change directories here.

Select files here.

Click here to copy.

12. Wait until the copying is complete.

13. Exit your FTP program.

14. Disconnect from your service provider.

Now you have a self-extracting compressed file on your computer. This file contains all the files that comprise Navigator. Skip ahead to one of the "Installing" sections later in this chapter for instructions on how to proceed.

Installing Navigator

Installing Navigator is a no-brainer. The file you just nabbed is a self-extracting zip file, so all you have to do to unzip it is run the program file. Simply run Windows Explorer (or File Manager, if you're using Windows 3.1), change to the folder or directory that contains the file you just downloaded (for example, N3230.exe or N1630.exe), and then double-click the file.

The Netscape Navigator Installation dialog box appears, telling you that the file you've just chosen to run will install Netscape Navigator. Click **Yes** to proceed. The compressed file extracts itself, placing the Netscape Navigator installation files on your hard drive. The Installation utility starts, and displays the Netscape Navigator Setup window with the Welcome dialog box in front.

The installation utility will lead you through the installation process by displaying a series of dialog boxes, asking you questions, such as "Where do you want us to put the files?" Respond to the dialog box questions to the best of your ability, or just keep clicking on the **Next** button till no more dialog boxes appear. At this point, Navigator is on your computer.

At the end of the installation, a dialog box appears, asking if you want to connect to the Netscape site to complete the installation. If you choose to do this, Netscape Navigator runs and attempts to connect you to a page where you can register your copy of Navigator. This step is optional, but if you choose to do it, you'll have to establish your Internet connection.

The Mac Edition...

Check This Out...

The Macintosh version of Netscape Navigator comes as an HQX file. When you download an HQX file using an FTP program, the FTP program automatically decompresses the file, and you can run the setup utility. However, if you downloaded the file using a Web browser, the Web browser does not perform this important step. To use the HQX file, you'll first have to decompress it using a program such as StuffIt Expander.

The Navigator Installation program installs Navigator for you.

Follow the on-screen instructions to complete the installation.

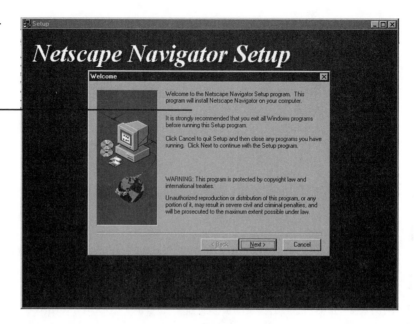

Day Tripping with Netscape Navigator

After you install Navigator, you should have a Netscape Navigator icon on the Windows Start menu and on the desktop (in Windows 95), or (if you're using Windows 3.1) in the Netscape program group. To run Navigator, first establish your Internet connection, and then double-click on the Navigator icon. Navigator runs and displays Netscape Communication's Home Page.

Netscape's Home Page is kind of boring, unless you're interested in looking at its other products and reading its boasts of world domination. So, let's start somewhere that's more interesting. Click inside the **Location** text box near the top of the Navigator window. Type **http://www.yahoo.com** and press **Enter**.

In a few moments, Navigator loads Yahoo's Home Page. This page contains an Internet search tool along with links to various categories of Web pages. Ignore the Search text box for now. Scroll down the page until you see a link for a category that catches your eye, and then click on the link. Yahoo displays a list of subcategories for the link you clicked on. Keep clicking on links until you find a specific page that interests you.

If you hit a dead end, click on the **Back** button to go back to a previous page and set out on a different trail of links. If you back up too far, click on the **Forward** button to move ahead one page.

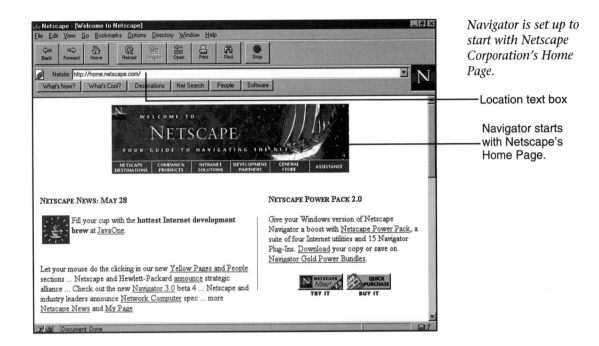

Navigator is set up to start with Netscape Corporation's Home Page.

Location text box

Navigator starts with Netscape's Home Page.

That's all you really need to know for now. Use these simple navigational tools to cruise the Web and get a feel for what's out there. If you run into trouble (for example, you can't seem to load a particular Web page), skip ahead to the next chapter, "What Could Possibly Go Wrong?" for condolences and fixes.

When you're ready to use more advanced navigational features, move on to Part Deux, "Mastering Navigator."

The Least You Need To Know

Now that Navigator's installed, you don't need to know much more. However, you should check Netscape's Web site every couple months or so to see if it has an updated version of Navigator. Simply run your TCP/IP program to connect to the Internet, run Navigator, and then open the **Directory** menu and select **Netscape's Home**.

This displays Netscape's home page (the main Web page), which displays news about and links to Netscape Communications Corporation's product line. Simply follow the links to download the latest version of Navigator.

Chapter 3

What Could Possibly Go Wrong?

By the End of This Chapter, You'll Be Able To...

➤ Translate an error message into plain English

➤ Determine what caused the error

➤ Find out the answer to the question, "Was it me?"

➤ Sidestep most connection problems

When I first ventured into the Web, I received all sorts of error messages:

```
Failed DNS Lookup.

Connection timed out.

Unable to Locate Document
```

I began to wonder. Was I doing something wrong? Did I inadvertently try to access classified Pentagon documents? Is my Internet service provider trying to tell me something?

You'll get many of these same error messages. I guarantee it. Just realize that it's usually *not* you, and you can't do much about most error messages. The purpose of this chapter is to desensitize you to these messages, and help you fix any problems that you can solve on your end. As for problems that are out of your control, why worry?

Why the Web Is Soooo Buggy

It's amazing that the World Wide Web works as smoothly as it does. Think about it. People all over the world have stitched together documents that refer to other documents on other computers all over the world. Now, say somebody deletes one of the documents or moves it to another directory. Maybe the link you click on has a typo, sending you to a page that doesn't exist. Or perhaps the network administrator on one of the Web servers decides to close down the network for maintenance. Any of these scenarios contains the formula for producing an error message.

But the Web is not the only thing under construction. The copy of Navigator you downloaded in Chapter 2 might also have a few bugs. Sure, it's a good program, and it'll get you around the Web, but the programmers who are developing it are constantly tweaking Navigator to make it run more efficiently. Until the program is perfected, it's likely that you, too, will encounter at least one of these bugs.

And that's not all. Now add your own human error into the equation. You might mistype a URL, try to skip around the Web too fast for it to keep up, or try to view a link before you've installed the proper helper application. When you take all these variables into account, you begin to realize how amazing it is that you can navigate the Web at all.

Navigator Can't Find the Server

If you spend an hour on the Web and you *don't* get this error message, you're probably doing something wrong. This reigning king of Web error messages is ambiguous; it can have any of several meanings. First, it might mean that the DNS (Domain Name Server) is having trouble matching the domain name of the server you're trying to access to its IP (Internet Protocol) number. Huh? (That's what I say. Look at the Techno Nerd Teaches, if you're interested in learning about the DNS.)

When Navigator can't find a server, it displays this dialog box.

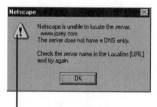

This message can mean anything.

More commonly, this error message *really* means that maybe you mistyped the URL of the desired server (or the person who created the Web page mistyped the URL for the link you clicked on). Try any of the following tactics to pull up the desired Web page:

➤ Did you remember to run your TCP/IP program before running Navigator? If you forgot, Navigator can't find the page, because it's not even connected to the Internet. Establish your Internet connection, and try again.

➤ If you typed the URL (in the Location text box), check your typing. One minor typo (an upper-case letter that should be lowercase, a slash mark that points the wrong way, or even a misplaced period) can cause the problem. Retype the URL and press **Enter**.

➤ If you received the error after clicking on a link, the URL behind the link may have a typo. Rest the mouse pointer on the problem link, and look at the URL in the status bar. If you see an obvious typo, retype the URL in the Location text box, and press **Enter**.

➤ This error message might also mean that you lost your connection with the service provider. In other words, your TCP/IP program hung up on you. Try some other links to make sure you're connected. If you keep getting this message no matter which link you click on, you've probably been disconnected. Go back to your TCP/IP program, and login again.

➤ If you're connected all right, but you keep getting this error message no matter which Web page you try to load, maybe your service provider's DNS server is down, or you have the wrong address for it. Contact your service provider to find out the correct address for the DNS server.

Techno Talk

The Trouble with DNS All servers on the Internet have a **domain name**— for example, **www.yahoo.com**, which is sort of understandable. Each server also has a unique IP (Internet Protocol) number, such as **128.252.135.4**, which is almost impossible for any person with an average IQ to remember. A special server, called a *DNS (Domain Name Server)*, matches the domain name to the IP number to find the server that has the requested data. As you innocently click on hyperlinks, the DNS is matching domain names and IP numbers to make sure you get where you're supposed to be.

Check This Out...

Common Courtesy If you find a Web page that has a link referring to a page that doesn't exist or that has a typo in it, let the Webmaster (the creator of the page) know about it. At the bottom of most Web pages is the Webmaster's e-mail address. Click on the e-mail address, and then use the dialog box that appears, to notify the Webmaster of the problem.

Navigator Can't Find the Document

Say you type a long URL or click on a link for a long URL that looks something like this...

```
http://www.yahoo.com/Entertainment/Movies/
```

...and you get a screen that looks something like this...

Web pages may move or disappear from a site.

The Web page you tried to go to is unavailable.

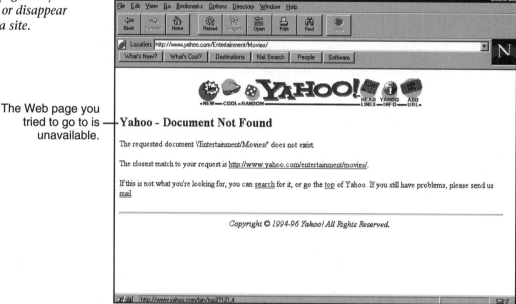

...then you're connected to the right Web server, but somebody moved or deleted the Web page you're trying to pull up. Try chopping the end off the right side of the URL, and enter the shortened URL into the Location text box. For instance, in the example above, you might try typing

> **http://www.yahoo.com/Entertainment**

If you still have trouble connecting, try chopping another portion off the right side of the URL (for example, type the URL without **/Entertainment**). You can chop all the way down to the domain name (for example, www.yahoo.com). This gets you in the general vicinity of the Web page you're looking for. You can then click on links to search for the specific Web page.

Document Contains No Data

Another ambiguous error message, this one usually means that the end is chopped off the URL. URLs typically end with a file name, telling Navigator which page, graphic, video, or sound file to open. For example, **http://home.netscape.com/newsref/ref/index.html** opens a Web page document file called index.html. Sometimes, if the file name is chopped off (as in **http://home.netscape.com/newsref/ref/**), Navigator might tell you that the document contains no data.

Because you do not know the name of the file, you can't just type it into the URL and press **Enter**. Instead, try chopping more off the right side of the URL. Type the chopped URL into the **Location** text box, and press **Enter**. Most Web servers display their home page whenever you connect to the server. You can then click on the links on this page to find a specific page.

Of course, this error message might also mean that the page you pulled up really is blank. However, Web people rarely stick blank pages on the Web. It's just not fun (or annoying enough) to inspire such an act.

Less Frequent Problems

Most of the problems you'll encounter in your Web wanderings are caused by some discrepancy between the URL you entered and the actual URL of the page you're trying to load. However, there are a few less common, more mysterious error messages:

➤ **403 Forbidden** You've been locked out. You tried to load a Web page that some-one doesn't want you to look at, or that you have to pay to look at.

➤ **Connection timed out** Your service provider's computer has given up searching for the item you specified. Try again later, and if you get the same message, you might consider giving up as well.

➤ **Connection Refused by Host** This just means that the site is probably too busy to let you in. Try again later.

➤ **Too Many Users** Standing room only; the Web site you're trying to get into is too crowded. You can't get the page now, but you might have some luck later (like at 3 a.m.).

➤ **TCP Error** This is a network problem, which you can't do much about. Try con-necting again later.

➤ **NNTP Server Error** NNTP (Network News Transport Protocol) is the language used to send and receive data for newsgroups. The problem here is that you are probably trying to connect to a newsgroup before selecting a newsgroup server. See Chapter 12 for details on how to select a Newsgroup server.

Finding Answers to Your Questions

If you're getting error messages that aren't covered here, or you have questions about other aspects of Navigator, go to the Web for additional information. The programmers at Netscape put together a bug list and a *FAQ (Frequently Asked Questions)* list. The bug list covers known problems in the program. The FAQ (pronounced "fack") list gives answers to the most commonly asked questions about Navigator.

Navigator makes it easy to access Navigator help on the Web. Simply open the Help menu, and click on the type of help you need. **Handbook** displays the documentation for using Navigator. **Release Notes** displays a list of bugs that were fixed with this release of Navigator, and a list of known bugs that have not yet been fixed. And **Frequently Asked Questions** displays a list of commonly asked questions about Navigator, along with the answers.

The Least You Need To Know

As you cruise the Internet with Navigator, you're going to hit some potholes and drive into a good share of dead ends. Don't let it get to you. If you hit a snag when you're wandering for fun, simply click on the **Stop** button and try a different link. If there's a page that you just have to access, keep trying.

Also, remember that you can take any of several paths to a page. If the URL you have doesn't work, try reentering a shorter version of the URL. Eventually, you'll clear the roadblock and be able to resume your expeditions.

Part Deux
Mastering Navigator

Anyone can fire up Navigator, plunge into the Web, and click link after link in a trail of frenzy, but only masters of the Web and Navigator can get where they're going in a hurry. If you're interested in government, maybe you want to visit the White House. Or maybe you're a movie buff, and you want to see trailers for the latest Hollywood flick. Or perhaps you just need a recipe for tonight's dinner. Whatever the case, this wandering business isn't going to get you where you want to be in a hurry.

In this part, you're going to learn how to take control of the Navigator and the Web. You'll learn how to find information; return to your favorite places; copy, save, and play movie and sound clips; and even configure Navigator to make it look and act the way you want it to! By the end of this part, you'll know everything you need to know to master Navigator and the Web.

Chapter 4

Weaving Through the World Wide Web

By the End of This Chapter, You'll Be Able To...

➤ Pick a page that will open automatically when you run Navigator

➤ Use a URL to "dial into" a specific hyperdocument

➤ Pick a page from a list of pages you visited

➤ List the URLs of four great search pages

Wandering the Web is as stimulating as wandering through downtown Chicago. You find museums, shops, peep shows, and cultural havens tucked into the most unlikely places. However, you'll eventually want to visit a specific site on the Web, to do research, or to find a cool picture or game that one of your friends has told you about.

When you need to get somewhere in a hurry, links may not be the most efficient way to reach your destination. They'll just pull you deeper into the Web, and take you off on some fruitless journey. In this chapter, you'll learn how to take control of the Web. You'll learn how to go to specific Web sites, search for information, and quickly backtrack when you get stuck.

Starting from Your Home (Page)

Whenever you start Navigator, it loads Netscape Corporation's Home Page (a clever advertising scheme). Chances are that you *don't* want to start here. You can tell Navigator to load a different page when it starts or load a blank page (so you can start from scratch). This page is called your *starting page*.

Ideally, this should be a page on your service provider's computer (or on your own computer), and it should contain links to your favorite Web documents. But you might not know the URL of your service provider's home page, and you probably haven't created your own home page yet (you'll do that in Chapter 20). So, for now, try setting up Navigator to load the Yahoo Home Page, a page with thousands of links to interesting pages. Here's what you do:

1. Open the **Options** menu and select **General Preferences**. This opens the Preferences dialog box.

2. Click the **Appearance** tab. Next to **Browser Starts With** are the options for loading a specific page when Navigator starts.

3. Click **Home Page Location**. This tells Navigator to load a specific page at startup, rather than loading a blank page.

4. Drag over the URL in the **Browser Starts With** text box, and then type **http:// www.yahoo.com**.

5. Click **OK** to save your change. Now, whenever you start Navigator, it will load the Yahoo home page, and you can use the links there to begin your wanderings.

You can tell Navigator to load a specific page at startup.

Select Home Page Location.

Type Yahoo's home page URL here.

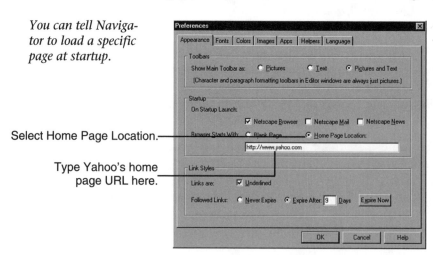

If, in your Web wanderings, you find a different Web page that you want to use as your home page (or if Yahoo moves its home page), simply repeat these steps. To save time, you can copy the URL from the Location or Go to text box by clicking inside the text box (to select the text) and pressing **Ctrl+C**. Then, display the **Preferences** dialog box, drag over the URL in the **Browser Starts With** text box, and press **Ctrl+V**. This inserts the URL you copied into the text box.

Home Page
A home page is sort of like one of those maps you find at a mall entrance. It's the first page that greets you when you connect to a Web site, and it usually contains links to all the other Web documents at that site.

Moseying Around the Navigator Screen

The overall Navigator screen should look pretty familiar… like all Windows applications, Navigator is in a standard window. It has a menu bar, a toolbar, scroll bars, controls for resizing and closing the window, and a status bar at the bottom that displays informative messages.

What makes this window so different are its contents. Notice that the page displayed here has one or more underlined, highlighted words or phrases. These are *links* that point to other pages or Web sites. Click a link, and Navigator loads the appropriate page, no matter where that page is stored (on the current server or on a server in Alaska, Sweden, or anywhere else). Links can come in all shapes and sizes; they can be text, icons, or even small graphics, but they all work the same way.

What's This Button For? You can quickly find out the name of any button in the toolbar. Just rest the mouse pointer on the button in question. A box appears, showing the button's name, and the status bar (at the bottom of the Netscape window) displays the button's role in life.

One other unique element on the Navigator screen is the big **N** with the flying comets. Look on the right side of Navigator window. This little eye-catcher isn't just for decoration. Comets fly across the **N** as your connection transfers data. This shows you when Navigator is busy fetching information for you.

Bird's eye view of Navigator.

Menu bar   Toolbar   The Navigator icon

Location (URL) of current document

Links

Document viewing area

Status bar

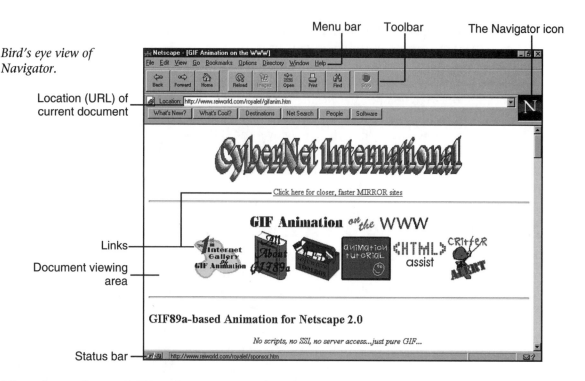

Navigational Tools of the Trade

Check This Out...

Back and Forward

If you enter a URL in the Location text box, Navigator assumes that you're taking off on an entirely new journey, and it loses track of the trail of links you clicked on. You may not be able to use the Back and Forward buttons to step back through previous pages.

You took a day trip on the Web in Chapter 2. Maybe you clicked on one or two links, clicked on the **Back** button to return to a site, and used the **Forward** button to pick up where you left off. Using these basic navigational tools is like trying to use your keyboard to steer and shoot in your favorite arcade game. They're just not designed for the quick turns and turbocharged movement you want on the Web.

The following sections show you some of the more advanced navigational tools that Navigator offers. Once you've mastered these tools, you'll be skipping along the Web like a spider on speed.

What's with the Purple Links?

You've encountered the blue, underlined links that take you places, but have you encountered any purple links yet? The purple indicates that you've already visited the page. By default, Navigator keeps track of the links you've visited for up to nine days. This allows you to see which pages you've visited, so you can avoid unnecessary return trips to those pages. After nine days, Navigator returns the links to their original blue.

You can tell Navigator to return the links to their original color. Open the **Options** menu, click on **General Preferences**, and click on the **Appearance** tab. Under Link Styles, click on the **Expire Now** button. You can also tell Navigator to **Never Expire** the links, or you can change the number of days Navigator keeps track of the links.

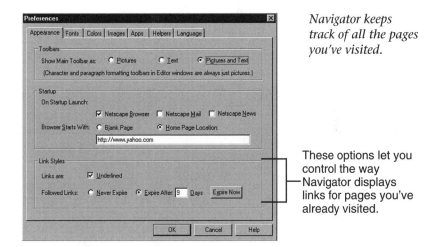

Navigator keeps track of all the pages you've visited.

These options let you control the way Navigator displays links for pages you've already visited.

You can also change the color used for links you've explored. Click on the **Colors** tab. Next to **Followed Links**, click on **Custom**, and then click on the **Choose Color** button, and select the color you want to use. (Some documents have codes that specify a color for links. To have Navigator override these color codes, make sure there's a check in the **Always Use My Colors, Overriding Document** box.)

Going Home

Although you can use the Back button to step page-by-page back to the first page Navigator loaded, there's a quicker way. Simply open the **Go** menu and select **Home**. An even faster way to go home is to click the **Home** button in the toolbar.

Recovering from Interrupted Transfers

Occasionally, you'll skip through pages before Navigator is done loading them. While Navigator is busy loading some huge image or a bunch of tiny ones, you see the link you want, and you click it. This terminates the transfer of the current page. If you go back to that page, only a small portion of it is loaded, and you might see a message at the bottom of the page indicating that the transfer has been terminated.

To have Navigator nab the rest of the page, simply click the **Reload** button in the toolbar, or open the **View** menu and select **Reload**. Navigator uses the URL to find the page and reload its contents.

Going to Places You've Been

Navigator lists the most recently loaded pages near the bottom of the Go menu. To quickly return to a page, open the **Go** menu, and click on the name of the page. When you exit Navigator, it erases the page names from the Go menu; however, you might be able to return to recently visited pages by selecting them from the **Location** drop-down list.

The Go menu contains the names of the most recently loaded pages.

Click on the name of the page you've visited.

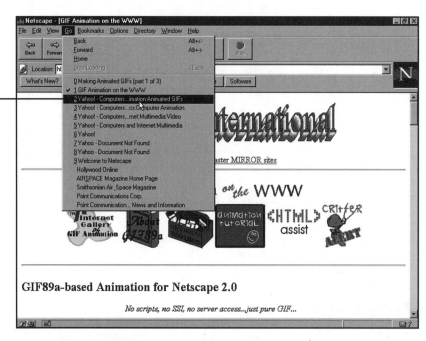

The History Log of Your Journeys

In addition to keeping track of pages on the Go menu, Navigator keeps a history list of the pages you've visited. You can display this list by opening the **Window** menu and selecting **History**. Or, display an abbreviated version of the list by opening the **Location** drop-down list (the Location text box doubles as a history list). From this list, select the page you want to revisit. You'll learn more about history lists in Chapter 5.

Menu Options

Although most of the navigational tools are conveniently placed on the button bar, you can also select them from the menus. The **Go** menu contains the **Back**, **Forward**, **Home**, and **Stop Loading** commands, and the **View** menu contains the **Reload** command. In addition, you can right-click inside the main viewing area to display a shortcut menu that offers many of the same commands, plus a few you haven't seen.

Touring the Web with URLs

So far, you've managed to avoid all the behind-the-scenes wizardry that enables you to jump from document to document. You click a link, and you're swept away to Switzerland. Three links later, and you're in a Cajun recipe database in Louisiana. You might start to wonder what's going on behind the scenes. More importantly, you might wonder how you can take more control of your wanderings.

Location, Go To, Netsite
You may have noticed that the **Location** text box (into which you type URLs) has an identity problem. When you are connected to a non-Netscape Web server, the name appears as **Location**. At a Netscape Web server, the Location changes to **Netsite**. And when you're typing a URL in the text box, its name is **Go to**.

The secret is to use *URLs (Uniform Resource Locators)*. URLs are addresses that specify the locations of the millions of pages and files that make up the Web. Each link you select (each starting point you choose) has a corresponding URL that kicks you out to the linked document.

What does this have to do with you? You'll learn later in this chapter how to enter URLs to load specific hyperdocuments… assuming, of course, you know the document's URL.

URLs Dissected

Each URL indicates the type of server, the server's unique *domain* (name), the directory in which the hyperdocument is stored, and the document's name. Let's look at a sample URL to see how it's made. Here's the URL for a Web page that deals with the Beat Generation author, Jack Kerouac:

```
http://www.charm.net/~brooklyn/People/JackKerouac.html
```

Techno Talk blah blah blah blah blah blah

Absolute and Relative References URL references can be *absolute* or *relative*. Absolute references specify the complete trail to the file, including the server's domain name, and a complete directory path. Relative references may give only the file name or the path and file name, assuming that you are logged in to the correct server and are in the right directory.

Let's dissect it. First, there's http. This stands for *HyperText Transfer Protocol*, which is a set of rules that govern the exchange of data on the Web. Every URL for Web servers starts with http (or https if you are at a secure site). If you see a URL that starts with different letters (for example ftp or gopher), the URL is for a different type of server: Gopher (gopher), FTP (ftp), WAIS (wais), USENET (news), or Telnet (telnet).

The next part of the URL (www.charm.net) is called the *domain name*. Each computer on the Internet has a unique domain name that distinguishes it from other computers on the Internet. That way, when the phone rings, all the computers don't answer at the same time. Domain names usually provide some vague indication of the establishment that runs the server. For example, guess who runs this one: www.whitehouse.gov. As you work with URLs, look for these common abbreviations: www (World Wide Web), edu (educational), pub (public), gov (government), and net (network). The URL might also specify the country (for example, jp for Japan).

Next comes the directory path (/~brooklyn/People) that shows the location of the file. Following that is the name of the document (JackKerouac.html). The .html is a file name extension that stands for *HyperText Markup Language*, a simple set of commands that tells Navigator (or whatever Web browser you're using) how to display the document. You'll get to work with HTML when you create your own home page in Chapter 20.

To complicate matters, some URLs do not end in a document name. For example, http://www.yahoo.com does not specify a directory or a file name. However, when you connect to the Yahoo Web server, it automatically loads the Yahoo home page by default. Many Web servers are set up to automatically load a home page.

Hitting the URL Trail

Opening an HTML document is like... well... opening a document. You enter the **File/Open Location** command, type the directory path and file name of the document, and then click **Open**. The only difference in opening an HTML document is that the "directory path" is a URL.

Practice entering URLs by taking the following guided tour of the Web:

1. Open the **File** menu and select **Open Location** (or click the **Open** button, or press **Ctrl+L**). The Open Location dialog box appears, prompting you to type the URL of the page you want to load.

The Open URL dialog box lets you type the location and name of a document.

2. Type the following URL: **http://ballet.cit.gu.edu.au/Movies/**. (Always type a URL exactly as shown. If you type **movies** instead of **Movies**, the domain name server won't know which page you want.)

3. Click the **Open** button. Assuming all goes as planned, you should now see The Internet Movie Database Browser at Griffith University in Australia.

The Internet Movie Database Browser.

Bypass the Open Location Dialog Box

A quicker way to enter a URL is to click inside the **Location** text box, type the URL, and press **Enter**. When you click inside the text box, the existing entry is highlighted. As you start typing, **Location** changes to **Go to**, and the characters you type replace the existing entry.

4. Repeat steps 1–4 for the following URLs:

http://www.pointcom.com/   Displays the Point Communications' Top 5% Web Sites list.

http://www.nasa.gov/   Connects you to NASA's (yes, the space program people) Web server.

http://www.w3.org/hypertext/DataSources/bySubject/ Overview.html   Displays The WWW Virtual Library, an index of topics ranging from Aboriginal Studies to Zoos.

http://www.bgsu.edu:80/~jzawodn/ufo/   Connects you with the UFO page.

This Page Has No Links!

Occasionally, you'll come across a Web page that does not use the standard blue text links. Instead, the page displays a Web navigational tool called a *map*, which uses graphics instead of text for its links. Below is a picture of a map on the Macmillan Computer Publishing home page.

Maps contain graphic links.

This map acts as a navigational tool.

Click an area of the map to go there.

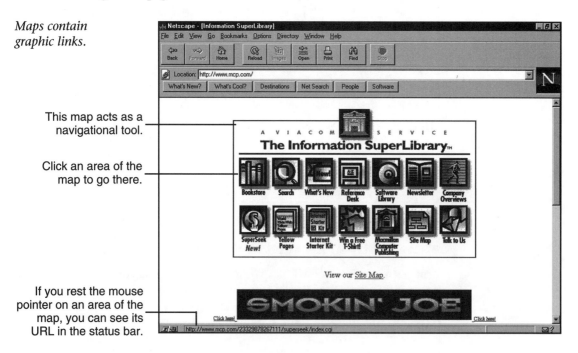

If you rest the mouse pointer on an area of the map, you can see its URL in the status bar.

If you happen upon a map, but you're not sure what it is, roll the mouse pointer to different areas of the map, while keeping an eye on the status bar. The URL displayed in the status bar changes as you move the mouse pointer over different areas. If you click an area, Navigator loads the corresponding Web page.

Sometimes, a simple graphic might look like a map. Don't let it fool you. If the URL in the status bar remains the same no matter which part of the picture you point to, the graphic is merely a picture, not a map.

Does It Seem S... L... O... W?

Hyperdocuments can be packed with pictures called *inline images*, no relation to inline skates. These buggers take forever to transfer over the phone lines and can slow your Navigator sessions down to a mere crawl. There is, however, a trick to speeding up Navigator. Open the **Options** menu and select **Auto Load Images**. In the next hyper-document you load, standard icons will appear in place of the images. To view a single image, you can click it. To view all images on the page, click the **Images** button (below Navigator's menu bar).

You can always switch back to having all the images displayed by opening the **Options** menu again, and clicking on **Auto Load Images**. However, as you wander the Web, you'll discover that you can get around a whole lot quicker by turning Auto Load Images off. When you find the page you were looking for, click the **Images** button.

Juggling Two or More Web Documents

You're surfin' now, but if you really want to hang ten on the Web, you can load several Web documents. Navigator is set up to allow you to open several Web documents at the same time—each in its own separate window.

To open another Navigator window, open the **File** menu and select **New Web Browser** (or press **Ctrl+N**). A new window opens, showing the contents of the first document you opened after starting Navigator. You can now use this window to open another Web document, by clicking on links, or by entering the URL of the document you want to open. To change from one window to another, open the **Window** menu, and click the name of the window you want to go to (they're listed at the bottom of the menu). (You can also switch windows by pressing **Alt+Tab** or using the Windows 95 taskbar.)

You can arrange the windows by resizing or moving them, minimizing one window while you work in the other one, or using Windows to arrange the windows for you. In Windows 95, you can quickly arrange windows by right-clicking on a blank area of the taskbar and selecting **Cascade**, **Tile Horizontally**, or **Tile Vertically**. In Windows 3.1, these same commands are on the Program Manager's Window menu.

*You can open two
or more Navigator
windows.*

Navigator windows
cascaded

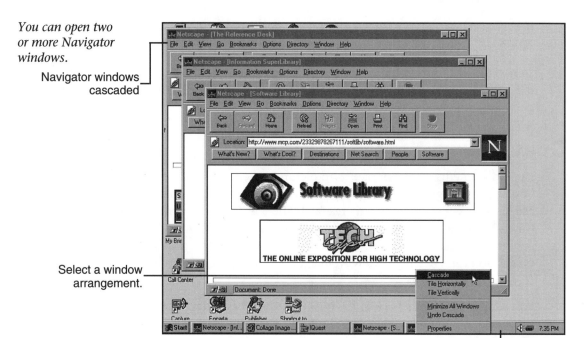

Select a window
arrangement.

Right-click a blank
area of the taskbar.

Right-Click a Link

Right-click a link inside the current Web document, and then select
Open in New Window. This opens the Web document that the link
points to and displays the document in a separate window.

Working with Window Frames

Occasionally, you'll come across a Web page that splits your Navigator window into two
frames—an upper and lower frame. Each frame has its own scroll bar, so you can view
two or more Web pages at the same time, as shown here. Frames are especially useful for
helping you move around in a long Web document. For example, one of the panes may
contain an outline of the document. Whenever you click on a link in the outline, the
other frame displays the page that contains detailed information about the topic.

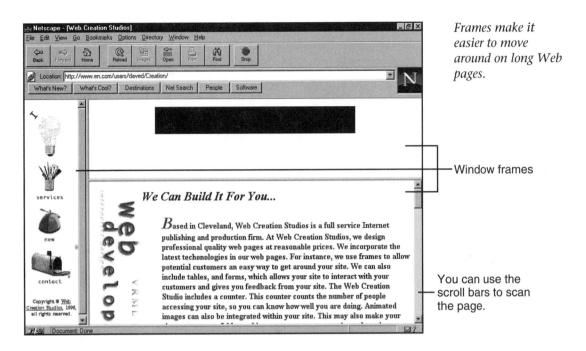

Frames make it easier to move around on long Web pages.

Window frames

You can use the scroll bars to scan the page.

You can't turn these frames on or off from your end. They're built into the Web page, and they tell Navigator to split the window in two. You can change the relative size and dimensions of the frames by dragging the borders that separate them. You can also move from one page to another by clicking on a link in any of the frames.

Check This Out...

Frame Commands

The View menu has several Frame commands. **Reload Frame** rereads the information in the selected frame. **Frame Source** displays the HTML-coded document that's behind the frame. **Frame Info** displays information about the frame's content, such as the date it was last modified.

Searching the Web

Although the Web allows for freewheeling, it does have several sites that can help you find specific information. These sites store indexes (also called directories and catalogues) of topics arranged in alphabetical order. You simply click the desired topic to go to its corresponding URL. Some sites also offer *forms* that you can fill out to search for specific topics in an index.

To use an index or search form, you simply enter the **File/Open Location** command, type the URL of the index or search tool, and then click **Open**. Try *WebCrawler*, one of the more popular tools for searching the Web. Enter the following URL:

    http://www.webcrawler.com/

Warning Message
Whenever you fill out a form on the Web, Navigator warns you that the information you're submitting could be intercepted by a third party. Because the information in a search is rarely confidential, simply confirm your desire to submit the information. You'll learn how to control these warning messages in Chapter 19, "Digital Certificates, Cookies, and Other Security Topics."

This displays a document called a *form* into which you can enter search instructions. Type the topic you want to search for in the text box (case doesn't matter). WebCrawler is initially set up to display the titles of pages it finds; to have it display summaries as well, open the **Search the web and show** drop-down list, and select **summaries**. Open the **for ____ results** drop-down list, and select the number of Web pages you want the search to present (10, 25, or 100); the larger the number, the longer the search will take. Click the **Search** button to start the search. The search displays a list of links to all the pages that match your search instructions; click a link to display its page.

If WebCrawler can't find a match, it displays a message telling you so. Try searching again using a different search phrase, something more unique. If WebCrawler found more pages than you chose to display, a button appears, such as **Get the next 25 results**. Click the button to view additional pages.

Remember, if you click a link that displays a page you don't want, you can click the **Back** button to go back to the list of pages that WebCrawler found. You can then click another link to try a different page.

If WebCrawler doesn't provide the expected (or desired) results, try another type of search tool. Here's a list to help you start:

    CUSI: **http://www.eecs.nwu.edu/susi/cusi.html**

    Lycos: **http://www.lycos.com/**

    SuperSeek: **http://www.mcp.com** (and then click on **SuperSeek**)

    Internet Yellow Pages: **http://www.mcp.com** (and then click on **Yellow Pages**)

    Alta Vista: **http://www.altavista.digital.com/**

    INKTOMI: **http://204.161.74.5:1234/query**

    Deja News: **http://www.dejanews.com/**

    Yahoo: **http://www.yahoo.com**

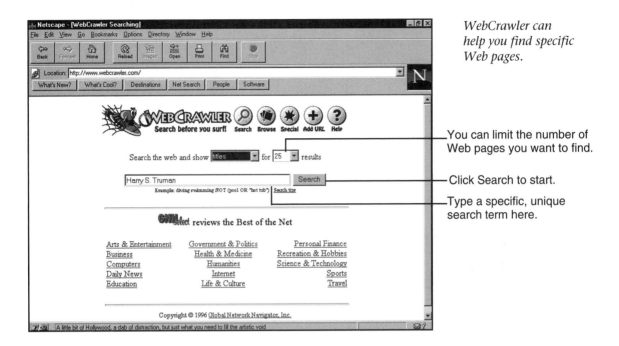

WebCrawler can help you find specific Web pages.

You can limit the number of Web pages you want to find.

Click Search to start.

Type a specific, unique search term here.

In addition, a company called Nexor provides a long list of Web search tools. To view this list, enter the following URL:

http://info.webcrawler.com/mak/projects/robots/active.html

Search for Unique Terms

Because there is so much information to index, Web seekers refuse to index certain common terms, such as New York Times, University, WWW, Web, and so on. So, don't even bother searching for such terms. Try to enter search instructions that are both specific and unique.

Searching for Information on a Page

Some Web documents look like the neighborhood landfill. The Webmaster did a mind dump, and you're buried in text. You have no clue where to look for the information you want. Fortunately, Navigator has a search tool you can use to look for words or phrases.

To use the tool, open the **Edit** menu and select **Find** (or press **Ctrl+F**, or click the **Find** button in the toolbar). Type the text you want to search for in the **Find what** text box, and then click the **Find Next** button. Navigator scrolls the screen to bring the first occurrence of the search text into view. You can click the **Find Next** button again to scroll to subsequent terms. Click **Cancel** when you're done. If you cancel a search, you can quickly search for the same text again by pressing the **F3** key. You won't get the Find dialog box, but if the text is on the current page, Navigator will find and highlight it.

What About the Movie Clips? The Sound Clips?

Although Navigator can display pictures and play some sounds on its own, the larger graphics—as well as movie and sound clips—require special *helper applications*. When you click a link for one of these clips, Navigator transfers the file to your computer, launches the helper application, loads the linked file into it, and starts to play the movie or sound clip. If you don't have the right helper applications, or Navigator can't find them, you get a dialog box asking you to pick an application.

Navigator may not be able to play a link you clicked.

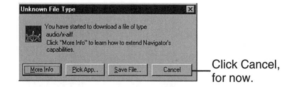

Click Cancel, for now.

For now, wander the Web without trying any of the special links. After you sign off, read Chapter 12 to learn how to download, install, and configure helper applications to work with Navigator.

The Least You Need To Know

Now that you know how to go places with URLs, you can skip to the back of this book for a list of nifty Web sites you can visit. While you're entering URLs and cruising, keep the following in mind:

➤ At the bottom of the Go menu is a list of the sites you most recently visited.

➤ Another way to go to recently visited sites is to open the **Location** drop-down list and then click the site's URL.

➤ There are three ways to enter a URL: type it in the **Location** text box and press **Enter**; click the **Open** button in the toolbar; or open the **File** menu and select **Open Location**.

➤ Type a URL *exactly* as it appears, or it won't take you where you want to go.

➤ "If you don't know where you are goin', you will probably not wind up there." —Forrest Gump

Chapter 5

Revisiting Your Favorite Pages

By the End of This Chapter, You'll Be Able To...

➤ Jump back to a page you just visited

➤ Slap a bookmark on a page, so you can quickly return to it

➤ Create a list of hot Web pages

➤ Swap Web page lists with your friends

You just clicked on a trail of 35 links trying to find the Elle MacPherson home page. You racked up an hour in Internet connect time charges. But now your eyes are getting droopy, and you don't have the energy to look at the 120 pictures of Elle you found. What do you do? Even if you could remember how to get back to this page, you wouldn't have the energy or desire to repeat the trip... well, maybe you would—it is Elle after all.

In this chapter, you'll learn how to go back to pages you've visited by selecting them from the history list and by creating bookmarks for your favorite pages. As a bonus, you'll also learn how to transform a list of bookmarks into a Web page, and how to trade bookmark lists with your friends, family, and colleagues.

Going Back in History (Lists)

As you carelessly click links and enter URLs, Navigator keeps track of the URLs for the pages you visited. Navigator tracks up to ten pages from the last time you used Navigator, and it tracks scads more during the current session. It adds each URL to a *history list*. When you use the Back and Forward buttons, you are actually moving up and down the history list to return to the documents you viewed.

But what happens when you visit ten sites and want to return to the fifth one? Clicking on the Back button five times is hardly the fastest way to return. To zip back, select the desired URL from the history list. The easiest way to do this is to open the **Location** drop-down list; then click the URL for the page you want to view, as shown here.

Click here to open the list.

You don't need a menu to view the history list.

History list

Click a URL to return to its page.

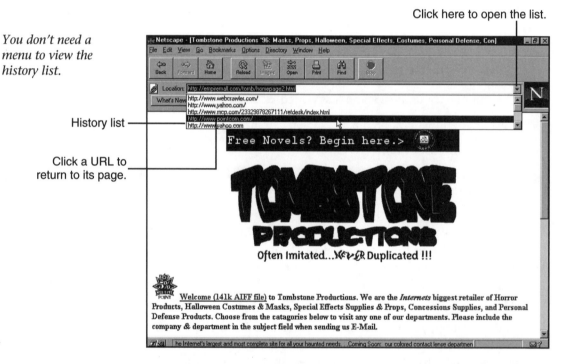

You can also get at the history list in a dialog box. To view the history list in this way, open the **Window** menu and select **History** (or just press **Ctrl+H**). This displays the History dialog box. To return to a page, click its URL in the history list, and then click the **Go to** button. Ignore the Create Bookmark button for now; you'll learn what it does later in this chapter.

Another way to revisit a page is to open the Go menu, and select the page from the bottom of the menu. Unlike the Location drop-down list (which displays only URLs), the Go menu displays the actual page names, so they might make more sense to you. The

History list that is displayed in the History dialog box gives you the best of both systems, displaying the page name and URL.

Making Shortcuts in Windows 95

In Windows 95, you can make shortcuts to your favorite Web pages. (Shortcuts are icons that sit on the Windows desktop.) To create a shortcut, right-click on the link for which you want to make a shortcut, and then click on **Internet Shortcut** to display the Create Internet Shortcut dialog box. Type a name for the shortcut in the **Description** text box, and click on **OK**.

The shortcut is placed on the Windows desktop, and appears as a Netscape Navigator icon. To load a page for which you've created a shortcut, double-click on the shortcut.

Make Navigator Your Default Browser

If you have more than one Web browser installed on your computer, you can use only one of them to create and use shortcuts. If you run Netscape Navigator, and a dialog box appears, telling you that this browser is not the default browser, click the Yes button to make Navigator the default browser; otherwise, you won't be able to use shortcuts.

Marking a Page with a Bookmark

You have this gargantuan book, over a million pages, and you find a page that has an interesting picture, or a mind-altering quote. You want to remember this page, and you'll probably want to return to it someday. What do you do? Create a bookmark for the page. A *bookmark* is an entry that you can select (from the Bookmark menu) to quickly return to a page you visited.

You can quickly create bookmarks for any page that's displayed, and for any URL you have (even if you haven't yet visited the page). All the bookmarks are dumped at the bottom of the Bookmarks menu, but you can group the bookmarks, place them on submenus, and even juggle them to place them in some order that you can follow.

To create a bookmark for a page that's displayed, take the following steps:

1. Open the page you want to display.

2. Watch the flying comets and the status bar to make sure the document has been completely transferred. If the document is in the process of being transferred, you can't mark it.

3. Open the **Bookmarks** menu and click **Add Bookmark** (or press **Ctrl+D**).

The bookmark is added to the bottom of the Bookmarks menu. When you add a bookmark in this way, the page name appears on the Bookmarks menu, and the URL remains behind the scenes. However, if nobody gave the page a title, the page's URL may appear on the menu. In either case, you can quickly revisit a page you've marked by opening the Bookmarks menu and clicking on the name of the page, or on its URL.

You can click a bookmark to quickly load a page.

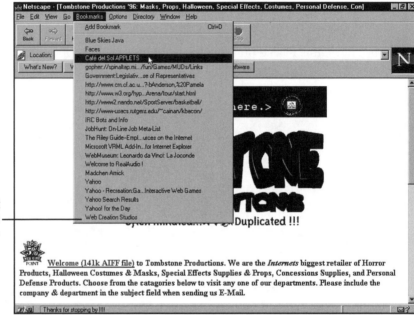

Bookmarks appear at the bottom of the Bookmarks menu.

If you have more bookmarks than will fit on the Bookmarks menu, you'll see the **More Bookmarks...** option at the bottom of the menu. Click this option, and a window appears showing all your bookmarks. You can double-click a bookmark to go to it.

Bookmarking a Link

If you see a link that you might like to visit later, you can create a bookmark for it without opening its page. Right-click the link to display a shortcut menu, and then click **Add Bookmark**.

Giving Your Bookmark List a Makeover

As you add bookmarks, they're dumped at the bottom of the Bookmarks menu and stuck with whatever name or complicated URL the Webmaster decided to use. As time passes, your Bookmarks menu becomes cluttered with all sorts of incomprehensible names and URLs that are listed in no logical order.

The good news is that you can take control of your bookmarks. In the following sections, you'll learn how to rename bookmarks, place them in logical groups, delete bookmarks you no longer need, and even create your own bookmark submenus. By the time you're done with these sections, you'll have a leaner, more efficient Bookmarks menu, one that even Al Gore would be proud of.

But, before we get into the nitty-gritty of remolding your Bookmarks menu, let's display the screen you use to edit the Bookmarks menu. Open the **Window** menu, and click **Bookmarks** (or press **Ctrl+B**). The Bookmarks window appears, showing the existing structure of your bookmarks.

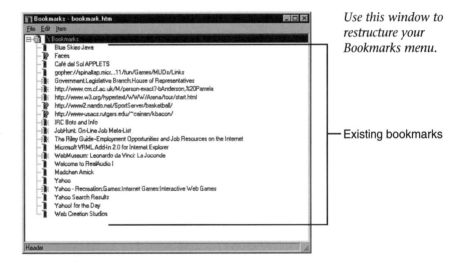

Use this window to restructure your Bookmarks menu.

Existing bookmarks

Renaming and Deleting Bookmarks

The first step in restructuring your Bookmarks menu is to give your bookmarks names that you can easily recognize. This is especially important if you have raw URLs on your menu. The easiest way to rename a bookmark is to right-click it and choose **Properties**. This displays the Bookmark Properties dialog box, with the Name entry highlighted. Type a new name for the bookmark, and click **OK**.

One word of caution: Don't change the **Location (URL)** entry. This is the URL that works behind the scenes to load the specific page. You can change the name of the bookmark, but changing the URL entry is the same as changing an address on a letter. If you give this bookmark the wrong address, Navigator won't be able to find the page.

You can give your bookmarks more recognizable names.

Do not change the URL.———

Type a new name for the bookmark.

You can ignore this. (It appears only if you open the Bookmark.htm file to edit it.)

If your bookmark list is cluttered with bookmarks you no longer use, delete them. Simply click the bookmark, and then press the **Del** key (or select **Delete** from the **Edit** menu).

Shuffling Your Bookmarks

Once you've renamed any bookmarks that needed it, think about rearranging your bookmarks. For example, you might want to place the bookmarks for all the sports pages together, and stick the bookmarks for entertainment sites next to each other.

To move a bookmark, click it, and then drag it up or down in the list. A highlight bar appears, highlighting the bookmark *below* which the bookmark you're dragging will be placed. When the bar is where you want the bookmark moved, release the mouse button.

Moving Bookmarks in the Old Days

If dragging the bookmarks is too easy for you, there's a more standard (and much more monotonous) way of moving bookmarks. The process consists of cutting and pasting the bookmarks using the Edit menu. I'm not about to encourage this method, so I'll let you figure it out for yourself.

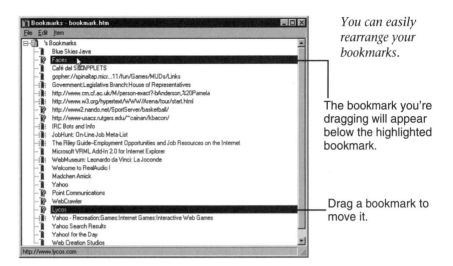

You can easily rearrange your bookmarks.

The bookmark you're dragging will appear below the highlighted bookmark.

Drag a bookmark to move it.

Grouping Bookmarks with Separators and Submenus

You've cleaned up your Bookmarks menu, deleted the fluff, and assigned names to faceless URLs. What more could you want? Well, if your list is still too long to fit on the Bookmarks menu, you might want to create some submenus and add separators to place your bookmarks in logical groups.

Separators are the lines that divide options on a menu into groups. If you open Navigator's File menu, you'll see two separators: one before the Print options, and one before the Close and Exit options. You can add separators to your Bookmarks menu. In the Bookmarks window, click the bookmark below which you want to insert the separator; then open the **Item** menu and click **Insert Separator**. Or, right-click on the bookmark below which you want to insert the separator, and click on **Insert Separator**.

Separators are great if you have only about ten to fifteen bookmarks, but if you have many more than that, you should consider creating submenus for related bookmarks. For example, you can create a submenu called Business that includes bookmarks for all your business-related Web pages. To create a submenu and place bookmarks on it, take the following steps:

1. Open the **Navigator Bookmarks** window, and click the bookmark below which you want the submenu to appear.

2. Open the **Item** menu and click **Insert Folder**. The Bookmark Properties dialog box appears, prompting you to name the folder.

3. Type a name for the folder, and press **Enter** (or click **OK**). A folder appears in the list of bookmarks. You can now drag bookmarks into this folder to place them on the submenu.

4. Click one of the bookmarks you want to add to this folder, and then **Ctrl+click** any additional bookmarks you want to add. The selected bookmark(s) appear highlighted.

   You can select a group of neighboring bookmarks by clicking the first one in the group and then **Shift+clicking** on the last one.

5. Move the mouse pointer over any one of the selected bookmarks, and drag it over the folder you created. The folder appears highlighted.

6. Release the mouse button. The bookmarks are now listed below the folder.

7. Repeat these steps to create additional submenus and group your bookmarks.

8. If you end up creating a submenu of a submenu, you can move the submenu up one level in the tree by dragging it to the top of the tree. This moves the submenu and all its bookmarks.

In the Bookmarks window, if you see a folder that has a plus sign (+) next to it, you can click on the plus sign to *expand* the folder (display its contents). The plus sign is then replaced by a minus sign (-), which you can click to hide the contents of the folder.

Use submenus to group related bookmarks.

Bookmarks appear under the submenu you created.

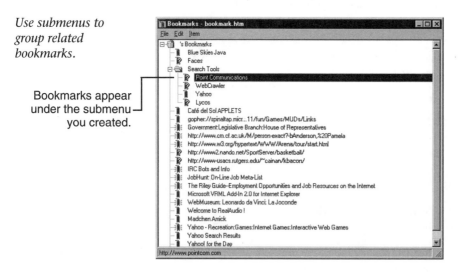

When you are done editing your bookmark list, open the **File** menu and select **Close**, or click the **Close** button in the upper right corner of the window (or press **Ctrl+W**). Your Bookmarks menu is immediately updated to reflect your changes. To open a submenu, simply open the **Bookmarks** menu, and rest the mouse pointer on the submenu's name. You can then click a bookmark to select it.

Your Bookmark List Is a Web Page!

Congratulations, you just created your first HTML (Web) document. You don't believe me? In the Navigator window, open the **File** menu and click on **Open File**. Use the dialog box that appears to open the file named Bookmark.htm (in Windows 95, the file is in the Program Files/Netscape/Navigator folder). You can also set the Bookmark.htm file as your starting Web page, as explained in Chapter 4.

When You Add Bookmarks Later...

If you add bookmarks later, the bookmarks are placed at the bottom of the Bookmarks menu. You can move them to one of your submenus by displaying the Navigator Bookmarks window again and dragging the bookmark(s) over the submenu name.

Another way to add bookmarks to a submenu is to tell Navigator on which submenu you want the bookmarks placed. Open the **Window** menu and click **Bookmarks**. Click on the name of the submenu on which you want the new bookmarks placed. Open the **Item** menu and select **Set to New Bookmarks Folder**. Now, whenever you display a Web page and then enter the **Bookmarks/Add Bookmark** command, the bookmark is added to the specified submenu, instead of to the bottom of the Bookmarks menu.

You can also choose to use a submenu's bookmarks as your Bookmarks menu. Open the **Window** menu, and click **Bookmarks**. Click on the name of the submenu you want to use as your Bookmarks menu, and then open the Item menu and click on **Set to Bookmark Menu Folder**. When you open the Bookmarks menu, you'll see only the bookmarks on the selected submenu.

To return your Bookmarks menu to its original condition, display the Bookmarks menu, and click on the folder icon at the top of the bookmarks list. Then, open the **Item** menu and click on **Set to Bookmark Menu Folder**. Open the Item menu again, and click on **Set to New Bookmarks Folder**. Now, the Bookmarks menu will look and behave the way it used to.

Right-Click Bookmark Control

Your right mouse button works in the Bookmarks window, as well. Right-click on a folder, and you can choose to cut, copy, paste, or delete the folder; use it as the Bookmarks menu; use it for new bookmarks; or insert a separator or subfolder. Right-clicking is a whole lot easier than trying to poke around in the pull-down menus.

Ugh! Adding Bookmarks Manually

By far, the easiest way to add a bookmark is to pull up a Web page, open the **Bookmarks** menu, and click **Add Bookmark**. If you're a masochist, however, you might like adding bookmarks yourself—by typing them in.

To insert a bookmark, first open the **Window** menu and click **Bookmarks**. This opens the Navigator Bookmarks window. Click the bookmark (or submenu name) below which you want the bookmark to appear. Then, open the **Item** menu, and click **Insert Bookmark**. A dialog box appears, prompting you to enter the name and location (URL) of the page. Type the page's name (or the name you want to give it), and then tab to the **Location (URL)** text box and type the URL for the page. Click **OK**.

The Page Moved!

If some joker on the Web moves a page, you may have to change the URL for one of your bookmarks. This is easy enough; click the bookmark; then open the **Item** menu and click **Properties**. This displays the dialog box showing the bookmark's name and location. You can then edit the item, as necessary.

An easier way to check for an update on your bookmark URLs is to have Navigator do it for you. Display the **Bookmarks** window, and then open the **File** menu and click on **What's New?** The What's New dialog box appears, asking if you want to check all your bookmarks or only the selected bookmarks. Click on the desired option, and then click on the **Start Checking** button. Navigator updates the URLs for your bookmarks. (This might take awhile, depending on the number of bookmarks you have and how busy each Web page is.)

Creating and Saving Additional Bookmark Lists

As you know, the bookmark list you created is a Web document file called bookmark.htm, but you can save the list under another name. For example, if you have hundreds of bookmarks, you might want to save them in separate files—one for entertainment, one for business, and one for research. Then, you can choose which bookmark file you want to use.

To save a bookmark file under another name, display the Navigator Bookmarks window (**Window/Bookmarks**). Open the **File** menu, and select **Save As** (or press **Ctrl+S**). Type a name for the bookmark file (you can leave off the extension), and click **Save**.

To specify which bookmark file you want to use (so its bookmarks will appear on the Bookmarks menu), open the **Window** menu, and select **Bookmarks**. Open the **File** menu and click on **Open**. Use the Open bookmarks file dialog box to select the drive, folder, and name of the bookmark file you want to use. Click **Open**. This opens the specified bookmark file. Now, when you close the Netscape Bookmarks window, the specified bookmark file is made active; its bookmarks appear on the Bookmarks menu.

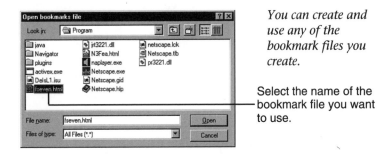

You can create and use any of the bookmark files you create.

Select the name of the bookmark file you want to use.

Trading Bookmark Lists with Your Friends

If you're reading all the little boxed tips throughout this chapter, you know that a bookmark list doubles as a Web page, which goes by the name of bookmark.html or bookmark.htm. You can open it in Navigator, and it even looks like a Web page. Because a bookmark is structured as a Web page, you can trade your bookmark lists with your friends and colleagues. You can send your bookmark file to a friend, who can then import it into her bookmark list. Or you can import a bookmark list you received from a friend. (You can also tell Navigator to use a specific bookmark file, as explained in the previous section.)

The bookmark.html or bookmark.htm file is in the NETSCAPE/NAVIGATOR directory, which is in the PROGRAM FILES folder in Windows 95. You can copy the file to a floppy disk or send it via e-mail. If you receive a bookmark file, you can add its bookmarks to your Bookmarks menu by performing the following steps:

1. Make sure the bookmark file is on your hard disk or on a floppy disk inside one of your floppy disk drives.

2. Open Navigator's **Window** menu and click **Bookmarks**. This displays the Navigator Bookmarks window.

3. Open the **File** menu and select **Import**. The Import bookmarks file dialog box appears, prompting you to select the bookmark file you want to import.

4. Change to the drive and folder that contains the bookmark file.

5. Click the name of the bookmark file you want to import, and then click the **Open** button. The bookmarks are appended (tacked on) to the end of your bookmarks list.

Here's a great tip that makes this book well worth the money you paid for it. You've created a Web page (your bookmarks file), so consider using it as your starting page. Open the **Options** menu, click **General Preferences**, and click the **Appearance** tab. Make sure **Home Page Location** is selected, and then type the path to your bookmark file in the text box. For example, type

```
file:///C¦/Program Files/Netscape/Navigator/Bookmark.htm
```

Notice that the "URL" starts with "file," indicating that the page is stored on your computer. There are three forward slashes after **file:**, followed by the drive letter and the pipe symbol (|), *not* a colon. Click **OK**.

Can't Get It to Work?

If you have trouble typing that **file:///C|** stuff, enter Navigator's **File/ Open File** command. Use the dialog box that appears, to find and open the bookmark.htm file. Navigator opens the file, and displays its URL in the **Location** text box. Click inside the text box, and press **Ctrl+C** to copy the URL. Then, click inside the **Home Page Location** text box, and press **Ctrl+V** to insert the copied URL.

The Least You Need To Know

Okay, I admit that this chapter probably contains about three times as much information about bookmarks than you really wanted. However, if you perform all the procedures in this chapter (including tips), you'll save yourself a lot of time you would spend searching for cool pages you've already loaded.

➤ Just keep in mind that you can add bookmarks to your Bookmarks menu by open-ing the page, clicking **Bookmarks**, and then selecting **Add Bookmark**.

➤ If you care to fiddle with your Bookmarks menu (no one says you have to), open the **Window** menu, and click **Bookmarks**.

Chapter 6

Going Multimedia with Helper Applications

By the End of This Chapter, You'll Be Able To...

➤ In 25 words or less, explain what a helper application does

➤ Tell the difference between a helper app and a plug-in

➤ Find and download a sound player, movie player, and picture viewer

➤ Get the helper applications you need right off the Internet

➤ "Play" any multimedia link simply by clicking on it

Navigator can take you around the world, connecting to computers in any of the contiguous and noncontiguous states, and with computers in foreign lands. It can play most audio files, and it can display some pictures. But if you click a link for a video clip or picture file, and you get this...

...then Navigator needs help. You see, Navigator is a Web browser, designed to "play" Web pages—pages with text and funky codes that make links appear blue. Navigator isn't designed to play multimedia or video clips, and although it can handle inline images (tiny graphics) and other small graphics files, it isn't a full-fledged drawing program.

To play the multimedia files that really bring the Web to life, Navigator needs help, it needs special programs called *helper applications*. In this chapter, you'll learn how to get helper applications off the Internet, install them, and set them up so that Navigator can use them.

Plug-Ins Versus Helper Apps

Don't confuse helper applications (helper apps) with plug-ins. A helper application is an independent program that Navigator calls into action when it needs help. A plug-in is a program that becomes an integral part of Navigator, extending Navigator's built-in capabilities. For details about getting and installing plug-ins, see Chapter 7, "Beefing Up Navigator with Plug-Ins."

How Do Helper Applications Help?

Helper applications are programs that perform the specialized jobs that Navigator by itself is unfit to manage. Whenever you click a link that Navigator can't play, Navigator loads the file to disk, and then summons (spawns) the helper application associated with that file. The helper application loads the file and plays it.

Sound simple? It's absolutely brainless, assuming you have everything set up correctly. However, setting up everything to run correctly takes some effort. You have to get and install the helper applications, and then tell Navigator which application goes with each type of file you might want to play.

Media Files That Navigator Can Handle

Navigator can play several types of media files without any outside help. It can display images in JPG and GIF formats, and it can play sound recordings in AU, AIF, MID, and WAV formats. To play other file types (for example, PCX images and AVI movie clips), you'll have to download and install either a plug-in or a helper app.

The choice between a helper app or plug-in is up to you. Helper apps are useful if you want a program that offers more features and allows you to open and play files without running Navigator. For example, with a helper app, you can download media files to disk, and then run the helper app later to play those files (without connecting to the Internet).

Helper Applica-tions Also known as *external viewers* (or *helper apps*), helper applications are programs that play the Web's multimedia files, including photos, sounds, and video clips. Typically, these programs run quickly and use little memory. However, you can set up robust applications, such as CorelDraw and Microsoft Word, to act as helper apps.

Plug-ins provide a less bulky way to play media files. Instead of running a separate program, the plug-in plays the file in Navigator. However, plug-ins typically provide fewer features than you'll find in helper apps.

Free and Inexpensive Programs That Fit the Bill

Sounds, pictures, and movies. Those are the three common types of multimedia files you'll come across on the Web. As mentioned in the previous section, Navigator can handle most sounds and pictures you'll encounter on the Web. However, you might want to use a helper app instead, if you prefer more control over the sounds and pictures you download, and if you want to play them off-line.

You will need helper apps or plug-ins for many of the other file types you'll encounter on the Web, including video clips. For example, you might need an *MPEG Viewer* to play video clips (.MPG or .MP2 files), an image viewer (such as PaintShop Pro) for displaying PCX images, and a real-time audio player (for playing real-time recordings). The following table lists common helper applications. You'll learn a quick way to download these files in the next section.

Common Helper Applications

Application	Plays	File Name
RealAudio	Real-time audio (RA) files	ra32_201.exe
TrueSpeech	Real-time TrueSpeech files	tsply311.exe
WHAM	AU, AIF, WAV sounds	wham133.zip
WPlany	AU, SND, VOC, WAV sounds	wplny.zip
LView Pro	GIF, JPG, BMP, TGA images	lview31.zip
PaintShop Pro	PCX, JPG, GIF, and much more	psp32bit.zip
MPEG Play	MPG video clips	mpegw32g.zip
NET TOOB	MPEG (MPG), AVI, MOV video	nettoob.exe
VDO Live	VDO video clips	plgply16.exe
AVIPRO	Video for Windows	avipro2.exe

Don't worry too much about nabbing an audio player. Most sound files you find on the Web end in .AU or .WAV. Navigator comes with an audio player that can handle the .AU files, and Windows Sound Recorder can handle .WAV files. These two programs (along with a couple woofers and tweeters) should be able to handle all your audio needs. You can probably skip the graphics viewer, too; although PaintShop Pro handles gobs more file types and provides lots of cool image enhancement tools than you'll find in Navigator.

Finding a Helper App Warehouse on the Web

Check This Out...

The File Names You See May Differ

Remember, the file names given here might change as the programmers update these programs. When searching for a specific file, be flexible and open-minded.

You can find links to most of the helper apps you need, along with information and ratings by pulling up Stroud's List, a helpful Web document kindly constructed by Forrest H. Stroud. To connect to this list, run Navigator and enter the following URL: **http://www.stroud.com**. If you can't pull up this page, go to Yahoo at **http://www.yahoo.com**, and search for **Stroud's**. This displays a list of links for various servers that mirror Stroud's List. Pick the server nearest you.

Scroll down the page to see the Main Menu, as shown in the following figure. (If you don't see the Main Menu on the opening page, click on the big graphic on the top of the page labeled **Stroud's Consummate Winsock Applications**.) This menu contains a list of Internet applications grouped by category. Click on the category for the type of helper app you need; for example, click on **Audio Apps** for sound file players, or **Graphics Viewers** for apps that display image files.

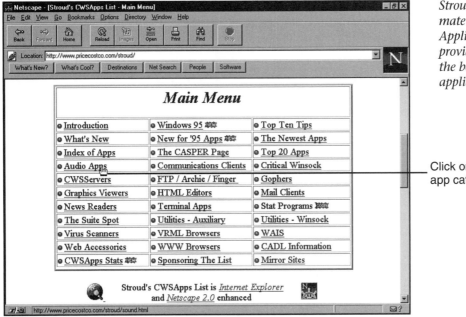

Stroud's Consummate Winsock Applications list provides links to the best Internet applications.

Click on a helper app category.

Check the Date

Stroud's List resides on several Web sites which update the list at different times. At the bottom of the Main Menu is a Mirror Sites link; click on it to view a list of the other sites. When you go to a mirror site, check the date at the top of the page to see when it was last updated. Try to find the site that was updated most recently.

Downloading from Stroud's

When you click on a category, Stroud's displays a list of the best and most popular apps in that category. Stroud rates each application and displays a brief description of it, including its size, version number, a link for downloading it and getting more information, and a link to a review of the program.

When you're ready to download the file, click on the link next to Location, and then follow the trail of links and on-screen instructions to download the file. Make sure you get the right version of the helper app (Windows 3.1, Windows 95, or Macintosh). Although Stroud's list may not distinguish between these operating systems when listing the helper apps, the download site typically displays a form that lets you specify your operating system, or displays links for the various versions.

From Stroud's List, you can download most applications.

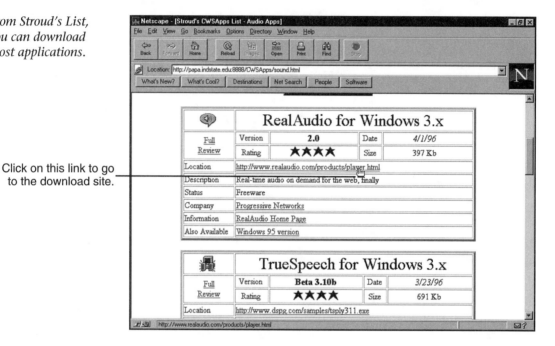

Click on this link to go to the download site.

Other Helper App Sites

Although Stroud's List is the best place to go for helper apps, there are other places that try to point you in the right direction. Check out the following pages:

http://pilot.msu.edu/user/heinric6/tools.htm
http://www.inf.bme.hu/htmldocs/pc_tools.html
http://131.74.26.2:8888/software.htm

Before You Download

Before you start downloading files and sticking them all over your hard drive, you should create a separate temporary directory or folder for your files. You might want to call it something like Helpers. You can then place all the original downloaded files in this folder. When you are done installing these helper apps, you can delete the Helpers folder and all the files it contains. Otherwise, you'll clutter your hard drive.

Get WinZip, too

When you're downloading files, be sure to get a copy of WinZip (for Windows) or StuffIt Expander (for the Mac). These utilities will help you decompress the other files you download. WinZip decompresses files whose names end in ZIP. StuffIt Expander can decompress Mac files that end in HQX.

Downloading Helper Applications with Navigator

You'll learn all about using Navigator to copy files from the Internet in Chapter 11, "Grabbing Files with FTP." However, we can't wait that long. You need helper apps, and you need them now.

So, you've been to Stroud's or some other helper app warehouse, and you've followed a trail of links to the download site. Your mouse pointer is perched over the link for downloading the file you need. What do you do? The following steps guide you through the process:

1. Click the link for the helper application you want. One of the following will happen:

   ➤ If you're lucky, the link points directly to the helper application you need, and Navigator tries to connect to the server where the file is stored and download the file. You'll see the Save As dialog box, asking you where you want the file stored. If you see the Unknown File Type dialog box, instead, click on the Save File button to display the Save As dialog box.

   ➤ If you're somewhat lucky, you'll be transported to an FTP site and offered a list of files to choose from. Click the link for the file you want. You should now get the Unknown File Type or Save As dialog box.

➤ If your luck has run out, and the site is too busy, you'll receive an error message. You'll have to try again later, or backup to Stroud's List and try downloading a different helper app.

Grabbing files through Navigator.

If you see this dialog box, you're in business.

Click the file you want. ———

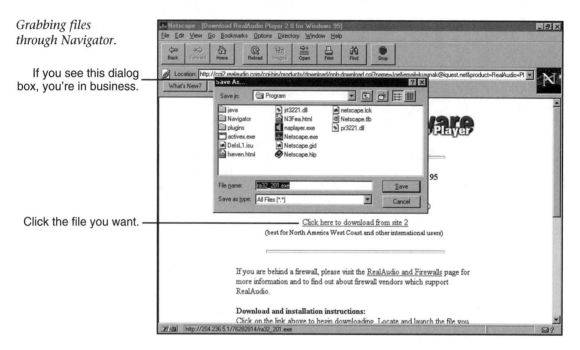

2. Use the dialog box to select the drive and folder in which you want to save the downloaded file, and then click **Save**. A dialog box appears, showing you the progress of the download.

3. Wait until the file is transferred to your computer (when the progress dialog box disappears).

4. Repeat these steps to download additional helper application files. If you were transported to an FTP site, you may have to use the **Back** button to go back to Stroud's List.

I'm not going to assume that everything proceeded as planned. If you couldn't connect to the computer that holds those precious helper application files, you have two options. You can try later (during the Letterman show, and at the crack of dawn are good times), or you can try downloading the files from somewhere else.

If you've tried several FTP sites, and you keep receiving error messages telling you that access has been denied, try typing your e-mail address and name in Navigator. Open the **Options** menu, select **Mail and News Preferences**, and click on the **Identity** tab. Type your name in the **Your Name** text box, and type your e-mail address in the **Your E-mail** text box. Click **OK**, and then try connecting to the FTP site. Many FTP sites require that you enter your e-mail address as a password.

Decompressing and Installing the Software

Some files you download come as self-extracting compressed files. These files end in EXE for PCs or SEA for Macs. To decompress the file, double-click on its name. The file decompresses itself and then usually runs an installation program that installs the application.

If the file ends in ZIP or HQX, you must use a decompression utility to unzip the file. In Windows, use WinZip. To install WinZip, first download the file and run it. WinZip comes as a self-extracting file that basically installs itself. To use WinZip to decompress your other files, take the following steps:

1. In Windows Explorer or File Manager, double-click on the zipped file you want to decompress. This runs WinZip. The WinZip window displays the names of all the files that are packed in the zipped file.

2. Click on the **Extract** button. The Extract dialog box appears, asking you to pick a folder or directory for the unzipped files.

3. Make sure **All Files** is selected, and then pick the drive and folder or directory into which you want the unzipped files placed.

4. Click the **Extract** button. WinZip decompresses the files and places them in the specified folder.

To decompress an HQX file using StuffIt Expander (for the Mac), drag the compressed file over the StuffIt Expander button, and release the mouse button. StuffIt Expander does the rest.

Once you've unzipped the helper application files you downloaded, read the installation instructions that came with each application for any quirky installation steps. (The instructions are usually in a file called README.TXT or INSTALL.TXT, which you can open in Windows Notepad or WordPad.) With some applications, you can simply unzip the application, create an icon for it, and start using it. Others may require that you run a separate Setup program (in File Manager or My Computer, look for a file called SETUP.EXE or INSTALL.EXE, and then double-click on it). When you're done, you should have an icon you can double-click to run the application.

Mapping Files to Their Helper Applications

I hate to break it to you, but installing the helper applications is only half the story. Now, you must tell Navigator which applications to run for each type of multimedia file you encounter on the Web. For example, if you click a movie link, Navigator must know whether it should run the audio player, the graphic viewer, or the movie player. You need to *associate* each file type you might encounter with a helper application that can load and play that file type.

You can associate program types to helper applications on the fly. If you click a link for a file that's not associated to a helper application, Navigator displays the Unknown File Type dialog box essentially saying, "What do you want me to do?" You can then click **Save to Disk** and worry about the file later, or click **Pick App** to associate this file type to a helper application. If you click **Pick App**, you're presented with the Configure External Viewer dialog box. Click the **Browse** button, and use the dialog box that appears to select the program file for the viewer (helper application) you want to use.

Where's Navigator's Audio Player?

Funny thing: Navigator may not know where its own audio player is located. In Windows 95, the Navigator installation program sticks the player in the Program Files/Netscape/Navigator/Program folder. You may have to associate AU files with this helper application.

If you don't like that idea, you can set up your helper applications ahead of time, and completely avoid the Unknown File Type dialog box. Navigator will automatically run the helper application when you try to load a file it cannot handle. To associate files, here's what you do:

1. Run Navigator (you don't have to be connected to the Web).

2. Open the **Options** menu and select **General Preferences**. The Preferences dialog box appears.

3. Click the **Helpers** tab. You now see the page of options you can select to specify how you want Navigator to handle various file types.

4. In the **File type** list, click the type of file you want to associate with a helper application. For example, you might click **video/mpeg** to associate MPEG video files with an MPEG Player. Here's a list of common file types and the helper applications that play them:

Extension	Helper Application
JPG	Lview
GIF	Lview
AVI	AviPro
MPG	MPEG
MP2	MPEG
AU	Naplayer (Netscape's sound player)
AIF	Naplayer
WAV	Windows Sound Recorder

5. Click inside the File Extensions text box, and type the file name extensions for any of the files you want this helper application to play. Leave out the periods, and separate the extensions with commas. For example, the names of most MPEG video files end in mpg, mpeg, or mpe. Navigator enters the most common file name extensions for you; just check to make sure.

6. Click the **Launch the Application** option. This tells Navigator that whenever you choose to load a file of this type, it should run the associated helper application.

7. Click the **Browse** button. The Select an appropriate viewer dialog box appears, prompting you to select the file that runs the helper application.

8. Change to the drive and folder (or directory) in which you installed the helper application.

9. In the file name list, click the executable program file (the file that launches the helper application), and then click the **Open** button. You are returned to the Preferences dialog box. In the **File type** list, under **Action**, the name of the specified helper application is inserted.

10. Repeat steps 4 to 9 to associate additional file types with their helper applications.

11. Click **OK** when you're done.

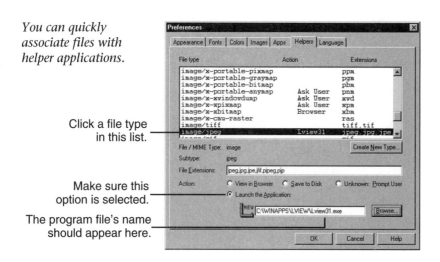

You can quickly associate files with helper applications.

Click a file type in this list.

Make sure this option is selected.

The program file's name should appear here.

Note the **View in Browser** option in the dialog box. This option tells Navigator to play the file itself. Navigator can play graphic files in the GIF or JPG format, but they won't look as clear as graphics displayed in a dedicated graphics program, such as LView Pro or Paint Shop Pro. This option is available only for certain file types. Navigator can't play video clips... yet.

Although the file type list includes most of the file types you'll commonly encounter on the Web—and then some—you may come across a file type that's not on the list and that requires a special helper application. In such a case, you can click the **Create New** button and create your own association. You'll get a dialog box asking for a Mime and Sub Mime type, which has nothing to do with Marcel Marceau.

MIME
Short for *Multi-purpose Internet Mail Extensions,* MIME is a protocol that controls all file transfers on the Web. Navigator uses MIME to recognize different file types.

Type the appropriate Mime and Sub Mime type in the text boxes. What's appropriate? The Mime type is the general type of file (audio, video, image). The Sub Mime type is a more specific abbreviation of the file type (for example, quicktime or jpeg). These entries don't matter much; they're more FYI (for your information). If Navigator can't recognize the Mime type of an incoming file, Navigator uses the file name extensions you enter to determine which helper application to run.

Click **OK** when you're done. You now have a new entry in the File Types list, and you can follow the previous steps to associate a helper application with the file type.

Playing Multimedia Links

Playing a multimedia link is as easy as clicking on the link. Navigator downloads the file and then runs the helper application, which loads and plays the file. All you have to do is sit back and watch.

Keep in mind that multimedia files can take loads of time to transfer, even if you have a direct (network) connection. The total time it takes depends on the speed of your connection, the size of the file, the amount of traffic on the server, the distance of the server from your computer, and the speed of your computer. Photos, graphics, video clips, and sound clips can be hefty. These files take a long time to transfer and consume a great deal of memory and disk space.

Saving Multimedia Files

Wait! Before you close that helper application, you might want to use the application's **File/Save** command to save the file to your disk. If you don't, when you close the application, you nuke the file. In Chapter 8, you'll learn how to save these files using Navigator.

Do It! Cinema, Sounds, and Photos

In your wanderings, you're sure to stumble across some Web sites that offer video and sound clips, photos, and on-screen art. Although I hate to spoil the thrill of discovery, I feel compelled to mention a few sites I stumbled across in my wanderings:

Internet Underground Music Archive: Stores sound clips of little-known bands. You can download short clips or entire songs.
http://www.iuma.com/

Kids Internet Delight (KID): Includes links to an MTV site and a movie database.
http://www.clark.net/pub/journalism/kid.html

MPEG Movie Archive: Contains animation clips, music videos, NASA images, auto racing pictures, and even clips of your favorite models.
http://www.eeb.ele.tue.nl/mpeg/index.html

Perry-Castaneda Library Map Collection: Offers maps of Africa, the United States, the Middle East, Europe, and maps of several major cities around the world.
http://rowan.lib.utexas.edu/Libs/PCL/Map_collection/Map_collection.html

Yahoo (a guide to the World Wide Web): Yahoo provides an index of cool Web sites, so you'll have to click a couple of links to get what you want. Click the **Entertainment** link, and then click **Comics**, **Multimedia**, or something else that catches your eye. You're sure to find some neat clips.
http://www.yahoo.com

You can download music clips of lesser-known artists.

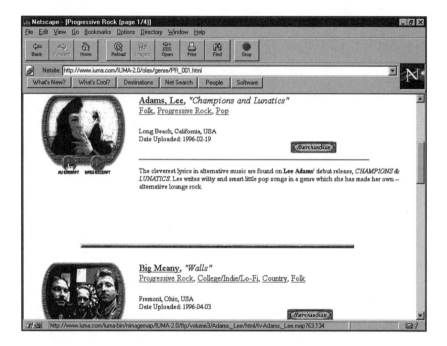

A Word About Sound and Video Quality

Eight-bit sound cards and standard VGA monitors just can't keep up with the sounds and clips stored on the Web. If you're still stuck with the old technology, maybe the Web will provide the incentive for you to upgrade.

If you have a Super VGA monitor and a 16-bit or better sound card, make sure they're set up to play at the highest quality. If you have your Super VGA monitor set to display only 16 colors, your pictures and video clips will look like snow storms. Make sure you set your monitor to display at least 256 colors. Also, check your sound card setup to make sure it's in 16-bit mode, stereo mode.

The Least You Need To Know

Now that you can watch movies and listen to sound clips, you probably already know everything you want to know. However, if you get bored with all that sensory stimulation, read the following review items:

➤ A helper application is a small, streamlined program that can play files which Navigator is incapable of playing.

➤ You might prefer using plug-ins instead. Skip to the next chapter to find out for yourself.

➤ To use a helper application, you have to get it, install it, and associate it with a specific file type.

➤ You can FTP from Navigator, but it's a big secret we won't talk about until Chapter 11.

➤ Assuming your helper applications are set up correctly, you can play a multimedia link simply by clicking on it.

➤ Sometimes, you're better off saving a file and then playing it later... especially if you get a juicy clip off one of the movie galleries.

Chapter 7

Beefing Up Navigator with Plug-Ins

By the End of This Chapter, You'll Be Able To...

➤ Increase Navigator's capabilities with plug-ins

➤ Shop for plug-ins from Stroud's List

➤ Install and uninstall plug-ins

➤ View virtual worlds with plug-ins and helper apps

In the previous chapter, you learn how to download and use helper apps to play file types that Navigator itself can't handle. If you were dazzled by all the helper apps available, and their capabilities, you probably overlooked the fact that these helper apps are a bit bulky and clunky.

Whenever you click on a link for a helper app, you wait while Navigator downloads the file, figures out which helper app it needs to play, and then opens the file in a separate window. If you click on many links that require helper apps, your screen starts to look like a game of 52-card pickup that got a little out of hand. And the Web starts to lose its appeal as a multimedia transport ship.

In this chapter, you'll learn how to use Navigator plug-ins to make playing media links in Navigator more transparent and smoother.

What Are Plug-Ins?

The helper app idea is an Internet version of division of labor. The Web browser specializes in displaying HTML pages, and each helper app plays its own special type of file. However, with the current trend toward downsizing, people started to think that they could eliminate the tasks that the helper apps were performing and make the Web browser do all the work.

The problem is that if you build all those capabilities into the Web browser, you're going to end up with a huge program that's barely able to creep along the Web, let alone cruise it. And it would take a couple days to download over a standard modem connection. Another problem is that if you ever had to update the helper app part of the browser, you'd have to scrap the entire browser.

To overcome these problems, developers came up with the notion of *plug-ins*, little gadgets that you can plug into the Web browser and easily update or remove later. The plug-in becomes an integral part of the browser. Because plug-ins typically provide fewer controls and rely on the browser for much of the display work, they're leaner and more transparent than their half-brother helper apps.

Gobs of Plug-Ins

Because Navigator is the most popular Web browser around, developers have gone wild creating plug-ins for it. Almost every helper app listed in Chapter 6 has a comparable Netscape Navigator plug-in. If you were using a less popular browser, such as Mosaic, you wouldn't find the same selection of plug-ins.

Finding Plug-Ins on the Internet

The best place to look for plug-ins on the Web is the same place you looked to find helper apps: Stroud's List. To go to Stroud's list, fire up Navigator and enter **http://www.stroud.com** in the **Location** text box. When you get there, click on the big Stroud graphic at the top of the page. Then, scroll down the page until you see the Main Menu, as shown in the following figure. (Another good place to grab plug-ins is Tucows at http://www.tucows.com.)

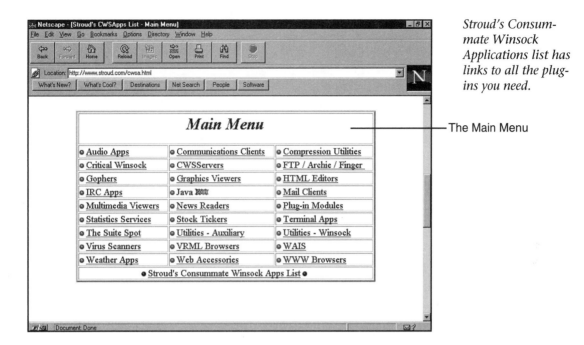

Stroud's Consummate Winsock Applications list has links to all the plug-ins you need.

——The Main Menu

Can't Load Stroud's?

Stroud's List is a busy place. If you can't connect to the original site at http://www.stroud.com, you might have to connect to a clone site. Go to Yahoo (http://www.yahoo.com) and search for **stroud's**. You'll get a list of sites longer than your arm. Click on the link for the site nearest you. (Some sites may look a little different from the Stroud's main site.)

From the Main Menu, click on the **Plug-in Modules** link. This takes you to a page that lists common plug-in modules. As of the writing of this book, all the plug-in modules listed were for Netscape Navigator. However, as Internet Explorer 3.0 becomes more popular, you might see links for Internet Explorer plug-ins. Make sure you get the Navigator plug-in.

75

Make sure the
plug-in is for
Netscape Navigator.

*Stroud's has an
entire page full of
useful plug-in
modules.*

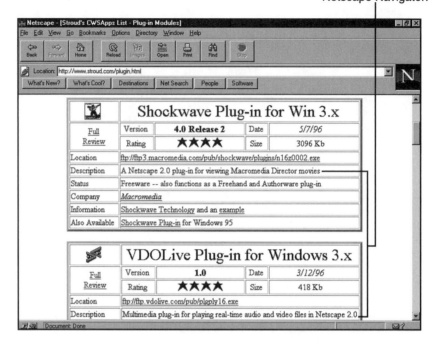

Although the Plug-in page offers links to many of the most popular Navigator plug-ins, the list is not very comprehensive. For example, the list does not include the plug-in version of FigLeaf, a graphics viewer that comes both as a helper app and plug-in. If you're looking for a plug-in version of one of your favorite helper apps, go back to Stroud's Main Menu, and click on a link for an application category. For example, you might click on Audio Apps for a sound player, Graphics Viewers for an image viewer, or Multimedia Viewers for video players. You might have to go to the app's information page to find out whether it is offered as a plug-in.

Stroud's list also rates the plug-ins, indicates whether the plug-in has been tested, and shows the size of the file you're about to download. Be sure to check out this information before downloading. You don't want to download a 4 megabyte file only to find out that it's not what you expected.

To read a brief review of the product and compare it to other products in its category, click on the **Full Review** link. When you find a plug-in you want, click on the Location link to download it. Many Location links don't function properly from Stroud's. Many companies want you to fill out a form with your name and e-mail address before you download the file.

If you have trouble connecting with the Location link, click on the link next to **Information**. This usually connects you to the product's home page, where you can find a link for the plug-in.

Netscape's Plug-In Page

Another good place to find out about the latest Navigator plug-ins is at Netscape. Open Navigator's **Help** menu, and select **About Plug-ins**. At the top of the page is a link called **click here** that takes you to a page that has links to plug-ins.

Installing and Uninstalling Plug-Ins

The best part about plug-ins is that you don't have to mess with file associations. You install the plug-in, and Navigator takes care of the rest. Yes, that's right, no more MIME/SUBMIME/PANTOMIME/MARCEL MARCEU garbage. You plug it in, and it works.

The only trouble is that plug-ins do supplant your helper apps and any other plug-in designed to handle the same file type. So, if you install the plug-in and you decide you'd rather use a helper app instead, you have to uninstall the plug in (fairly easy), and then reassociate the file type with your helper app (a pain).

Installing a Plug-In

Installing a plug-in is easy. When you download the plug-in, you end up with a self-extracting, usually self-installing file on your hard drive. Before running the file, shut down Navigator. While you're at it, close your other programs, too, just in case anything bombs during the installation. In most cases, you can run the self-extracting, self-installing file, follow the on-screen instructions, and you're done.

In a few cases, the self-extracting file might not be self-installing. After decompressing the file, you may have to go into the directory where the extracted files are stored and run **Setup.exe** or **Install.exe**. If you extract a file, and it places DISK directories on your drive (disk1, disk2, disk3, and so on), the DISK1 directory usually contains the Setup or Install file.

Most plug-ins can install themselves.

Follow the on-screen installation instructions.

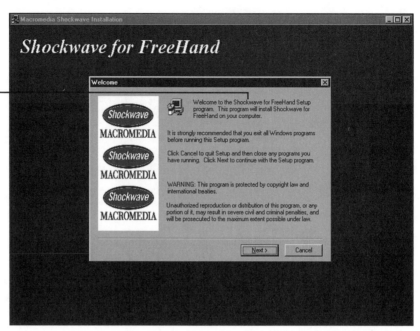

Delete the Original File

When you're done installing the plug-in, you can delete the file you downloaded and the installation files. However, before doing this, you might want to keep the original file you downloaded for awhile, until you are sure the plug-in works. You might also want to keep the original file so you can try out different plug-ins and then install the best plug-in.

Uninstalling Plug-Ins

Plug-ins typically come with their own uninstall utility. To remove a plug-in in Windows 95, open the **Control Panel**, and double-click on the **Add/Remove Programs** icon. Click on the name of the plug-in you want to uninstall, as shown in the following figure, and then click on the **Add/Remove** button.

Windows 3.1 does not have an Add/Remove Programs feature, so you'll have to rely on the plug-in's uninstall utility. Change to the directory that contains the plug-in's program files, and double-click on its uninstall icon. Follow the on-screen instructions to complete the operation.

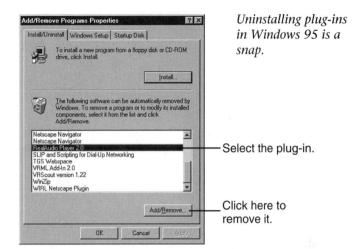

Uninstalling plug-ins in Windows 95 is a snap.

Select the plug-in.

Click here to remove it.

Which Plug-Ins Are Installed?

To find out which plug-ins are installed, open Navigator's **Help** menu and click on **About Plug-ins**. A page appears, listing all the plug-ins you've installed, including information about which file extensions they're linked to.

Listening to Real-Time Audio

Real-time audio is sort of a misnomer. You'd think that with real-time audio, you could plug into a radio station on the Web, and listen while deejays juggle their favorite tunes. That's not quite what real-time audio is all about.

Real-time audio simply lets you start listening to a sound clip before the clip has *completely* downloaded to your computer. As soon as the clip starts reaching your computer, a real-time audio player can start playing it. The audio clip isn't live. There's always at least a couple seconds delay between the time the clip is recorded, placed on a Web site, and downloaded to your computer. Usually, the delay is much longer.

Even though real-time audio may not live up to the vision you have of it (what does, really?), it is fun to play with, and it has inspired several broadcasting companies to place their recordings on the Web.

The Standard Metaphor

Real-time audio is more like a CD player than it is like an AM/FM radio. You click on an audio link, and it begins to play.

Grabbing a Real-Time Audio Plug-In

One of the most popular real-time audio plug-ins for Navigator is RealAudio, available at **http://www.realaudio.com/**. This URL calls up RealAudio's home page, where you'll find a link for downloading RealAudio Player. Don't look for a link for the plug-in version, because one RealAudio file contains the files needed for both the plug-in and helper app version.

Before you can download the file, RealAudio requests your name and e-mail address. You'll also need to supply information about your computer, including the operating system you're using, the type of processor, and your Internet connection speed.

Although RealAudio is one of the best real-time audio players around, there are others. If you have the time, check out the following players (Crescendo isn't a real-time audio player, but I thought I'd throw it in there anyway):

TrueSpeech: Comparable to RealAudio, TrueSpeech delivers real-time audio to your computer. You can get a copy at **http://www.dspg.com/**.

Internet Wave: Internet Wave is another real-time audio player that comes with an added bonus: a free evaluation copy of Internet Phone, a program that allows you to make long-distance voice calls without paying long-distance phone bills. (It's not as easy as it sounds, but the concept is interesting.) Catch the Wave at **http://www.vocaltec.com/home.htm**.

Crescendo: This audio plug-in from LiveUpdate plays MIDI (Musical Instrument Digital Interface) files. MIDI files contain codes that tell your sound card how to create a music clip. Although MIDI files cannot store voice recordings, they can store elevator music versions of your favorite tunes. You can get the Crescendo plug-in at **http://www.liveupdate.com/dl.html**. After installing it, visit the MIDI Jukebox at: **http://www.pensacola.com/~sunstar/jukebox.html**.

Sound Card Required

To use most audio players, you need a sound card with speakers. If you don't have a sound card, buy one. If you're too poor (or too cheap), you can pick up a PC Speaker driver that boosts the speaker that's built-in to your computer. However, the PC speaker is no match for a good, stereo sound card, and the driver may not work with some audio players. Pick up the PC speaker driver at **http://www.ncsa.uiuc.edu/SDG/Software/WinMosaic/Viewers/Speak.htm**.

Installing and Using RealAudio

After you've downloaded the RealAudio file, run the file, and follow the on-screen installation instructions to install it. You'll be given the option of installing RealAudio as a plug-in or helper app. Be sure to install it as a plug-in.

After installing, go back to RealAudio's home page, where you'll find links to real-time sound recordings at NPR, ABC, PBS, and other broadcasting sites. Use these links to test out your new plug-in. The RealAudio player appears, as shown below. You can use the Pause/Play and Stop buttons to control the playback. Drag the Volume slider at the right up or down to increase or decrease the volume.

Pause/Play —

Stop —

You can control the playback and volume.

— Volume

Watching Real-Time Video

Like real-time audio, real-time video allows you to start playing a video clip before it has been completely downloaded. Although the video clips you're watching aren't genuinely live, you get the impression that they are, and you get video on demand.

Navigator itself doesn't support real-time video, but there are several plug-ins that do. In the following sections, you'll learn how to download one of these plug-ins (StreamWorks) and use it to start viewing video clips on the Web.

Snatching and Installing a Real-Time Video Player

One of the most popular and powerful real-time video players on the Web is VDOLive. This plug-in allows Navigator to download and play both real-time video *and* audio files. The main attraction of VDOLive is that you'll find lots of files on the Web that VDOLive can handle. In addition, VDOLive is one of the best performing real-time video players available, allowing you to experience real-time video even over a relatively slow 14.4 Kbps modem connection.

To download a copy of the VDOLive plug-in, connect to VDO's Web page at **http:// www.vdolive.com/download/**. From this page, click on the **VDO Live Video Player** icon, and follow the trail of links and download instructions to copy the file (plgply32.exe).

Once you have the file on your hard drive, run it, and follow the on-screen installation instructions.

If after trying VDOLive, you want to test some other video players, download one or more of the following players. They don't all offer live video, but some provide support for additional file types that VDOLive may not be able to handle.

NET TOOB: NET TOOB is a high-performance video player that offers support for a wide range of video file types, including MPEG, AVI, QuickTime, FLC/FLI, and real-time audio and video files. You can download NET TOOB at **http:// www.duplexx.com**. After installing NET TOOB, return to this site for some demo clips.

StreamWorks: From Xing Technologies, StreamWorks is a capable real-time audio and video player. Although a bit on the slow side, StreamWorks is a decent choice for users who have a 28.8 Kbps modem connection or faster. You can pick up StreamWorks at **http://204.62.160.251/sw-winclient/info/dl_winclient.shtml**.

VMPEG Lite: Although it doesn't offer support for a wide variety of video formats, VMPEG Lite is one of the best viewers for MPG video. You can download a copy from **ftp://papa.indstate.edu/winsock-l/Windows95/Graphics/vmpeg17.exe**. (You'll learn more about FTP in chapter 11.)

Playing Real-Time Video Clips with VDOLive

Once you've installed VDOLive, return to VDO's home page at **http:// www.vdolive.com/**, where you will find links to movie clips that VDOLive can play. Follow the trail of links to a video clip that catches your eye, and click on it. The figure below shows a video clip from the movie *Casino*. Yes, these movie clips are as dark and dinky as the ones you get off your CD, and as choppy, but it's video on demand, so jump up and down, act real excited, and then go out and rent the movie.

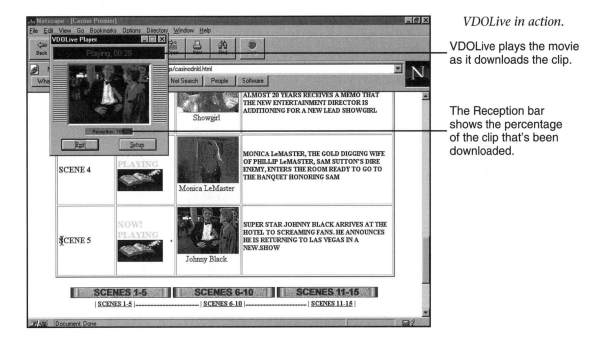

VDOLive in action.

VDOLive plays the movie as it downloads the clip.

The Reception bar shows the percentage of the clip that's been downloaded.

Exploring Virtual Worlds

The most exciting innovation on the Web is VRML (pronounced "vermal" and short for Virtual Reality Modeling Language). VRML allows developers to create three-dimensional worlds you can explore. Instead of connecting to a two-dimensional Web page, where you experience only text and snapshots on a flat screen, VRML allows you to walk through three-dimensional worlds.

Most of the current VRML offerings are not very impressive. Some simply display a cylinder or cube that you can spin in space. Other worlds, however, offer complete landscapes that you can walk or fly through, examining objects along the way. Still other sites present hotlinks, where you can click on an object to fly off to another VRML world or connect to a standard HTML Web page.

The future of VRML and technologies like it is impressive. Developers are quickly working to develop three-dimensional chat rooms, shopping centers, offices, and probably even red-light districts, where Internet users can explore, work, and have fun.

The following sections show you how to use one of the most powerful VRML Navigator plug-ins on the Web—WIRL. For details about maneuvering in WIRL, and for a list of alternative VRML players, see Chapter 18, "Becoming a Java (and VRML) Junkie." In Chapter 18, you'll also learn how to use Netscape's hot new real-time VRML player, Live3D.

Downloading and Installing WIRL

One of the newest and best VRML viewers on the Web is WIRL, and you can download it at **http://www.vream.com/3wirl.html**. This is a fairly hefty file, so it takes about 30 minutes to download over a 28.8 Kbps connection. Be sure to download the file into a temporary directory; do not download it to the main Netscape Navigator directory.

The file you downloaded is a self-extracting compressed file. First, exit Navigator. Then, run the file to decompress it, and follow the on-screen instructions to complete the installation. At some point, the installation program will ask you where Netscape Navigator is located on your computer (assuming that the installation program can't find the file). Use the resulting dialog box to find and pick the Netscape.exe file.

When the installation is complete, a dialog box appears, asking if you want to launch WIRL. If you select Yes, Navigator starts, connects to WIRL's demo page, and displays a sample world.

Exploring VRML Worlds with WIRL

Once you've installed WIRL, all you have to do is click on a link for a VRML file. The names of these files typically end with the WRL extension. If the URLs for VRML worlds don't immediately come to mind, check back at http://www.vream.com/3wirl.html for links to 3D demos. The following figure shows one of these demos being played in WIRL.

At the bottom of the Navigator window are the WIRL control buttons. To walk through virtual space, click on the running man button, and then drag inside the viewing area. To move the object, click on the hand button and drag in the viewing area.

The buttons on the right side of the toolbar act a little differently. To maneuver with these buttons, rest the mouse pointer on the desired button (a description of the button appears), and then hold down the mouse button. A small control pad pops up. Drag the mouse over the arrows on the control pad to move through space, change your perspective, or manipulate the object.

You can play with virtual worlds off-line by entering Navigator's **File/Open File** command, and selecting the **Worlds.htm** file in the **VREAM/WIRL** directory. This displays a page full of links to virtual worlds that are included with WIRL. The second figure on the next page shows a cool virtual piano you can play by clicking on the keys.

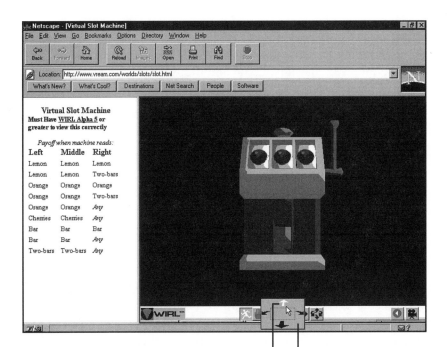

WIRL plays a 3D demo.

Drag the mouse over the desired arrow or control.

Hold down the mouse button on a button to display the control pad.

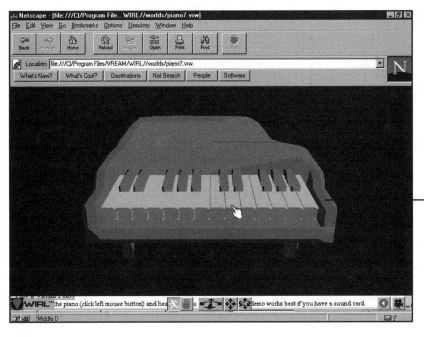

You can view the virtual piano at WIRL's Demo Page.

Don't miss the virtual piano.

Getting Shocked!

Multimedia presentations have become the latest time-wasting device in corporate America. Media specialists, middle management, and ambitious hourlies are all trying to impress each other with their fancy presentations and multimedia training programs, while the Japanese figure out better ways to build cars.

Okay, okay, I'll get off the soap box.

At any rate, multimedia presentations have finally hit the Web. A company called Macromedia, maker of programs such as Macromedia Director and FreeHand, have made it possible for multimedia developers to quickly and easily publish their presentations electronically on the Web. Along with its superior file-compression technology, Macromedia presentations are becoming more popular and more accessible.

Downloading and Installing Shockwave

To view Macromedia presentations on the Web, you need a special program called Shockwave, which Macromedia offers for free. You can find the beginning of the download link trail on Macromedia's home page at **http://www.macromedia.com/Tools/ Shockwave/**. Once you've found a link for downloading the file, click on it, specify the directory in which you want the file stored, and then wait patiently while Navigator downloads it.

This gives you a self-extracting file. Run it. After the file extracts itself, you should have three new directories on your hard drive: Authware, Director, and FreeHand. Each directory contains its own Setup.exe file. (You need a separate plug-in to play AuthorWare, Director, and Freehand files.)

Exit Navigator, and then poke around on your computer to find out where Navigator's executable program file is stored. This is usually one of the following folders or directories:

      Windows 3.1: C:\NETSCAPE

      Windows 95: C:\Program Files\Netscape\Navigator\Program\

Make a note of the directory, and during the installation steps, make sure that Shockwave installs its plug-ins in this same directory. If you install the plug-ins in a different directory, Navigator may not be able to find them when it encounters a Shockwave file.

Once you've figured out the location of Navigator's program file, run the Setup file in each of the new Shockwave directories, and follow the on-screen instructions to complete the installation.

Playing with Shockwave

Once you've installed Shockwave, fire up Navigator and return to Macromedia's home page at **http://www.macromedia.com/Tools/Shockwave/**. Here, you'll find a link for a list of sites that have Shockwave demos. The following figure shows the Mission Impossible site.

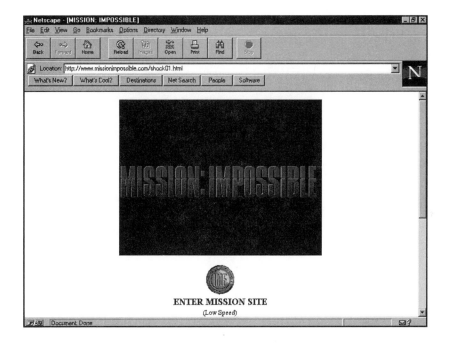

This site is based on the movie version of Mission Impossible.

No Macromedia sites will look the same. The presentation (or "movie"), not Shockwave, determines the controls displayed. When you visit shocked sites, be prepared to be... er... shocked.

The Least You Need To Know

If you have lots of free hard disk space and a couple days off work, you can have fun with plug-ins. Just remember that you can get most of the plug-ins you need from **http://www.stroud.com** or one of the mirror sites. After you download a file, run it; this decompresses the file and installs it. Oh yeah, one last thing: in most cases, you can return to the site from which you downloaded the plug-in to play some demos specially designed for that plug-in.

In the next chapter, you get to do more mundane activities, such as saving files and printing them.

Chapter 8

Saving and Printing Your Finds

By the End of This Chapter, You'll Be Able To...

➤ Save multimedia files to disk for your future enjoyment

➤ Save a hyperdocument and open it later

➤ Print a hyperdocument and make some minor page adjustments

➤ Take a behind-the-scenes look at a hyperdocument

The Web is like some big computerized flea market. You snake through the aisles picking up interesting facts, stories, bits of poetry and fiction, movie clips, sound clips, and even the occasional picture of your favorite actor or actress. You pull this stuff up in Navigator or in a helper app, give it a quick look, and then like some overstimulated kid at Christmas, you drop the item to hurry to another site.

But then it happens. You find it. A movie clip that sucks the breath right out of you. A document that answers your most profound questions. You gotta have it. What do you do? In this chapter, you'll learn various ways to preserve the treasures you discover on the Web. You'll learn how to save all your discoveries, print your favorite documents, and even see the skeletons that hang behind the HTML documents.

Saving and Playing Clips and Pictures

The method of choice on the Web is to grab the loot, disconnect, and then play with the newly acquired toys later. If you have an Internet service provider who charges by the hour, you don't want to waste precious time viewing clips while you're still connected. Besides, it's considered bad manners to loiter at Web sites; other users are trying to connect.

There are a couple ways to download files (copy files to your hard disk) on the Web. Here's my personal favorite: Right-click the link for the item you want, and then click the **Save Link as** or **Save Image as** option. This opens the Save As dialog box, which prompts you to select the drive and folder (or directory) in which you want to save the file. You can also give the file a new name. Make the appropriate selections, and then click **Save**. The reason I like this method is that it gives you the greatest flexibility: You can click to view, or right-click to download. You don't have to worry about setting any options.

Right-click a link to display the shortcut menu.

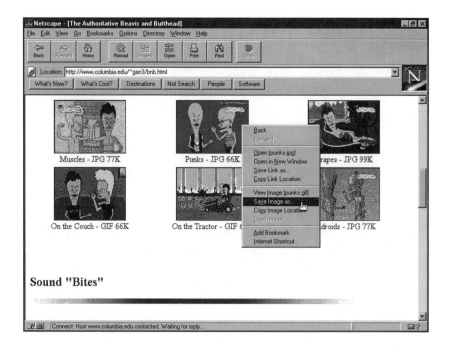

My second favorite method for saving clips and pictures is to use the helper app or plug-in. Click the link to open the file in the helper application, and then use the helper application's **File/Save** command to save the file. With this method, you don't have to make any long-term commitments. You get to preview the clip before you save it to disk. Some helper applications, such as Navigator's audio player, save the file automatically in your TEMP folder or directory, and offer no **File/Save** option. Other applications will play the file, disappear, and dump the file.

If you become a serious download junkie, there's one more approach to downloading files that might appeal to you. Remember in Chapter 6 where you associated particular file types to helper applications? Well, there's an option in the Preferences dialog box (on the Helpers tab) called Save to Disk. Instead of associating a file type to an application, simply click the file type, and then click **Save to Disk**. Whenever you click a link for this file type, Navigator will display the Save As dialog box, prompting you to specify where you want the file saved.

Reassociating File Types

If you turn on the **Save to Disk** option for a particular file type, you entirely foul up the association with the helper application. If you decide later that you want to associate a file type with its helper application, skip back to Chapter 6.

Once you've saved a file to disk, you can open the file and play it in one of your helper applications. Run the helper application, and use its **File/Open** command as you would in any application. Then, if you have a sound or movie, use the application's controls (they'll vary, of course) to play the file.

What About Hyperdocuments?

Ever wonder what's behind one of those hyperdocuments? I'll show you. Load your favorite page. Now open the **View** menu and select **Document Source**. You should see something like the hyperdocument pictured here. Not much to look at, eh? This is the original HTML document that's stored on the server. All those bracketed codes tell Navigator how to display the document without turning you to stone.

Behind the scenes with a hyperdocument.

```
Netscape - [Source of: http://www.indiana.edu/~kglowack/Athens/Athens.html]

<HTML>
<HEAD>
<TITLE>Ancient City of Athens</TITLE>
</HEAD>
<BODY>
<H1>The Ancient City of Athens</H1>
<img src="http://www.indiana.edu/~kglowack/Athens/City.GIF" alt="">
<P>
<H4>All images ©1995 by Kevin T. Glowacki & Nancy L. Klein
<BR>Department of Classical Studies
<BR>Indiana University, Bloomington, In 47405</H4>
<HR>
<B>THE ANCIENT CITY OF ATHENS</B> is a photographic archive of the archaeological and architectu
<P>
<i>©Copyright</i>
<BR>All of the images presented here are from the personal slide collection of Kevin T. Glowacki
<P>
<UL>
<B>
<LI><A HREF="http://www.indiana.edu/iub/">Indiana University Bloomington Home Page</A>
<LI><A HREF="http://www.indiana.edu/~classics/home.html">IU Classical Studies Home Page</A>
<LI><A HREF="http://www.indiana.edu/~classics/AIA/AIA.html">Archaeological Institute of America,
<LI><A HREF="http://www.indiana.edu/~classics/AIA/internet/internet.html">Archaeological Resourc
</B>
</UL>
<HR>
<H2>Topography & Monuments of Ancient Athens</H2>
<UL>
<P>

<A HREF="http://www.indiana.edu/~kglowack/Athens/keram.html"><IMG SRC="http://www.indiana.edu/~k
<LI><A HREF="http://www.indiana.edu/~kglowack/Athens/keram.html">The Kerameikos: </A> Kerameikos
<P>
```

Why would anyone ever want to view one of these documents? Two reasons. First, sometimes, there's a rebel URL in the background (one with a typo in it). You click the link (which you can see), but the URL (which you can't see) isn't pointing to the page you want to go to. In such a case, you can enter the **View/Document Source** command to take a peek at the URL. You can even highlight the URL (by dragging over it), and then copy it (by pressing **Ctrl+C**). Then, close the View Source window, click inside the **Location** text box, and paste (**Ctrl+V**) the URL. You can then edit the URL to correct it (assuming it has an obvious typo).

The other reason you might want to view a source document is to learn how to code a hyperdocument (which can come in handy when you design your own home page in Chapter 20).

You can also save hyperdocuments as hyperdocuments or as text files, but don't expect too much. In Navigator, you might see a Web page with a bunch of fancy graphics, but when you save the file, all you're getting are the text and/or codes that appear on the page. Now that you've been warned, you can take the following steps to save a Web page:

1. Display the Web document you want to save.

2. Open the **File** menu, and select **Save As** (or press **Ctrl+S**). The Save As dialog box appears, prompting you to specify a drive and folder or directory.

3. Select the drive and folder in which you want the file saved.

4. To change the name of the file (you don't have to), drag over the entry in the **File name** text box, and type the desired file name.

5. Open the **Save as type** drop-down list, and click the desired format in which you want the file saved:

    > **Source (*.htm,*.html)** retains all the Web page codes that were inserted in the file. You can then open the file in Navigator, and it will look something like a Web page (minus the cool graphics).

    > **Plain text (*.txt)** strips out all the Web page codes and saves just the text. This is good if you find some text that you want to paste into a document you're creating (for example, to lift a quote).

6. Click **Save**. The file is saved in the specified format and is stored in the drive and folder you selected.

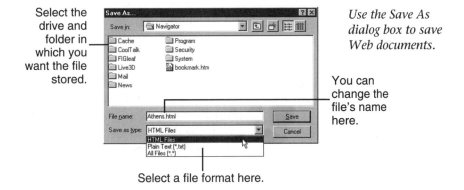

Select the drive and folder in which you want the file stored.

Use the Save As dialog box to save Web documents.

You can change the file's name here.

Select a file format here.

Taking a Peek at the Locals

Your computer has files too, you know, and Navigator can open them for you… assuming they are HTML (Web) or text documents, or that you set up a file association for that file type. (This makes it convenient to view files that you downloaded earlier.) To open a file that's on your hard disk, open the **File** menu and select **Open File** (or press **Ctrl+O**). Specify the location and name of the file you want to open (you can list all files in the folder by selecting **All Files (*.*)** from the **Files of type** drop-down list). Click **Open**.

If you select a file that's associated to another (helper) application, Navigator runs that application, which then loads and plays the selected file. If you select an HTML or text document, Navigator opens it just as if it were stored on a Web server. If the HTML document contains links, you can click those links to open them (assuming you are connected to the Internet with your TCP/IP software).

Making Paper—Printing

The World Wide Web is as close to paperless electronic publishing as you can get. However, you might encounter a document you want to print: maybe a Navigator help screen or an interesting quote or story. There's no trick to printing a document from Navigator. Simply display the Web document you want to print, open the **File** menu, select **Print**, and answer the dialog box that appears.

If you want to get fancy about printing, however, you can do more. You can select some page setup options to specify how you want the document to be positioned on the page and to indicate the type of information you want printed (the page's URL, for example). You might also want to preview the page before you print it. The following sections explain all this in detail.

Entering Your Page Preferences

Check This Out...

More Control If you want more control over the printing, go into your Windows printer setup (in the Windows Control Panel), and enter the desired settings.

If you print a Web document now, you get a basic 8.5-by-11-inch page with a header and footer, and half-inch margins all around. However, you can change the page settings to reposition the text on the page or select the type of information you want printed in the header and footer.

To change the page settings, open the **File** menu and select **Page Setup**. The Page Setup dialog box appears. The settings are fairly self-explanatory, so I'm not going to bore you with the details. Just enter the desired settings, and then click **OK**.

Previewing Pages Before You Print

You can never be sure how a Web page will appear in print. Will the sparkling graphics you see on your screen transfer to paper? How will the lines and bulleted lists look? In Navigator, you can quickly see how a page will appear in print by opening the **File** menu and selecting **Print Preview**. This opens the Print Preview screen, which displays the first page of the current Web document. You can then click the following buttons to control the page display:

> **Print**   Opens the Print dialog box, which allows you to send the document to your printer. Enter your print settings, and then click **OK**.

Next Page   Displays the next page of the document (assuming the Web document consists of more than one page).

Prev Page   Opens the previous page of the document, if you clicked on the **Next Page** button.

Two Page   Displays two pages of the document side-by-side.

Zoom In   Makes the page bigger, showing more detail. You can also zoom in by moving the mouse pointer over the area you want to see in more detail and then clicking the mouse button.

Zoom Out   Returns the page to its smaller view, giving you a bird's eye view of the page.

Close   Closes this window and returns you to the Navigator window. Be sure to use this button rather than the Close button in the title bar; otherwise, you'll close Navigator altogether.

Enter the desired page settings.

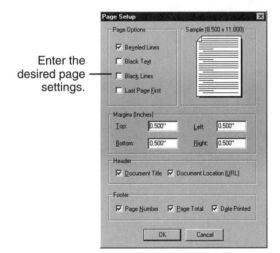

You can control how Navigator prints the page.

Be sure you click this Close
button to return to Navigator.

*You can preview a
document before
printing it.*

The mouse pointer
lets you zoom in on
an area of the page.

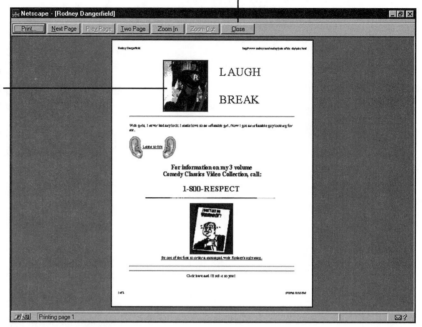

The Least You Need To Know

As you ready yourself for a download binge, try to remember the following:

➤ To quickly download a file, right-click its link, and then click the **Save** option.

➤ If you plan on downloading several files, open the Preferences dialog box, and turn on **Save to Disk** for the file type you want to download (instead of view).

➤ To view a coded hyperdocument, open the **View** menu and select **Document Source**.

➤ To open files stored on your hard disk, open the **File** menu and select **Open File**.

➤ To print a hyperdocument, open the **File** menu and select **Print**.

Chapter 9

Corresponding with Electronic Mail

By the End of This Chapter, You'll Be Able To...

➤ Send a letter without licking a postage stamp

➤ Put your e-mail address on your business card

➤ Grab mail from your mailbox

➤ Write to a Webmaster to offer suggestions

The U.S. Postal Service has made all sorts of improvements in an attempt to make their service more attractive. You want me to name one? Okay, they released the Marilyn Monroe stamp. Oh yeah, and they came out with those self-adhesive stamps, so you can still taste your coffee after applying the stamp.

But the mail is still slow. A letter you send today usually takes several days to reach its destination. Fortunately, the Internet has provided an alternative: *electronic mail* (*e-mail* for short). This postage-free alternative sends e-mail across the states, or to the other side of the world, in a matter of minutes or hours instead of days. In this chapter, you'll learn how to send and receive e-mail directly from Navigator.

You Have To Set It Up First

As with anything on the Internet, e-mail requires some setup before you can use it. You have to enter your return address, specify an e-mail server (sort of like a P.O. Box number), and enter your name. Although this takes a little longer than it takes to lick a postage stamp, it's almost as easy (and you only have to do it once).

To enter the necessary e-mail information, open the **Options** menu and click **Mail and News Preferences**. The Preferences dialog box pops up on your screen. Click the **Appearance** tab, and change any of the settings to control the way messages appear. The only tricky option here is the Fixed Width Font or Variable Width Font. A fixed width font gives each character the same amount of space, an anorexic "i" gets the same space as a corpulent "m." A variable width font gives each character the room it needs.

Next, click the **Composition** tab, and change any of the following options to specify how you want mail and newsgroup messages handled:

> **Send and Post** allows you to specify the type of file transfer protocol to use for mail messages. **8-bit** handles most types of mail servers. If you have trouble transferring a particular mail message, try changing this to **Mime Compliant**.

> **Mail Messages** lets you specify an e-mail address of someone to whom you want to send a copy of all your e-mail correspondence. You can leave this blank for now.

> **News Messages** lets you specify an e-mail address of someone to whom you want to send a copy of all the messages you post to newsgroups. Again, you can safely leave this blank.

> **Mail File** and **News File** allow you to specify a file in which to save the mail you send and the messages you post to a newsgroup. This file does not need to exist. Just type a path to the folder in which you want the file saved followed by the file's name (no extension is needed).

> **Automatically quote original message when replying** tells Netscape Mail to insert a copy of the original message in your reply. Mail inserts an angle bracket (>) before each line in the copied message to indicate that it's a quote. This helps the recipient remember what he sent to you. If you turn this off, you can still insert a copy of the original message in your reply by clicking on the **Quote** button.

Now, for the important options. Click the **Servers** tab, and enter the following information:

> **Outgoing Mail (SMTP) Server**   The name of your e-mail post office, which is on your service provider's computer. You should have received this name from your

service provider, and it should look something like **iway.com** or **mail.iway.com**. If you are unsure of this, call your service provider.

Incoming Mail (POP) Server   The name of your service provider's POP (Post Office Protocol) server. This name usually starts with pop, as in **pop.iway.com**.

POP User Name   This is the part of your e-mail address to the left of the @ sign. Don't enter the @ sign or any information to the right of it.

Maximum Message Size   Keep this set to **None**. If you decide later to limit the size of messages you receive, you can select the Size option, and then type the maximum size (in kilobytes) of incoming messages. Any part of the message over the limit will be kept on your mail server. This setting helps prevent you from getting huge mail messages from practical jokers who want to mess up your hard drive.

Mail Directory   The path to the folder on your hard drive in which you want incoming mail messages stored. Initially, Navigator is set up to use the Program Files/Netscape/Navigator/Mail folder, but you can change it.

Removed from the server and **Left on the server**   Allow you to specify whether you want messages deleted from your server's computer after Navigator retrieves them. Keep this set to **Left on the server** until you're sure that this e-mail thing works. Later, change this to **Remove from the server**, so you don't clutter your service provider's computer with your junk mail.

Check for Mail   Netscape Mail is set up to automatically check for mail every 10 minutes (assuming you're connected to the Internet). If you prefer to check for mail manually, set this option to **Never**.

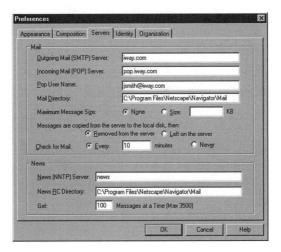

Before you can use e-mail, you need to enter some informa-tion about yourself.

Only two tabs left. Click the **Identity** tab to enter the following information about yourself:

> **Your Name** is your name, duh.
>
> **Your Email** is the e-mail address assigned to you by your service provider. This usually consists of your username followed by the @ sign, followed by the server name (for example, **jsmith@iway.com**).
>
> **Reply-to Address** is the e-mail address that will appear when you post messages to newsgroups. Leave this blank for now.
>
> **Your Organization** is an optional entry. You can type the name of your company or just leave the text box blank. If you plan on insulting someone through e-mail, don't link your company with the insult.
>
> **Signature File** is another optional entry. A signature file is a small text file that is automatically attached to the end of the letters you send. It can include your name, address, and phone number, your e-mail address, and any interesting quips you want to add. You can create the file in Windows Notepad or your word processor, and save it as a text file. Then, use the **Browse** button on this tab to tell Navigator where the file lives.

Finally, click the **Organization** tab. This tab contains options that tell Navigator how to sort your e-mail messages. The sort options are fairly straightforward; you can sort messages by date, subject entry, or the name of the sender. You can also have mail and news messages *threaded*. If you turn on the threading options, you'll see a copy of the message you sent whenever someone sends you a response to your message. This is good if you have Alzheimer's. When you're done setting your options, click **OK**.

You're now ready to e-mail!

Pronouncing an E-Mail Address

If you want to be cool, you have to be able to pronounce your e-mail address properly. If your address is jsmith@weidner.cyber.edu, you would say, "jsmith at weidner dot cyber dot edu." Just remember that @ = "at" and . = "dot." E-mail addresses are usually in lowercase, so you don't have to specify case unless one or more characters is uppercase.

Writing (and Sending) an E-Mail Message

Once you've entered your e-mail settings, you can start churning out e-mail messages. Open the **File** menu and click **New Mail Message** (or press **Ctrl+M**). The Message Composition dialog box appears. Notice that Navigator automatically enters your name and e-mail address next to **From**, at the top of the dialog box. (If the From text box is not displayed, open the **View** menu and click **From**.) To complete the dialog box, you must address your message and then type it.

Click inside the **Mail To** text box, and type the e-mail address of the person to whom you're sending the message. For example, you might type **cmiller@aol.com**. Click inside the **Subject** text box, and type a brief description of the message. Now, click inside the big message area at the bottom of the dialog box, and type your message. Assuming you want to send only the message you typed, click the **Send** button to send it. If you want to attach a file or grab some text from the Web page that's displayed, read on.

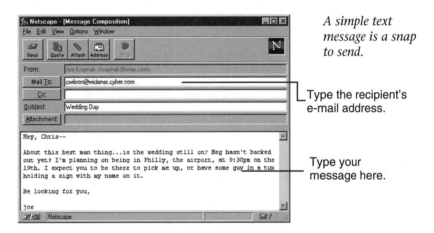

A simple text message is a snap to send.

Type the recipient's e-mail address.

Type your message here.

To send a file along with your e-mail message, click the **Attachment** button (or the **Attach** button in the toolbar). The Attachments dialog box appears, asking you to select the file you want to send. Pick one of the following options:

Attach Location (URL) Sends the Web document that's currently displayed in Navigator. Just click on the **OK** button. You can then select **As Is** to send it as an HTML document (a Web page) or select **Convert to Plain Text** to send the Web document as a text file.

Attach File   Sends a file that's on your hard disk (such as a graphic or sound file or a document you created). Use the dialog box that appears, to select the drive, folder, and name of the file you want to send, and then click on the **Open** button. (You can send more than one file by clicking on the **Attach File** button again.)

After selecting the file(s) or Web page you want to send, click the **OK** button. You're returned to the Message Composition dialog box, and the file's name(s) is inserted in the **Attachment** text box.

When you're ready to send your message (along with any attached file), click the **Send** button. Navigator sends the message. Because the message may take any of several paths on the Internet, it may arrive in seconds, minutes, or hours. Mail typically bounces around several Internet sites before reaching its destination (especially if there's a lot of traffic).

If you want to compose mail off-line (when not connected to the Internet), you can use the Deferred Delivery option to place outgoing messages in the Outbox until you're ready to send them. To turn this option on, the Message Composition window must be displayed. Open the **Options** menu, and select **Deferred Delivery**. As you create and send messages, they are stored locally on your hard drive in the Outbox. When you're ready to send mail, open the **File** menu and select **Send Message in Outbox** in the Netscape Mail window (or press **Ctrl+H**).

C/O Webmaster

As you browse the Web, you'll often encounter a link that allows you to write to the person who created a particular Web page (the Webmaster). If you click the link, Navigator automatically opens the dialog box that allows you to send an e-mail message.

Finally, a Browser That Can Read Mail!

Traditionally, Navigator has always been better at sending than receiving e-mail. Before Navigator version 2.0 came along, Navigator had no way to access incoming e-mail messages. If you wanted to check your mail, you had to use a specialized e-mail program, such as Eudora. But now Navigator comes with its own built-in e-mail reader that makes receiving e-mail as easy as sending it.

To read incoming e-mail messages, start Navigator's E-Mail program. Open the **Window** menu, and click **Netscape Mail**. A dialog box appears, prompting you to type your e-mail password (this is usually the same as your login password, supplied by your service provider). Type your password and click **OK**. Navigator checks your electronic mailbox. If you haven't received any mail, a dialog box appears, telling you that your box is empty (I hate when that happens). Click **OK**.

The Netscape Mail window appears, as shown in the next figure. Notice that the window is divided into three *panes*. The left pane shows two folders: **Inbox** for incoming messages, and **Outbox** for deferred delivery. The first time you send a message, Navigator will create a **Sent** folder (which contains copies of all the messages you've sent). The first time you delete a message, Mail creates a **Trash** folder. The right pane displays the contents of the active folder; initially, you have only one message, a sample message called **Mozilla**. This is a message that comes with Navigator (Mozilla is Netscape's mascot). The bottom pane displays the contents of the selected message.

You can change the relative sizes and dimensions of the panes by dragging their borders. You can also change the width of columns in a pane by dragging the right column marker.

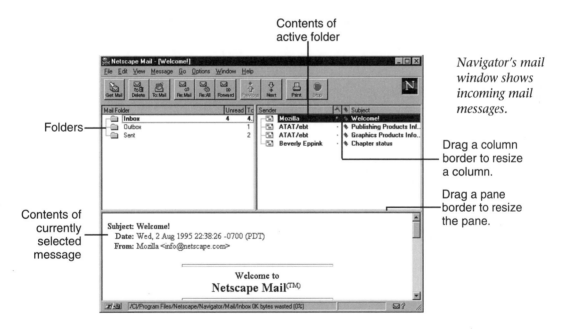

Contents of active folder

Folders

Contents of currently selected message

Navigator's mail window shows incoming mail messages.

Drag a column border to resize a column.

Drag a pane border to resize the pane.

Checking the Mail

When you first connect to your e-mail server using Netscape Mail, it automatically grabs any new messages and stuffs them into your inbox. If you want to check for mail yourself, you have three options: click the **Get Mail** button in the toolbar, press **Ctrl+T**, or open the **File** menu and select **Get New Mail**.

However you choose to do it, Navigator nabs any new messages, activates the Inbox folder, and displays the names of all the messages in your inbox. The names of messages you've already read appear in normal type. Names of new messages (messages you haven't read) appear bold. To read a message, click its name. The contents of the message then appear in the bottom pane.

You can continue to read messages by clicking on their names, but to save time, you can click the **Next** or **Previous** button in the toolbar to scroll through unread messages in the list. You can also use the commands on the Go menu to scroll through the messages: Next Message, Previous Message, First Unread, Next Unread, or Previous Unread.

Use the Next or Previous button to
view other unread messages in the list.

*Netscape Mail lets
you read incoming
e-mail messages.*

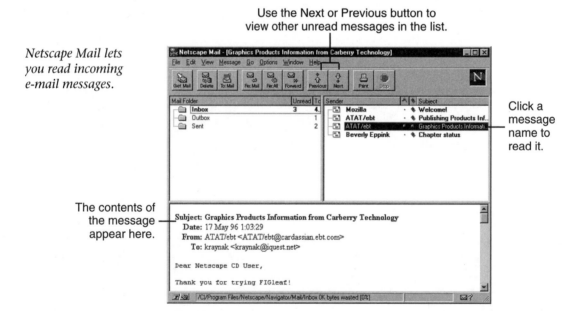

Click a
message
name to
read it.

The contents of
the message
appear here.

Responding to Messages

As you read your mail, you will undoubtedly want to respond to a message, especially if you're caught up in a flame war with your ex. (For a complete description of flame wars, skip ahead to "Behave Yourself: E-Mail Rules and Abbreviations.")

To respond to an e-mail message, first click the message to which you want to respond. Then, click the **Re: Mail** button in the toolbar (or press **Ctrl+R**, or open the **Message** menu and select **Reply**). The dialog box that appears looks a lot like the dialog box you saw earlier in this chapter (when you sent your first e-mail message). The only difference is that the Send To and Subject text boxes are already filled in for you.

If you left the automatic quote option on as explained earlier, a copy of the message to which you're responding appears in the message area with an angle bracket (>) before each quoted line. If you turned this option off, you can quote the message by clicking on the **Quote** button in the toolbar (or by opening the **File** menu and selecting **Include Original Text**). You can delete parts of the quote by using the **Del** or **Backspace** key. (You should rarely quote an entire message, because then the message becomes too long and redundant.)

You can also use the **Attachment** button to send a file along with your response. When you're ready to send the message, click the **Send** button.

Use the Attach button to send
a file along with the message.

These text
boxes are
filled in for
you.

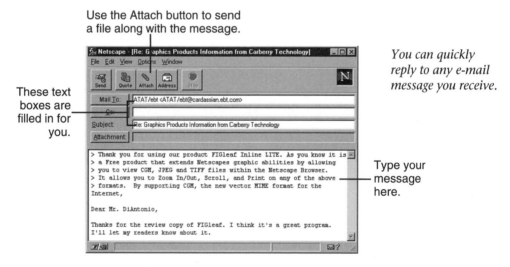

*You can quickly
reply to any e-mail
message you receive.*

Type your
message
here.

Right-Click Menus

You can save a lot of time in the Mail window by using your right mouse button. To reply to a message, right-click on its description, and click **Reply**. To delete a message, right-click and select **Delete**. Try right-clicking on various items in the Mail window to see which options are available for each item.

105

Organizing Messages with Folders

As the mail starts pouring in, you'll soon become a prolific writer, even if you never had any intentions of becoming a prolific writer. Soon, your landfill (folders) will be heaping with messages and ongoing dialogs with friends, relatives, and colleagues. You need some way to organize this opus… and clean it up.

Fortunately, Netscape Mail contains all the management tools you need to group, delete, copy, and move messages. It even comes with the equivalent of a trash compactor, which you can use to compress messages, so they take up less space.

The first step in reorganizing your messages is to create a folder. For example, you might create a folder for each person you frequently correspond with or one for business and one for personal messages. To create a folder, open the **File** menu (in the Mail window) and select **New Folder**. Type a name for the folder, and click **OK**. The new folder appears in the left pane. You can now copy and move messages to this new folder, as explained in the next section.

Selecting, Moving, Copying, and Deleting Messages

Whenever you receive a message, the message is added to the Inbox folder. When you send messages, they're added to the Sent folder. These folders quickly become over-crowded, making it nearly impossible to find a specific message later. To help, you can create folders, as explained in the previous section, and then move the messages to the folders you created.

Before you can move messages, you must select them. You can select a single message by clicking on its name. To select additional messages, hold down the **Ctrl** key while clicking on their names. You can select a range of neighboring messages by clicking on the top message in the range, and then holding down the **Shift** key while clicking on the bottom message in the range. The Edit menu offers some fancy commands to select messages:

Select Thread   Selects all messages that have the same title.

Select Flagged Messages   Selects all messages that you've flagged. To flag a message (mark it as important or as a message you want to respond to later), select the message, open the **Message** menu, and click on **Flag Message**.

Select All Messages   Selects all messages in the currently open folder.

You don't select messages for the sheer joy of selecting them; you usually want to do something to the messages, such as delete them or move them. The easiest way to move messages is to select the messages you want to move, and then drag them over the folder into which you want them placed. To copy messages, hold down the **Ctrl** key while dragging (although I can't imagine why you would want two copies of a message cluttering up your disk).

You can also move the selected messages, by opening the **Message** menu and clicking on **Move**. This opens a submenu that contains the names of all your folders. Click the name of the folder to which you want to move the messages. You can use the **Copy** option on the **Message** menu to copy messages to another folder.

To delete messages, first select them, and then click the **Delete** button in the toolbar, or press the **Del** key. The deleted messages are sent to the TRASH folder, which Netscape Mail creates automatically when you first delete a message. If you delete a message by mistake, you can move it from the TRASH folder to one of your other folders, as explained in the previous paragraph. If you delete a message from the TRASH folder, it's gone for good.

Taking Out the Trash

You can quickly nuke all the messages in the TRASH folder. Open the **File** menu and select **Empty Trash Folder**.

Sorting Out Your Messages

Long lists of messages can become somewhat unwieldy. To help, Netscape Mail can sort the messages for you by date, subject, and even by sender. To sort your messages, double-click the folder whose messages you want to sort, open the **View** menu, click **Sort**, and choose one of the following options:

Again   Sorts the messages again if messages were added since the last time you sorted them.

Thread Messages   Indents responses to original messages, so you can quickly see which messages are related.

Ascending   Sorts messages in ascending order. For example, if you sort by date, earlier messages will be listed first. If you sort by subject, messages are sorted alphabetically, starting with A.

By Date   Sorts messages by date. If you turn Ascending off, recent messages appear first in the list.

By Subject   Sorts messages alphabetically by their descriptions. With Ascending off, messages that start with Z would be listed before messages that start with A.

By Sender   Sorts messages alphabetically by the sender's name.

Compacting Folders To Save Space

Text messages typically take up little space. However, if you have a bunch of messages in a particular folder, they can put a dent in your hard disk. To save disk space, consider compressing your stuffed folders. Compressing really doesn't change the messages at all— you can still read them; they just take up less of your storage space.

To compress a folder, click it, and then open the **File** menu and select **Compress Folder** (or press **Ctrl+K**). To compress all of your folders, select them by using Ctrl+click or Shift+click before entering the Compress Folder command. Any messages you store in a compressed folder are automatically compressed.

Making an E-Mail Address "Book"

Internet e-mail addresses are about as easy to remember as international phone numbers. They can be a combination of long usernames, disjointed numbers, and domain names that snake across the screen, all separated with dots. Nobody expects you to remember these addresses, but if you don't enter them precisely as they appear, your mail will never reach its destination.

The solution to this problem is to create an e-mail address book. To make an address book, open the **Window** menu (in Navigator or in Netscape Mail), and click **Address Book**. The Address Book window appears.

To add an e-mail address to your book, open the **Item** menu, and click **Add User**. The Address Book dialog box appears. The Nick Name text box allows you to enter a person's username. As you establish electronic relationships, nick names become an important way of knowing people. In the **Nick Name** text box, type the person's nickname as a combination of lowercase characters and numbers (this entry is optional); you cannot use any uppercase characters, periods, or other funky symbols. Click inside the **Name** text box, and type the person's full name (you can include uppercase characters). This name will appear in your address book.

Now for the important entry. Click inside the **E-Mail Address** text box, and type the person's Internet e-mail address, just as you would type it if you were sending the person a message. You can type additional information in the **Description** text box, such as the person's phone number and mailing address. (If you open your address book in Navigator as a Web page, the description information will appear.) To start a new line in this text box, press **Ctrl+Enter**. When you're done, click **OK**.

The Address Book shows a list of people you've added.

Changing an Address Book Entry

If your friend or relative moves or picks a new e-mail address, you'll have to change it. Open the **Address Book** window, or right-click the person's name, and click **Properties**. This opens the same dialog box you used to add the person to your address book.

To delete a person from your address book (sorry it didn't work out), click the person's name, and press the **Del** key (or open the **Edit** menu and select **Delete**).

Now that you have an address book, how do you use it? When you display the dialog box for sending an E-Mail message, click inside the **To** text box, and then click the **Address** button in the toolbar. This displays your list of e-mail addresses. Click the address to which you want to send this message, and then click **To**. This inserts the selected e-mail address into the Mail To text box. Click on the **OK** button when you're done. Then, take any additional steps to send the message.

Displaying Your Address Book as a Web Page

Inserting addresses from your address book instead of typing them is a big time-saver, but if you really want to save some time, open your address book as a Web page. The names you entered in the address book appear as links; to e-mail someone, you simply click the link, and then type your subject and message. What could be easier?

109

To display your address book as a Web page, open the **File** menu and select **Open File** (or press **Ctrl+O**). The Open dialog box appears. Select the drive and folder where your address book is stored (in Windows 95, the address book is stored in PROGRAM FILES\NETSCAPE\NAVIGATOR), and then double-click its name (address.htm) in the file name list. This opens the address book as a Web page, showing the names you entered as links. Click a link to display the dialog box you use to send e-mail.

Displaying the address book as a Web page makes it easy to send mail.

When you click a link, this dialog box appears.

Navigator inserts the person's e-mail address into the Mail To text box.

Click the future recipient's link.

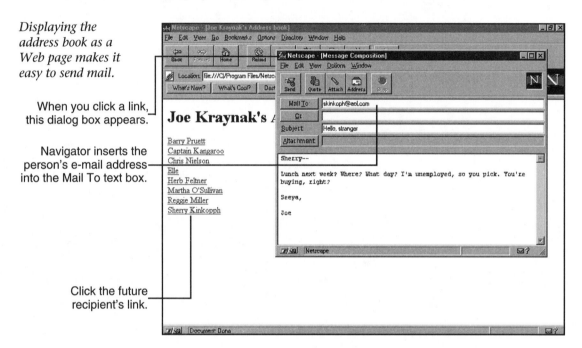

Behave Yourself: E-Mail Rules and Abbreviations

To avoid getting yourself into trouble by unintentionally sending an insulting e-mail message, you might want to consider the proper protocol for composing e-mail messages. The most important rule is to NEVER EVER TYPE IN ALL UPPERCASE CHARACTERS. This is the equivalent of shouting, and people become very edgy when they see this text on their screen. Likewise, take it easy on the exclamation points!!!

Secondly, avoid confrontations in e-mail. When you disagree with somebody, a personal visit or a phone call is usually more tactful than a long letter that painfully describes how stupid and inconsiderate the other person is being. Of course, if you're breaking off a relationship, sometimes e-mail is the best way to do it. The person becomes so irritated, that he or she will refuse to speak, write, or otherwise communicate with you.

Flame Wars

When you strongly disagree with someone on the Internet, it's tempting to *flame* the person, to send a stinging, sarcastic message. It's even more tempting to respond to a flaming message with your own barb. The flame war that results is usually a waste of time and makes both people look bad.

:-) Emoticons: A Symbolic Internet Language

If you want to look as though you're an e-mail veteran, then pepper your messages with any of the following *emoticons* (pronounced "ee-mow-tick-cons"). You can use these symbols to show your pleasure or displeasure with a particular comment, to take the edge off a comment that you think might be misinterpreted, and to express your moods.

:) or :-)	I'm happy, or it's good to see you, or I'm smiling as I'm saying this. You can often use this to show that you're joking.
:D or :-D	I'm really happy or laughing.
;) or ;-)	Winking
:(or :-(	Unhappy. You hurt me, you big brute.
;(or ;-(	Crying
:l or :-l	I don't really care.
:/ or :-/	Skeptical
:# or :-#	My lips are sealed. I can keep a secret.
:> or :->	Devilish grin
;^)	Smirking
%-)	I've been at this too long.
:p or :-p	Sticking my tongue out
<g>	Grinning. Usually takes the edge off whatever you just said.
<vbg>	Very Big Grin
<l>	Laughing
<lol>	Laughing Out Loud

111

<i>	Ironic
<s>	Sighing
<jk>	Just kidding. (These are my initials, too.)
<>	No comment

Common Abbreviations, To Save Time

In addition to the language of emoticons, Internet chat and e-mail messages are commonly seasoned with a fair share of abbreviations. The following is a sample of some of the abbreviations you'll encounter and be expected to know:

AFAIK	As Far As I Know
BRB	Be Right Back
BTW	By The Way
CUL8R	See You Later
F2F	Face To Face (usually in reference to meeting somebody in person)
FAQ	Frequently Asked Questions. Many sites post a list of questions that many users ask, along with answers to those questions. They call this list a FAQ.
FOTCL	Falling Off The Chair Laughing
FTF	Another version of Face To Face
FYA	For Your Amusement
FYI	For Your Information
HHOK	Ha Ha Only Kidding
IMO	In My Opinion
IMHO	In My Humble Opinion
IOW	In Other Words
KISS	Keep It Simple, Stupid
LOL	Laughing Out Loud
MOTOS	Member Of The Opposite Sex
OIC	Oh, I See

PONA	Person Of No Account
ROTF	Rolling On The Floor (presumably in laughter)
SO	Significant Other
TIC	Tongue In Cheek
TTFN	Ta Ta For Now

The Least You Need To Know

If you really want to get into this e-mail thing, read Paul McFedries' book, *The Complete Idiot's Guide to E-Mail*. However, if you just want to send and receive e-mail messages through Netscape Mail, you have to know only two things:

➤ To send an e-mail message, open Navigator's **File** menu and click **New Mail Message**. The rest of the steps are pretty obvious.

➤ To check your e-mailbox, open the **Window** menu and click **Netscape Mail**.

Chapter 10

Customizing Navigator To Make It Your Own

By the End of This Chapter, You'll Be Able To...

➤ Turn screen items, including messages and toolbars, on or off

➤ Get rid of that dingy gray document background

➤ Wake up your documents with fancy typestyles

Navigator has just moved in with you, toting along its old look and all its old habits and forcing you to conform. But now you're going to get your chance to mold Navigator into the Web browser of your dreams. Do you use that button bar just above the viewing area? Of course not. No one does, so get rid of it. You don't like the way the text looks? Change it! Consider this chapter your guide to Navigator empowerment. In the coming sections, you'll learn how to revamp Navigator to look and behave the way you want it to.

Turning Screen Things On and Off

Let's go into this customizing thing as slowly as possible, starting with some simple customization options. The easiest way to customize Navigator is to select checkmark options from the **Options** menu. This technique allows you to turn the toolbar on or off, show or hide the Location text box, and control other screen items.

The strategy here is fairly simple: You want to hide any screen objects that you don't use, giving Navigator more room to display actual Web pages. Open the **Options** menu, and select any of the following items to turn them off (if they're on) or on (if they're off):

Show Toolbar   Displays the buttons that appear directly below the menu bar. The Back and Forward buttons are priceless, so you may want to keep this one. But if you learn the hot-key combinations for entering these commands, you can do away with the button bar.

Show Location   Displays the Location text box. Because this text box makes it so easy to enter URLs, you might want to keep it on, too. However, if you develop a complete list of bookmarks for all your favorite sites, you might be able to live without it.

Show Directory Buttons   Displays the buttons below the Location text box that take you directly to Navigator Corporation sites. Yeah, who needs it? If I weren't writing this book, I wouldn't use it, either.

Show Java Console   Displays a window that shows what's going on behind the Java applets you're playing. Unless you're a total geek, keep this off.

Auto Load Images   When this option is on, Navigator loads any graphics that are on the Web pages. When this option is off, Navigator displays icons in place of the images, which results in pages loading faster but looking worse. If you're in a big hurry and you don't care about pictures, turn this off.

Document Encoding   Don't touch this one for now; it allows you to change the code style in the event that you connect to a Chinese, Japanese, or Korean server. Usually, if you hit a Japanese site, you just click the Back button, and that solves the problem. However, if you're one of the few multilingual people in the States, this submenu can help.

Hot-Key Alternatives

If you turn off some of the screen elements, use the following key combinations:

Ctrl+L	To enter a URL
Alt+<	To display the previous Web page
Alt+>	To display the next Web page
Esc	To stop loading a page
Ctrl+R	To reload
Crtl+I	To load images

If you exit Navigator now, and then restart it, any screen objects you turned off stay off. If you used an older version of Navigator, you might remember having to save your changes.

Giving Navigator a Makeover

Turning screen items off is pretty drastic. It's sort of like knocking out a wall in your house or demolishing an entire wing. But what if you just want to add a fresh coat of paint? You can do that in Navigator by changing the font used to display Web document text or changing the background colors. To change the appearance of Navigator, open the **Options** menu and select **General Preferences**. This displays the general Preferences dialog box.

As you can see from the picture, this dialog box has a bunch of tabs, a few of which you have already encountered. We'll skip the Helpers tab, since you spent enough time there in Chapter 6. We'll also ignore the Language tab, which has advanced options you can afford to ignore. And we'll skip the Apps tab, which you'll use for Telnetting (in Chapter 14). Now that you've whittled down the list to four tabs, let's see what's on them.

A Peek at the Appearance Options

As soon as you open the Preferences dialog box, the Appearance tab jumps to the front, so let's deal with its options first:

Show Main Toolbar as Allows you to control the appearance of the buttons in the toolbar. You can choose **Pictures** (for small buttons with pictures on them), **Text** (for skinny buttons with words on them), or **Pictures and Text** (for big buttons with pictures and words).

117

On Startup Launch   Gives you the option of starting Navigator (Netscape Browser), Netscape Mail, and Netscape News automatically when you start your computer in Windows 95.

Browser Starts With   Lets you specify which page you want Navigator to load when you start it. You can select **Blank Page** if you don't want Navigator to load a page. Or select **Home Page Location**, and then type the desired page's URL in the text box. This can be the URL for a file on your hard disk, as explained in Chapter 5.

Links are   This option lets you turn off underlining for links. Hey, the links are blue, anyway, so what do you need underlining for?

Followed Links   As you know, Navigator keeps track of the URLs for the Web pages you've visited and displays the links for those URLs in a different color. You can use the Followed Links options to specify how far back you want Navigator to "remember" those URLs. **Never Expire** tells Navigator to remember forever. **Expire After ___ Days** specifies the number of days Navigator should remember. The **Expire Now** button erases Navigator's memory.

The Preferences dialog box lets you change the look of Navigator.

Click a tab to view its options.

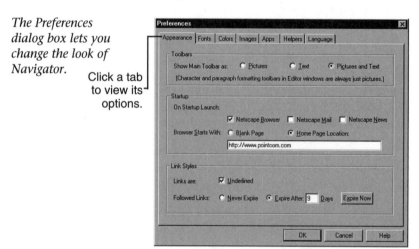

Dressing Your Text in the Right Font

If you took a peek at the source document in Chapter 8, you know that Web pages consist of a bunch of text and codes. Sometimes, the codes actually outnumber the text. These codes tell Navigator (or whatever Web browser you might use) how to display a document. It specifies the colors to use, the background, and the style of the text. However, codes give general orders like "make this text bigger," and "emphasize this text." The browser (Navigator for instance) interprets the codes... and there's a lot of room for interpretation.

Because of this, you can pick the fonts you want to use to style the text. With the general Preferences dialog box displayed, click the **Fonts** tab.

To refresh your memory, a fixed font gives each character the same amount of room. A slender "i" gets the same space as a wide-body "w." Proportional fonts are more communistic—"to each, according to his needs, from each, according to his abilities." In other words, each character gets only the room it needs. Fixed fonts are usually used to display file names at FTP sites. Proportional fonts are used for most of the text you see on Web pages.

To change a font, click the **Choose Font** button next to the Proportional or Fixed Font option. A dialog box appears, allowing you to select the type style and size you want to use. Make your selections, and then click **OK**.

Taking Your Crayolas to the Screen

You've taken it for granted—that dingy gray background that sits behind each Web page you look at is intentional, placed there by one of Navigator's many color settings. How would you like to turn that background white or display a background picture of Carol Channing starring in *Hello, Dolly!*?

Pick a typestyle.

You can control the look of the text on-screen.

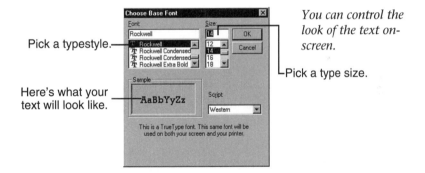

Pick a type size.

Here's what your text will look like.

Carol Channing and Cal Ripken

You need a bit of trivia to wake you up. Did you know that Carol Channing has missed only one day of work while performing in *Hello, Dolly!* for the past 30 years? That smashes Cal Ripken's attendance record.

Okay, maybe you don't want Carol Channing staring out at you from behind every Web document you load, but the point is that you can take control of the Navigator background and the colors that Navigator uses to display text and links. Simply click the **Colors** tab, and change any of the following options:

Links   Controls the colors of the links you haven't yet tried. If you like blue links, don't change this setting. If you would prefer some other color, click **Custom**, and then click the **Choose Color** button. In the dialog box that appears, click the desired color, and click **OK**.

Followed Links   Sets the color for links that you've already tried. Perform the same steps to change this color setting as you performed for the Links setting.

Text   Sets the color for the rest of the text (nonlink text) that makes up a Web page. Black is a good setting, but if you pick a dark background, you should pick a lighter shade of text.

Background   Lets you pick a background color for any Web page that does not have a background color (some Web pages contain codes that display a specific color, giving you no choice). The Default setting gives pages a white background, which makes the text easy to read. To pick a different color, click **Custom**, and then use the **Choose Color** button to display a dialog box that lets you change the background color.

Optionally, you can pick a graphic image to act as your Navigator background. Click **Image File**, and then use the **Browse** button to pick the JPG or GIF image file that you want to use as the background. Be careful with this one; some images can make the text unreadable.

Always Use My Colors, Overriding Document   Tells Navigator to use your colors and background setting even if the Web page you load is set to display a different color or background.

You Can Control Pictures, Too

Check This Out...

Power Tip
Select the **Default background** option, and turn on **Always Use My Colors, Overriding Document**. This speeds up Navigator, because it won't try to download any fancy backgrounds that the Web pages try to send you.

Up to this point, you've been setting the options for boring stuff such as text and backgrounds. But what really makes a Web page come alive are its pictures. To control the way Navigator displays pictures, click the **Images** tab.

The Images tab doesn't give you a whole lot of options (two, to be exact). The Choosing Colors options specify how Navigator displays the colors that make up inline images and other graphics it displays. Leave this option set to **Automatic**; this setting will pick the best option for displaying colors in most images. **Substitute Colors** and

Dither sometimes make the graphics look blotchy. Experiment. If you encounter a graphic that looks bad on-screen, try one of the other options.

Mr. Dithers

Dithering is used in graphics to help smooth the areas on the picture where colors and shades meet. When you turn dithering off, you force the graphics program (or the program that displays the image) to form harsh boundaries between shaded and colored areas. This gives you a sort of early '70s Jimi Hendrix album cover look.

The Images option that can really make a difference in how Navigator performs is the **Display Images** option. You can choose to have images displayed while Navigator receives them or after receiving them. Personally, I don't like the way Navigator gradually displays images. I keep trying to focus in on what I'm getting before the picture actually arrives. However, if you choose **After Loading**, you won't be able to click a graphic link until Navigator is done loading *all* the graphics on the page… and this can take awhile. Pick your poison.

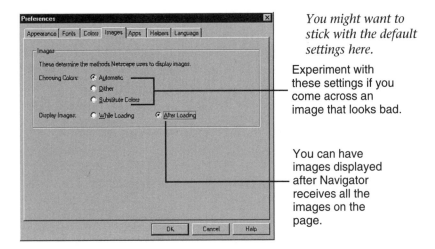

You might want to stick with the default settings here.

Experiment with these settings if you come across an image that looks bad.

You can have images displayed after Navigator receives all the images on the page.

Turning the Security Warnings On and Off

If you've filled out any search forms or order forms in your Web wanderings, you know that whenever you click the button to start the search or submit the form, a bossy dialog box appears warning you that someone might see what you just did. I don't know about you, but that always startles me and makes me glance over my shoulder. Although you can turn the warnings off, you might want to keep them on at least until Chapter 19, where I'll explain the risks in detail.

Tinkering with Some Additional Settings

You've played with the look of Navigator, but what about how it behaves? How much RAM should it use for those Web pages? How much disk space should it use? And how many connections should it manage at the same time? These settings can seriously affect Navigator's performance, so let's take a look at them. Open the **Options** menu, and click **Network Preferences**. This displays the network Preferences dialog box, which contains options you can use even if you have a lowly modem connection.

Establishing a Strong Cache Flow

The first tab, **Cache**, has the most important options. A *cache* is memory or disk space that Navigator (or any other program) uses to temporarily store data. In Navigator's case, the cache is used to store Web pages you've already loaded, so if you go back or forward to a page, Navigator doesn't have to reload the page from the Web site. The minimum numbers for the disk and memory cache are already entered for you; don't go any lower. If you have scads of disk space or memory, you can increase the numbers so Navigator will "remember" more pages.

Another reason you might want to increase the cache is if you're playing huge files with plug-ins or helper apps. For example, if you're downloading large Shockwave files, you may want to increase the cache, so Navigator will have room to store them.

Clear That Cache!

The buttons next to the disk and memory cache settings (**Clear Memory Cache Now** and **Clear Disk Cache Now**) are useful if you have trouble running your other Windows programs, because your system is low on memory. These buttons clear the cache, freeing that storage space for other use.

You should leave the Disk Cache Directory setting as is, unless you have a good reason to change it. When you installed Navigator, it created a CACHE folder for you, which is as good a place as any to store the cache.

The last option (second to last, anyway), **Verify Documents**, lets you specify how often you want Navigator to check a Web document you've loaded against the original. The less often Navigator has to verify documents, the faster Navigator will run. **Once per Session** is a good, safe setting. **Every Time** is excessive and will slow down an already slow process. **Never** is good if you want to speed up Navigator; you can always reload the page if it doesn't transfer right the first time (just press **Ctrl+R**).

Allow Persistent Caching of Pages Retrieve through SSL is another one of those security options you can ignore for now. When this option is off, Navigator does not cache pages at a secure Netscape site. This prevents nosy coworkers from flipping through Web pages you've visited.

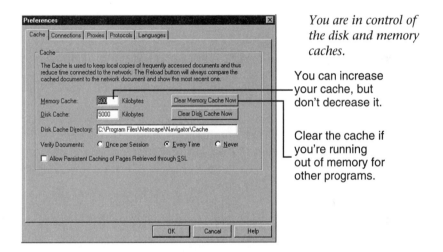

You are in control of the disk and memory caches.

You can increase your cache, but don't decrease it.

Clear the cache if you're running out of memory for other programs.

You Gotta Have the Right Connections (But How Many?)

The second tab in the network Preferences dialog box lets you control the flow of data from the remote computer to your computer. Initially, Navigator is set up to open four "channels" to the remote computer, which allows Navigator to grab several files at once. If you watch your screen and status bar as Navigator loads Web pages, you'll notice that Navigator grabs a little text, and then part of a picture, and then part of another picture, in an attempt to build the entire page at once.

If you increase the number of simultaneous connections, you'll slow down each individual connection, but you'll allow Navigator to load more parts of the page at once. It's a toss-up, but if you have a fast network connection, go ahead and crank up this setting.

If your computer is connected to the Internet through a network cable, you can also play with the **Network Buffer Size** setting. As you increase this number, Navigator allows more data to enter the connection at one time. However, if you crank this setting up too high, more data than your computer can handle may come rushing in, and it will foul up the transmission and leak all over the keyboard. Experiment with the setting, but increase it by only one or two kilobytes at a time.

A Word About the Proxies Tab

I know, you're curious about that Proxies tab. Go ahead and click on it. You see that the No Proxies option is selected. In case you're wondering, a proxy is a server that acts as a sort of a middleman. If you're connected to the Internet through a network connection (instead of a modem), your network may have something called a *firewall* that protects the network from unauthorized access. The problem with these firewalls is that they may limit your access to some Internet features. Proxies act as bridges over the firewalls, allowing information to pass freely between the Internet and your network.

If you're connected to the Internet with a modem, leave No Proxies on. If you have a Network connection, ask your network administrator if you need to use proxies. If you do need proxies, the network administrator can tell you which options you need to select, and how to enter information about the proxies.

The Least You Need To Know

You don't need to know a whole lot about customizing Navigator. Just remember that the Options menu is your key to changing Navigator, that the first four options open dialog boxes, the next five options allow you to turn settings on and off, and that the last option is fairly useless for most people.

Now, play around some more until Navigator looks and behaves the way you want it to.

Part 3
Stretching the Web with Navigator

You've surfed the Web. You clicked links, typed URLs, set up your helper applications, downloaded files, and even sent and received some e-mail. You probably have two or three different bookmark files by now. Given the most obscure topic, you can probably find at least five Web pages with relevant information. Face it, you've mastered Navigator. You've whipped the Web. Now, you need a new quest.

In this section, you'll learn how to use Navigator and the World Wide Web to explore the Internet. You'll learn how to find and transfer files from FTP sites, to read messages in newsgroups, to connect to gopher servers, and more. You'll even learn how to use Navigator (with some help from a telnet program) to use other people's computers. By the end of this part, you'll be able to use Navigator as your sole Internet tool.

Chapter 11

Grabbing Files with FTP

By the End of This Chapter, You'll Be Able To...

➤ Fake your way through a conversation about FTP

➤ Stumble into FTP sites without even trying

➤ Use Navigator to download files from FTP sites

➤ Find specific files when you know their names

➤ Identify common file types on the Internet

Chances are you've already downloaded files from FTP sites using Navigator. The process is simple. You find a link for the file you want to download, click on the link, and specify the name of the file and where you want it stored. So why have a whole chapter on it? Because there's more you *can* know about accessing FTP sites through Navigator— information that can help you find specific FTP sites, connect to those sites, and navigate through their directory structures to download the files you want.

FTP: What's It All About?

Techno Talk

FTP FTP stands for File Transfer Protocol, a set of rules that govern the transfer of files between computers. True geeks use this acronym as a verb, for example, "I FTP'd to the to ftp-dot-netscape-dot-com to nab all my helper applications."

When the Internet started out, it wasn't much more than a gigantic file warehouse. Businesses and individuals stored files on various Internet servers, where other people could come and copy (download) those files. It was like a huge swap meet for computer geeks.

As the Internet grew and diversified, it had to assign specific jobs to different servers. World Wide Web servers were given the task of storing hyperdocuments, newsgroups were set up to act as bulletin boards, and FTP servers became the file warehouses. What does this have to do with you? You can connect to many public-access FTP servers; once there, you can copy programs, text files, graphics, and anything else that can be stored electronically.

Connecting to FTP Sites

In Chapter 2, you learned a couple of ways to connect to the Netscape FTP site to download the copy of Navigator you're now using. If you're a masochist, you probably like to connect to sites and transfer files the old-fashioned way: using the UNIX shell. You type cryptic commands at a clueless prompt and hope you get what you want.

An easier way to perform FTP file transfers is to use a special FTP program. With one of these—such as WS_FTP for Windows—you can transfer files simply by copying them from one panel to another in a dialog box. In addition to ease-of-use, an FTP program offers two important benefits: it allows you to copy the file directly to your computer, and it transfers files fairly quickly.

The third and easiest way to FTP is to use Navigator. You simply type the URL of the FTP site, and Navigator presents you with a graphical representation of the files and directories on the server. To open a directory, you click on its link. To download a file, you simply click on its name.

128

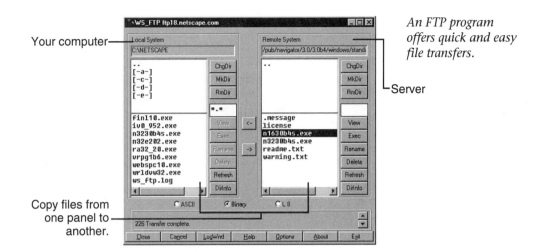

Your computer

An FTP program offers quick and easy file transfers.

Server

Copy files from one panel to another.

FTP Sites That Anyone Can Use

You'll encounter two types of FTP servers: those that let anyone transfer files (*anonymous* sites) and those that don't. To connect to an anonymous site, you usually log in as **anonymous** and then use your e-mail address as your password. As long as you have entered this information into Navigator, it will use the information to automatically log in to FTP sites for you.

Nonanonymous sites require you to enter a username and a password. To connect to one of these sites, you must contact the network supervisor of the site beforehand (usually by sending the supervisor an e-mail message or by calling that person). That person will provide you with a login name and password... assuming she agrees to give you access.

If you have trouble connecting to FTP sites, make sure you've entered your e-mail address in Navigator. You probably already did this in Chapter 9, but to refresh your memory, you open the **Options** menu, click **Mail and News Preferences**, and then click the **Identity** tab. Enter your name and e-mail address. (Most FTP sites won't give you access without an e-mail address.) Then, open the **Options** menu, select **Network Preferences**, click on the **Protocols** tab, and make sure **Send EMail Address as an Anonymous FTP Password** is checked.

Know the Rules

If you ruffle the administrator at an anonymous FTP site, you will quickly lose your anonymity. The administrator can use your e-mail address to lock you out. You'll try to log on as anonymous, and you'll get an **access denied** message or something similar. When you first access a site, read its rules. On most anonymous FTP servers, the only rule is, "Don't connect during business hours."

Using URLs to Access Specific Sites

Picture this. You work for a local underground newspaper. A friend sends you an e-mail message telling you of a great FTP site where you can get the latest dirt about members of Congress and presidential hopefuls. You decide to do a little muckraking, but how do you get to that site?

You connect to FTP sites the same way you connect to HTTP sites: type the site's URL in the **Location** text box, and press **Enter**. Always precede the URL for an FTP site with **ftp://** to indicate to Navigator that you want an FTP site, not a Web page. For example, you would enter **ftp://ftp.netscape.com** to connect to Netscape's FTP site.

You can also use the **File/Open Location** command, and then type the URL in the dialog box that appears, but that's an extra step. If the FTP site won't let you in, check to make sure you typed the URL correctly. If you still can't get in, don't be surprised. The site may not allow anonymous access, or access during high-traffic hours. Either that, or the site may be simply too busy to handle your requests.

Stumbling Around in FTP Sites

Chances are you stumbled unknowingly into a couple of FTP sites already. If you looked in the Location text box, you would see that the URL started with **ftp://** rather than **http://**. Another sign that you just stepped out of the Web is that you'll see tiny document and folder icons next to the link text. If you see any of the following icons, it's a sure sign you're in FTP country.

 A directory or folder. It may contain files and additional directories or folders.

 A text file. Navigator can probably read and display the file.

 A file that Navigator can't read and that has no helper application or plug-in associated to it. The file might be a compressed file or a program file.

A sound file. If you set up a helper application for sound files, you may be able to play this one.

 A movie file, usually a file with an .mpg extension.

 A graphic, usually GIF or JPG.

The folder icons represent directories. To change to a directory, click on its link (not on the icon). You may see additional directories. Continue clicking on links until you find the desired file. You can move up the directory tree by clicking the **Up to a higher level directory** link at the top of the tree. If there is no Up to a higher directory link, click the single period (.) to move to the root directory, or the double period (..) to move up one directory.

> **Don't Forget About Bookmarks** When you find a great FTP site, create a bookmark for it. Open the **Bookmarks** menu and click **Add Bookmark**. You can then quickly return to a site that was too busy to give access.

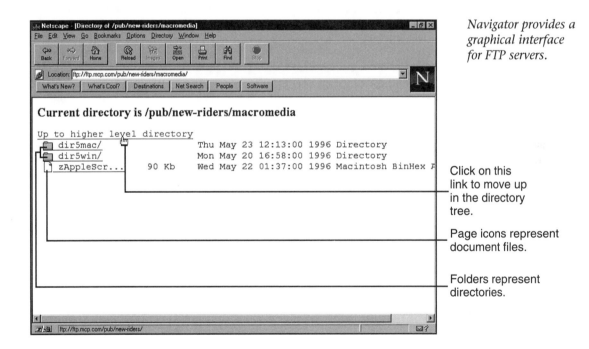

Navigator provides a graphical interface for FTP servers.

Click on this link to move up in the directory tree.

Page icons represent document files.

Folders represent directories.

continues

Viewing and Getting Files

Once you find the desired file, you have to make a decision: do you want Navigator to "play" the file or download it. Navigator can display plain text files, and can play any other file types for which you installed helper applications. So, if you installed a GIF viewer (for example), and you come across a graphic file with the GIF extension, you can click on the link as you would click on any multimedia link in a Web document. Navigator downloads the file and then runs the associated helper application, which plays the file.

If you encounter a program file, a compressed file, or any file that Navigator is not set up to play, you must download the file to your disk. Then you can work with the file outside Navigator. Navigator displays a special icon for most files it can't play; the icon looks like a box with 010 on it, indicating that the file is binary.

To download a file, right-click on the file's link to display a shortcut menu, and then click the **Save Link as** option. The Save As dialog box prompts you to name the file, and select the drive and folder where you want it stored on your hard drive. Enter the requested information, and then click **Save**.

ZIP, TAR, and Other Compressed Files

Many files you find at FTP sites are *compressed* in some way, so they take up less storage space and travel more quickly over Internet connections. PC files are commonly compressed into a .ZIP format, requiring you to *uncompress* the files with WinZip or PKZip. Most Mac files are compressed into .SIT or HQX format, so you'll want to stay away from those files. Here's a list of other compressed formats you might encounter:

  .Z   Compressed with a UNIX compression program.

  .z   Compressed with a UNIX pack program.

  .shar   Archived with UNIX shell archive.

  .tar   Compressed with UNIX tar.

  .pit   Compressed with Macintosh Packit.

  .zoo   Compressed with Zoo210.

  .arc   Packed with PKARC for DOS.

  .exe   Self-extracting .ZIP file for a PC.

.**hqx**   Mac BinHex.

.**sea**   Self-extracting .SIT file for the Mac.

When downloading files, make sure you get files that can run on your platform: DOS or Windows. In other words, if you have a PC running Windows, don't bother downloading a Macintosh .SIT or .SEA file. Most sites also have the shareware utilities you need to decompress the files. Look for a /UTIL directory—that's where you'll usually find them. If you can't find the decompression utilities you need, check Stroud's List at **http:// www.stroud.com** or Tucows at **http://www.tucows.com** for links to helpful utilities.

Using Archie to Sniff Out Files

When word gets out that an anonymous FTP server has cool files, every user with a modem and a SLIP account tries to connect and grab some free stuff. The administrator then closes the server or restricts access, and the online locusts swarm to another server. The good news is that the files you want are probably stored on other (*mirror*) servers in addition to the swamped location. A mirror server is a duplicate of the original server, although the site may not be updated as frequently as the original server. If you can't get the file at its original location, you can get it at the mirror site.

Archie Archie is a system that periodically creates an inventory of the files on many FTP servers. When you search for a file using Archie, you are actually searching through the file directory that Archie created. You're not searching the FTP servers themselves, although some searches can take so long that they give that impression.

But how do you find these mirror sites? Many high-traffic sites contain links to take you to mirror sites. If you see a link for a server closer to you, click on its link rather than trying to download from the original FTP site. You can also find mirror sites by using a program called Archie, which is sort of like a Web robot for FTP servers. Instead of sniffing out Web sites, however, Archie helps you find the FTP servers on which a file is stored.

Performing an Archie search in Navigator is easy. You display an Archie Request Form, fill out the form, and submit it. Archie acts as an automated librarian; it finds the files that match your search instructions, and displays a list of servers on which the file is stored. To display and fill out an Archie Request Form, perform the following steps:

1. Run Navigator.

2. Click inside the **Location** text box, and type one of the following URLs:

   http://hoohoo.ncsa.uiuc.edu/archie.html
   http://www-ns.rutgers.edu/htbin/archie
   http://www.wg.omron.co.jp/AA-eng.html

3. Press **Enter**, and wait for the Archie Request Form to appear. The form you see varies depending on the URL you entered in Step 2.

4. Enter the name or partial name of the file you're looking for. (If you type a partial name, make sure you enter a setting to search for a substring instead of an exact match.)

5. Enter any other information or settings as desired. For example, most Archie search forms ask if you want the search to be case-sensitive.

6. If you're given a choice, click the **By Host** or **By Date** button to select a sorting preference. By Host tells Archie to sort the found files by host name. By Date lists newer files first.

7. If you see a **Priority** or **The impact on other users can be** drop-down list, select how pushy you want to be. Not Nice At All tells the Archie server to drop everything to search for your file. Select Nicer to be at least sort of nice. (Choosing Not Nice At All is sort of like cutting in line to see Santa. Don't do it unless you're in a big, big hurry.)

Check This Out...

Be Specific
The first thing you'll want Archie to do is sniff out all the JPEG and MPEG video files on the Internet. Resist the temptation. Archie is designed to look for specific files. Don't clog Archie's arteries with vain searches. Archie won't help you with these overly general searches, anyway.

8. If you're given a choice of Archie servers to use, open the drop-down list, and select the Archie server you want to use for this search. A closer server may be faster in off-hours, whereas a distant server (one located in a time zone where it is evening or early morning) might work better during business hours.

9. If you see a text box that allows you to limit the number of copies of the file you want Archie to find, type a number in the text box. Archie searches can take a long time, so I usually type **30** in this text box.

10. Click the **Start Search** button (or its equivalent). Archie searches can take awhile, so don't expect a list of files to pop up immediately.

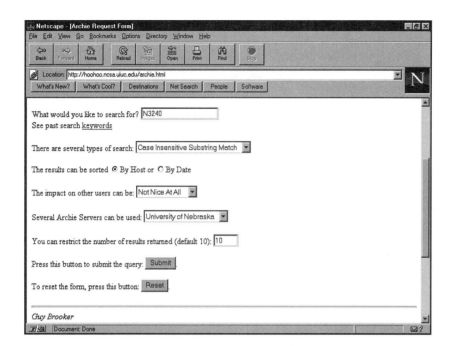

An Archie Request Form.

At this point, you can probably go get a cup of coffee… and drink it. The only thing slower than an Archie search is an Archie search through Navigator. When you come back from your break (assuming Archie is done), you can expect one of two things. If Archie found items that match your entry, you get a list of the items. You can then click on one of the listed links to connect to an FTP server and download the file. If Archie failed to find a file that matched your entry, you'll see the Archie form; you won't see any message telling you that the search failed.

The Monster FTP Site List

The Archie search technique may be a little too specific for your liking. If you prefer wandering aimlessly through FTP sites, I have the perfect place for you. It's an exhaustive directory of FTP sites listed alphabetically.

To view this list, click inside the **Location** text box, and type the following URL. The FTP Interface page appears, displaying links for the various alphabetical groupings of FTP sites. Click on a link to view a list of sites.

```
http://www.ncsa.uiuc.edu/SDG/Software/Mosaic/Interfaces/ftp/ftp-
interface.html
```

*The Monster FTP
Site List.*

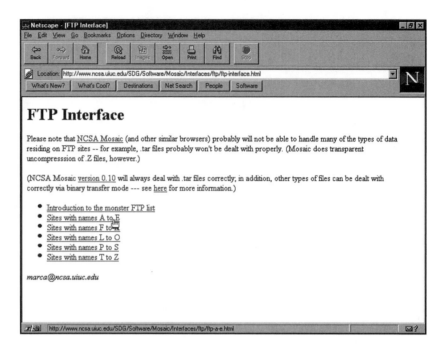

Uploading Files

In addition to grabbing loot off of FTP sites, you can also copy files to some sites (upload files). This allows you to post your favorite shareware, show off graphic images of yourself, and pass along the latest information (assuming you have authorization to upload files to a site).

You can upload files in either of two ways. The easiest way is to go to the FTP site and directory in which you want to place the file, and then drag the file's icon (from Windows Explorer or File Manager) into the Navigator viewing area.

If you don't like that method, you can use the **File/Upload File** command, and use the dialog box that appears to copy the file to the FTP server.

A Cool Trick

You can have Navigator display the directories and files on your hard disk. This gives you the opportunity to "play" files from your hard drive that you may have downloaded from the Internet. In the **Location** text box, type **file:///** followed by the path to the drive and directory you want to access. Your entry might look like this:

```
file:///c¦/data/letters
```

Make sure you use three forward slashes after **file:** and that you use a vertical line (|, the pipe symbol) after the drive letter instead of a colon.

When you press **Enter**, Navigator displays a listing of all the files and subdirectories in the directory you specified. You can then copy files to another drive and directory: Right-click on the file, and use the dialog box that appears to specify a name and destination for the file.

You can access these files through Navigator, just as you can on an FTP site. For example, if you have a text file, you can click on it to open it in Navigator. If you have movie clips, graphics, or sound files, and you set up helper applications for those files, you can click on the file to have Navigator run the appropriate helper application and play the file. You can even set up a program such as Microsoft Word as a helper application to play .DOC files.

The Least You Need To Know

Before Navigator (BN), FTPing was one of the clumsiest Internet features. However, with Navigator's graphical interface, you should have no trouble connecting to anonymous FTP sites and downloading files. As you set out on your downloading venture, keep the following points in mind:

➤ Try to connect to FTP sites in the evening or on weekends.

➤ Before you FTP, make sure you've entered your e-mail address in Navigator.

➤ If you know the name or partial name of the file you want, perform an Archie search to find FTP sites where the file is stored.

➤ Here's the URL for a popular Archie Request Form:

   http://hoohoo.ncsa.uiuc.edu/archie.htm

➤ To connect directly to an FTP site, type its URL in the **Location** text box, and press **Enter**. The URL for FTP sites cleverly starts with **ftp**.

EXTRA!! EXTRA!! READ ALL ABOUT IT.

@NEWS

Chapter 12

Reading and Posting Newsgroup Messages

By the End of This Chapter, You'll Be Able To...

➤ Tell the difference between a newsgroup and newspaper

➤ Have a general idea of what's in a particular newsgroup just by looking at its URL

➤ Navigate a newsgroup by clicking on links

➤ Connect to and read messages in at least five newsgroups

If you've never encountered newsgroups, you might have a somewhat distorted image of what they are. Maybe you think that newsgroups provide up-to-the-minute online news... news on demand. You click a link to get the latest sports scores, click another link to see a national weather map, and click still another link to view CNN Headline News.

That's not quite what Internet newsgroups are all about. A *newsgroup* is more of a discussion group, an electronic bulletin board on which users exchange messages. For example, you might post a message in a body art newsgroup asking for instructions on how to pierce your belly button. Other people will read your messages, and some of those people will post responses, telling you just what to do. They might even offer to do it for you!

Check This Out...

USENET Most newsgroups are part of a larger organization called USENET, which is short for user's network. USENET sets the standards by which the various newsgroups swap information.

There are thousands of newsgroups on the Internet, dealing with just about any topic you can think of... everything from Christianity to body art to dog training. In the past, you needed a special program called a newsgroup reader in order to read and post messages. Now, with Netscape Navigator, you can read and post messages directly from your Web browser.

Before You Can Read Newsgroups...

To read messages posted in a newsgroup, you have to tell Navigator which newsgroup server you want to use. Hopefully, your service provider already supplied you with the domain name of its newsgroup server. If you don't have this information, get on the phone to your service provider (yes, again), and find out. Because there are no public newsgroup servers, you have to use your service provider's newsgroup server.

Check This Out...

When in Doubt, Guess

If it's 2 a.m., and you can't get ahold of your service provider, guess the domain name of your service provider's news service. You can usually just add "news." to the beginning of your service provider's domain name entry. For example, if the general domain name is iquest.com, the news server address should be news.iquest.com.

Once you have the information you need, open the **Options** menu and select **Mail and News Preferences**. Click the **Servers** tab. Now, click inside the News (NNTP) Server text box, and type the domain name of your service provider's newsgroup server. Don't change the entry in the News RC Directory, unless you have some good reason for changing it. This entry tells Navigator where to store information about the newsgroups you decide to read. Click **OK** to save your changes.

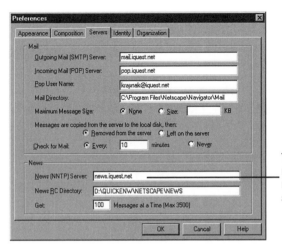

Specifying a newsgroup server in Navigator.

Type the domain name of your newsgroup server here.

Connecting to a Newsgroup

Enough preliminaries. The only way to see how a newsgroup looks in Navigator is to bring one up. You connect to a newsgroup the same way you connect to any server: you can either click a link that points to a newsgroup, or type the newsgroup's URL in the Location text box, and press **Enter**. The URL must start with **news:**. Here are some URLs to try:

news:alt.comedy.british

news:misc.forsale

news:sci.anthropology

news:sci.military

> *Check This Out...*
>
> **Where Did It Go?** If you get a message saying that the newsgroup no longer exists, you may have mistyped its URL... or the newsgroup may no longer exist. Also, some less active newsgroups may have no messages. In that case, you'll get a message saying that the newsgroup is empty.

When you connect to a newsgroup, Navigator runs a special newsgroup reader. It's sort of a helper application that's built into Navigator. The newsgroup you chose to connect to is listed on the left, along with a count of new messages and messages you haven't yet read. On the right is a list of the messages that have been posted. To read a message, skip ahead to the "Reading Newsgroup Messages" section later in this chapter.

You may not be able to connect to all newsgroups. There are over ten thousand newsgroups, but your service provider may subscribe to only a few thousand. Check with your service provider to find out which newsgroups are available. Your service provider can probably send you a list of newsgroups along with their URLs.

A list of messages in the
selected newsgroup

*Navigator lists the
messages in the
specified newsgroup.*

Newsgroups ────

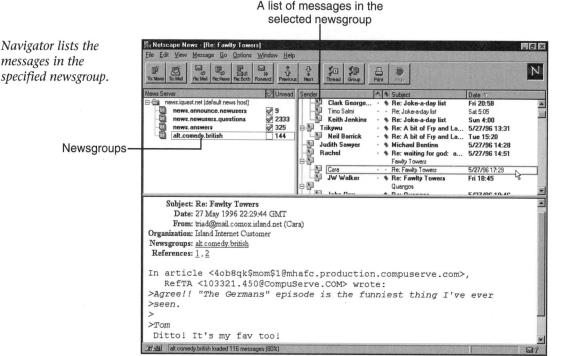

Dissecting Newsgroup Addresses

Maybe you noticed the unique format of newsgroup addresses. (Then again, maybe you didn't.) These addresses can tell you a lot about the newsgroup's focus; most are made up of two to three parts.

The first part of the address indicates the newsgroup's overall subject area: **comp** stands for computer, **news** is for general information about newsgroups, **rec** is for recreation (hobbies, sports, and so on), **sci** stands for science, **soc** is for social topics, **talk** is for controversial debates, **misc** is for general topics such as jobs and selling, and **alt** is for topics that may offend some people, and... well... you get the idea.

The second part of the address indicates, more specifically, what the newsgroup offers. For example, **comp.ai** is about computers, specifically covering artificial intelligence. If the address has a third part (most do), it focuses even further. For example, **comp.ai.philosophy** discusses how artificial intelligence can be applied to philosophical questions, which is probably a philosophical question in itself. **rec.arts.bodyart** discusses the art of tattoos and other body decorations.

Chain Letters

If you're wondering how the Internet broadcasts messages throughout the world, just think of it as a huge chain-letter system. Whenever someone posts a message in a newsgroup, the message is stored on that person's newsgroup server and is sent out to other newsgroup servers. These newsgroup servers send copies of the message to other newsgroup servers; the process continues until all the participants in the particular newsgroup have received the message. This usually takes no more than a couple of hours.

Searching for Newsgroups

You can make Navigator display a list of all the newsgroups in a specified category. Simply enter the newsgroup category followed by the asterisk. For example, to display all the newsgroups in the sci category, type **news:sci.*** in the Location text box, and press **Enter**. You can narrow the search by adding a subcategory name to your entry. For example, enter **news:sci.space.*** to display the names of all newsgroups that deal with space exploration.

To view the names of all the newsgroups (this can take awhile), type **news:*.*** in the Location text box, and press **Enter**. Or when the newsgroup reader window appears, open the **Options** menu and click **Show All Newsgroups**. A dialog box appears, telling you that this will take some time. Click **OK** to proceed.

Download a List of Newsgroups

You can download lists of newsgroups from various FTP servers. Try the following site:

ftp://pit-manager.mit.edu/pub/usenet-by-group/news.answers/active-newsgroups

You'll find two files called **Part1** and **Part2**. Assuming you are FTPing from Navigator, right-click one of the files, and use the dialog box that appears to save it as a text file (give it the **.txt** extension). Then repeat the step for the second file. All together, these two files make up a newsgroup address book of about 40 pages!

Reading Newsgroup Messages

Okay, now that you know all about connecting to newsgroups, you're probably dying to read some messages. Take a gander at Navigator's newsgroup window. It's divided into three panes:

➤ The left pane displays the names of the newsgroups.

➤ The right pane displays the names of messages in the selected newsgroup.

➤ The bottom pane displays the contents of the selected message. (You can change the relative sizes of the panes by dragging the bars that separate them.)

Navigator's newsgroup window is divided into three panes.

This pane shows the names of newsgroups and newsgroup categories.

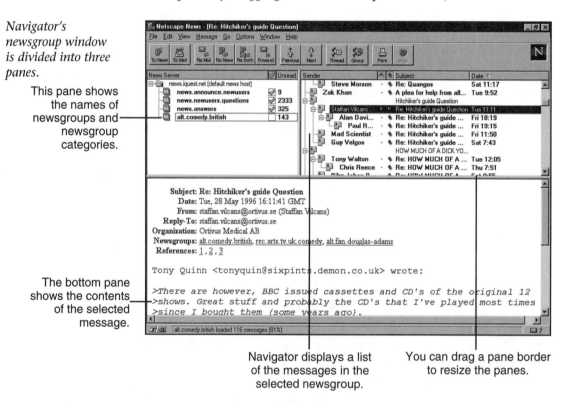

The bottom pane shows the contents of the selected message.

Navigator displays a list of the messages in the selected newsgroup.

You can drag a pane border to resize the panes.

Let's start with the left pane. If you chose to display all the newsgroups, the contents of the left pane look something like a directory or folder tree, listing newsgroups and newsgroup categories in alphabetical order. Newsgroup categories appear as folders. To open a folder (and display the newsgroups in it), click the folder. The names of the newsgroups in the folder appear. Next to each newsgroup are two numbers, indicating the number of messages in the newsgroup and the number of messages you haven't yet read.

If a newsgroup has no numbers next to it, either your service provider does not recognize the newsgroup or the newsgroup is empty. In either case, don't waste your time with these newsgroups. When you see a newsgroup in which you are interested (and one that has some messages in it), double-click its name. Navigator retrieves the message descriptions and displays the names of the messages in the right pane.

Speaking of the right pane, it does not simply display a list of messages in chronological order. It displays messages as ongoing conversations. The first message in a topic of conversation is listed first. If another person responded to the first message, the response is indented from the topmost message, to indicate that it is related. This method of displaying messages in called *threading* and is designed to make newsgroup discussions easy to follow.

> **Check This Out...**
>
> **Sorting Messages**
> Netscape News can sort the newsgroup messages by date, subject, or sender. Open the **View** menu, click **Sort**, and select the desired sorting option. Be sure to keep the **Thread Messages** option on, so you can easily see which messages belong to a separate discussion.

To read a message, click the name of the message in the right pane. This displays the message contents in the pane at the bottom of the window. The contents may be a text file or a graphic, and it may take Navigator some time to decode the message, so the information can be displayed. You can continue to read messages by double-clicking their names. Or you can use the options on the **Go** menu to move from message to message:

Next Message displays the contents of the next message. (Or click the **Next** button in the toolbar.)

Previous Message displays the contents of the previous message in the list. (Or click on the **Previous** button in the toolbar.)

First Unread displays the contents of the first message that you haven't read in the newsgroup.

Next Unread displays the contents of the next message that you haven't read in the newsgroup.

Previous Unread displays the contents of any previous message that you haven't read.

You can also search for newsgroups or messages. To search for a newsgroup, click inside the pane that displays the newsgroup names, and then open the **Edit** menu and select **Find**. Type the name of the newsgroup, and then press **Enter**. To search for a message in a newsgroup, click inside the pane that lists the message titles, and then open the **Edit** menu and select **Find**. Type one or two words that might appear inside the message description you're looking for, and press **Enter**.

Replying to Newsgroup Messages

Before you post messages to a newsgroup, familiarize yourself with the newsgroup. Hang out, and read existing messages to obtain a clear idea of the focus and tone of the newsgroup. Reading messages without posting your own messages is known as *lurking*. Newsgroups encourage lurking, because it provides you with the knowledge you need to respond intelligently and to avoid repeating what was already said.

If you read a message and decide to respond, make sure the message is selected, and then open the **Message** menu and select one of the Reply options: **Post Reply** (to post a response in the newsgroup, where everyone can read it), **Mail Reply** (to respond to the person privately with an e-mail message), or **Post and Mail Reply** (to reply privately with e-mail and post the message in the newsgroup).

If you select **Post Reply**, Navigator displays the dialog box shown here, allowing you to type your response. Notice that the From, Newsgroups, and Subject text boxes are already filled in for you. Don't change any of this information. Simply type your response in the large text box at the bottom of the dialog box, and click the **Send** button. Your reply is then posted to the newsgroup, where everyone can open and read it.

You can quickly reply to any newsgroup message.

Click on the Send button.

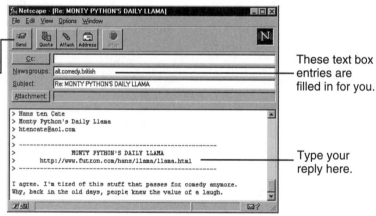

These text box entries are filled in for you.

Type your reply here.

Newsgroup Etiquette

To avoid getting verbally battered in a newsgroup, follow a few simple rules. Don't insult any person or attack any topic of conversation. Post messages that pertain to the newsgroup and topic of conversation (read the entire conversation before adding your own two cents). And don't advertise in a newsgroup unless the newsgroup is especially designed for advertising. Oh yeah, DON'T SHOUT by using all capital letters in your message.

Starting a New Discussion

As you gain experience in a particular newsgroup, you might decide to venture out and start your own conversation. For example, if you're into hot rods, and you need a bumper for your '64 Corvette, you might want to post a message asking if anyone knows where you can find the bumper.

To start a conversation, first activate the newsgroup in which you want to post your message. Then, open the **File** menu and select **New News Message**. The dialog box that appears is very similar to the dialog box you use to reply to messages, except in this dialog box, the Subject text box is blank. Click inside the Subject text box, and type a description for your message.

Now, click inside the big text box at the bottom of the dialog box, and type your message. When you're done typing, click the **Send** button. Your message is posted in the active newsgroup. You can now check the newsgroup on a regular basis, to see if anyone has replied to your message. And don't be surprised if you receive replies via e-mail!

Receiving and Sending Files in Newsgroups

What's cool about newsgroups is that they allow you to trade files (in addition to text messages) with other newsgroup members. The only trouble is that these files are usually encoded, so they can be transferred over the phone lines. Whenever you send a file, the file has to be encoded, and whenever you receive a file, you have to decode it before you can open or use it. Fortunately, Netscape News can handle the coding and decoding for you.

In most cases when you come across a file that has been uploaded to a newsgroup by another user, the file is usually in numbered parts. You'll see a list of messages something like

    dog.gif (0/4)
    dog.gif (1/4)
    dog.gif (2/4)
    dog.gif (3/4)

The first part of the message, dog.gif (0/4) usually contains a brief description of the file. The remaining parts of the message contain the coded version of the file that was uploaded. If you click on dog.gif (1/4) message, Netscape News grabs all parts of the file, decodes them, and displays the file (in this case, a graphic file) in the message area.

Other times, you'll see a link for the file in the message area (at the bottom of the screen). If you click on the link, and Netscape News or one of your helper applications can play the file, Netscape News automatically downloads the file and plays it. If News or one of your helper applications cannot play the file, a dialog box appears, allowing you to save the file to your hard disk.

You can also send a file along with the message you post. In the dialog box you use for posting your message or reply, click the **Attach** button. Use the dialog box that appears, to select the document or file you want to send, and then click the **Attach** button.

The Least You Need To Know

You've just read one of the shortest chapters in the book... and you want less?!! Okay, here goes:

➤ Newsgroups are discussion groups.

➤ To connect to a newsgroup, type the group's URL in the Location text box, and press **Enter**.

➤ Navigator lists the messages in a newsgroup from newest to oldest and threads messages on a specific subject to keep them together.

➤ To see a list of messages in a newsgroup, double-click the newsgroup's name in the left pane of the Netscape News window.

➤ To read a message, click its name in the right pane of the Netscape News window.

➤ To reply to a message, first open the message you want to reply to, and then open the **Message** menu and click **Post Reply**.

Gophering from Navigator

gopher n. 1. Any of various short-tailed, burrowing mammals of the family Geomyidae, of North America. 2. (Amer. colloq.) Native or inhabitant of Minnesota: the Gopher State. 3. (Amer. colloq.) One who runs errands, does odd jobs, fetches or delivers documents for office staff. 4. (computer tech.) Software following a simple protocol for tunneling through a TCP/IP internet.
—*Copied from the University of Minnesota Gopher site.*

You're chin deep in the information age, swallowed up by a bottomless pit of facts, files, and data... and you don't know where to start. You need help. You need an automated online tool that can run around and find files for you, an electronic rodent that can tunnel through the Internet and sniff out interesting subject areas and useful resources, a hunter that can track down information on all the various types of Internet servers. You need Gopher.

Gopher is an indexing system that enables you to access various Internet services through menus. Whenever you connect to a Gopher site, it presents you with an opening menu. When you select a menu item, the server presents you with *another* menu containing additional options and/or files. These options may send you off to another Gopher server, an FTP server, a newsgroup, or other Internet servers. You proceed through the menus until you find the file you want... or reach a dead end.

You may already have used Gopher menus through your service provider or by using a Gopher menu program, such as the one shown here. As you can see, the Gopher menus are text-based. In this chapter, you'll learn how Navigator can provide you with a more graphical interface, one that contains links similar to those in a Web document.

A Windows Gopher program gives the Gopher site a slick look, but it's still text-based.

The folders here indicate that clicking on the option displays a menu.

Click on an option to view the next menu or a list of files.

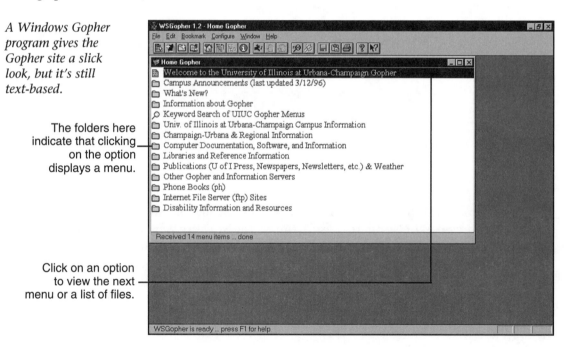

Gopher Guts

Here's how Gopher works: Each Gopher server has a huge index of Internet resources, including the names and locations of thousands of files. You have Gopher menu software (on your hard drive) that provides a way for you to access the servers' indexes. Whenever you connect to a Gopher server, it sends index information to your menu software, which uses that information to build a menu system. All this goes on behind the scenes. The only things you see are the menu options, which you select to access various Internet resources.

Gopher and FTP: What's the Difference?

Before you connect to a Gopher site, I have to warn you: the screen is going to look almost identical to the screens you encountered at FTP sites. The difference is in how the two types of servers function.

When you connect to an FTP server, you're limited to the files stored at that site. Accessing an FTP site is almost like accessing a gigantic hard disk drive. None of the links will kick you out to a different site or help you find resources on another server. You use links only to change directories and download files.

Like FTP servers, most Gopher servers contain files you can download. The similarity ends there. Gopher servers also provide links to other servers on the Internet. For example, you might click on a menu option and find yourself halfway around the world, on a Gopher server or a telnet site in another country. Gophers are designed to give you easy access to *all* Internet resources.

Connecting to a Gopher Site

You may have stumbled into a Gopher hole without realizing it, because some Web documents contain links to Gopher sites. You click on a link, and Navigator takes you to the site. So how can you tell you're at a Gopher site? First, look in the **URL** text box. If the URL starts with **gopher** rather than **http**, you're at a Gopher site. In addition, the Gopher page may have a heading such as **Gopher Menu**, which is a pretty good indication that you're in Gopherland. The third sign is that Gopher sites use menus like the one shown here.

Sure signs that you've reached a Gopher site.

"gopher" appears here.

Gopher Menu title

Gopher menu items

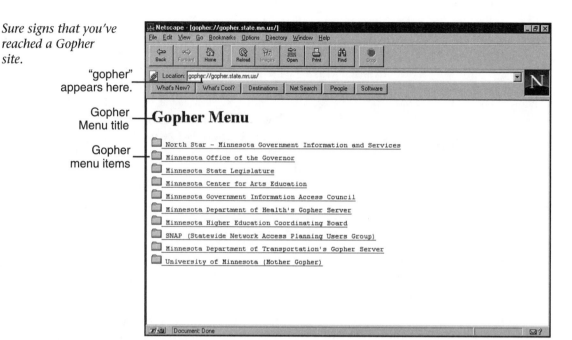

If you haven't encountered a Gopher, what are you waiting for? Check out a couple sites, just to see what you're getting yourself into. If you know the Gopher site's URL, type it in the **Location** text box and press **Enter**. For example, to go to the original Gopher, at the University of Minnesota, type the following URL, and press **Enter**:

gopher://gopher.micro.umn.edu

Romping Around in a Gopher Server

There's no trick to getting around in a Gopher server. You simply click on the desired links to follow a trail of menus. Use the Back and Forward buttons to display the previous or next screens, just as you would with Web documents. The following icons can provide clues as to what the Gopher menu options provide. Note that most of these icons are identical to icons you encounter at FTP sites, and that not all Gopher screens will contain these icons:

 A directory or folder. It may contain files and additional directories or folders.

 A searchable index. This usually displays a search screen that has a Search text box at the bottom. Type your search instruction in the text box, and press **Enter**. Refer to the following section for details.

Telnet site. Telnetting allows you to connect to a remote computer and control it from your keyboard. See Chapter 19 for details.

 A text file. Navigator can probably read and display the file.

 A file that Navigator can't read that has no helper application associated to it. The file might be a compressed file or a program file.

 A sound file. If you set up a helper application for sound files, you may be able to play this one.

 A movie file, usually with an MPG extension.

 A graphic, usually with a GIF or JPG extension.

To test out any of these multimedia file types, visit the Gopher+ Example Server at **gopher://mudhoney.micro.umn.edu:70/11/gplustest**.

The topmost choice in most gopher menus is **About this Gopher**. Click on this link to find out information about the current Gopher, including general descriptions of what's stored on the Gopher and the types of services it offers. Some Gophers may also have restrictions you should read about before using them. To read this document, click on its link. Navigator loads and displays its text.

Searching Gopherspace with Veronica

Browsing the Internet with Gopher can be fun, but when you need specific information in a hurry, browsing just won't do. You need a way to search out only those Gopher sites that have the information you want. You need Veronica.

With Veronica, you type search strings that tell Veronica what to look for and how many items to find. Veronica searches its huge index of Internet resources and then assembles a menu of servers that match your search string. For example, you can enter a search string to have Veronica find all sites that contain information about IBM and Apple.

Archie, Veronica, and Jughead

The fact that the names **Archie** and **Veronica** stir up images of comic-book characters is no coincidence. Archie (short for "archive") started it all. Veronica, Archie's comic-book girlfriend, followed. There's even a search program called Jughead, which is a limited version of Veronica.

153

The first, and possibly most time-consuming, step in searching with Veronica is to access a Veronica server. What makes this step so difficult is that Veronica servers are in high demand; you may not be able to gain access when you need it most. The easiest way to access Veronica is to connect to a Gopher server that has a Veronica link, and then click on that link. If you have trouble finding a Gopher that offers Veronica, use your favorite Internet search tool (**http://www.yahoo.com**, **http://www.webcrawler.com**, and so on) to search for **veronica**.

Select a Veronica site.

Veronica sites ‒

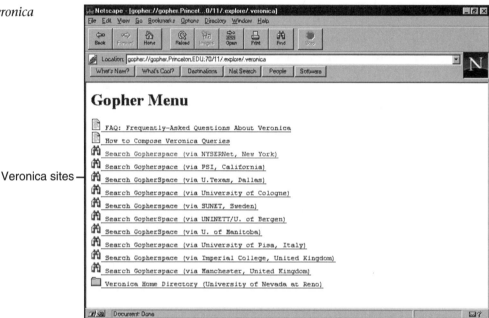

Sometimes, the list of Veronica sites are divided into two groups: one allows you to search all gopherspace, and one searches only for directories. For a quick search that turns up fewer finds, select one of the **Directory Only** options. For a more thorough search, select a **Gopherspace** option. Regardless of which choice you make, Veronica displays a form that allows you to enter your search string.

Click inside the text box, type the words you want to search for, and press **Enter**. For example, type **spanish literature**, and press **Enter**. Veronica looks for all entries that have "spanish" and "literature" in the title, but not necessarily in the order in which you typed the words—Veronica also turns up any occurrences of "literature" and "spanish." Make your search string as specific as possible, and read the following sections to take more control of your searches.

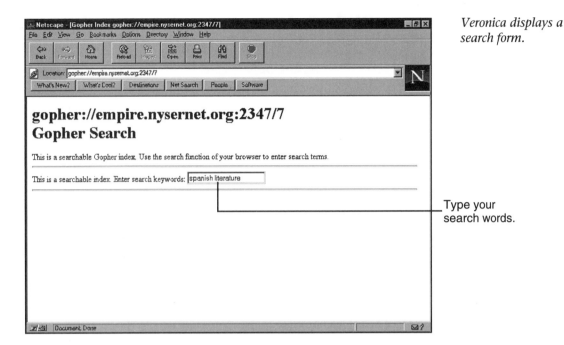

Veronica displays a search form.

Type your
search words.

Searching with "And," "Or," "Not," and Wild Cards

The preferred search method (mine, anyway) is to keep it simple. Type one to three well-focused words, and press **Enter**. Veronica does, however, allow you to enter more complex search strings by using wild-card entries and link terms called *Boolean* operators.

The only wild-card entry you can use is an asterisk (*), and you can use it only at the end of a word. For example, you can type **book*** to have Veronica find "book," "books," and "bookstore." But if you type b*k, Veronica will void the search, slap your fingers, and tell everyone that you don't know how to type a proper search instruction.

You can also use Boolean operators ("and," "or," and "not") to narrow or broaden a search. The "and" operator is fairly useless. If you type three words as your search string, Veronica automatically inserts "and" between them, so don't bother typing "and." The "or" operator is also pretty useless because it broadens the search, when your primary goal is to *narrow* it. For example, if you type **spanish or literature** as your search string, the search will be too broad to do any good. The "not" operator is somewhat useful for preventing some items from being included in the search. For example, to be politically correct, you could enter **tuna not dolphins**.

To put together some fancy searches, use parentheses to group your search items. For example, if you want to find listings for only Polish and French literature, you might enter **literature (polish or french)**. This is one way to make use of the "or" operator.

Narrowing a Search with Switches

Unless you specify otherwise, Veronica limits the number of items it finds to 200, and searches for all file types. You can use the -m<*number*> and -t<*type*> switches to change these defaults. Simply type the switch before or after your search string.

The -m<*number*> switch tells Veronica the maximum number of items to list. For example, -m5 tells Veronica to list no more than five items. (Don't type the brackets < and >.) And -m1000 specifies 1000 items. Use the -m switch without a number to have Veronica list all the items it finds, no limit. When typing this switch, make sure there is no space between the -m and the number.

The -t<*type*> switch indicates a file type. For example, -t0 finds only text files, -ts finds sound files, and -tg finds GIF images. You can combine file-type symbols by typing their codes, without spaces, after the -t. For example, -t0gs finds text files, GIF images, *and* sound files. Here's a list of file-type codes:

0	Text File
1	Directory
2	CSO name server
4	Mac HQX file
5	PC binary
7	Full Text Index (Gopher menu)
8	Telnet Session
9	Binary File
s	Sound
e	Event (not in 2.06)
I	Image (other than GIF)
M	MIME multipart/mixed message
T	TN3270 Session
c	Calendar (not in 2.06)
g	GIF image
h	HTML, HyperText Markup Language

In addition to these codes, you can include text after the -t switch to limit the search further. For example, type **-ti mac** to find non-GIF images that have "mac" in their titles.

Searching a Single Server with Jughead

Veronica is an ambitious search tool. It searches for all Internet resources that match your entry, regardless of whether those resources are stored on the current server or on another, remote server. Jughead is a similar, though less ambitious tool, which searches only for those resources that are stored on the current server.

Most of the time, you'll use Jughead without ever knowing it. You might select a menu item, such as **Search Gopher titles at the University of Minnesota**. You get a search form that looks just like the form you would get through Veronica. The only difference is that instead of searching all Internet resources, the search is restricted to the resources at the current site. Although Jughead allows you to type a search string, your options are limited. You can type only two words, and you can't use the **-t**<*type*> switch.

Making Bookmarks for Your Gopher Sites

Once you've found a great Gopher site, it's tempting to poke around and get lost in the menu system. You get lost in the play, you sign off, and an hour later you can't remember where you've been. To get back, you have to perform another search, which may not generate the same results. So, before you weave through the menu system, add a bookmark for the gopher site. Open the **Bookmarks** menu and select **Add Bookmark**.

Create a Gopher Submenu

Consider creating a separate Gopher submenu on the Bookmarks menu. You can then add the URLs for your favorite Gopher sites to this submenu. Refer to Chapter 11 for details.

Playing and Grabbing Files

The ultimate goal in a Gopher session is to find a file and then play it or save it. You've done the first part; you found a file that looks promising. Now for step two. You can download a file from a Gopher site the same way you download files in FTP. Right-click on the file's link. This opens a dialog box, and you know what to do from here.

Navigator can display text files without saving them to disk. In addition, if you set up helper applications for specific file types, you can play those files without downloading them. To open a text file or play another file type, click on the file's link, and then wait for Navigator to download and play the file.

The Least You Need To Know

To make this section a bit more interesting, I'm presenting the review material as a list of riddles and questions. The answer for each riddle or question follows it immediately, so don't peek.

➤ What do you get when you cross a Web document, an FTP site, and a menu?

Answer: A Gopher.

➤ If Gopher and FTP had a fight, who would win and why?

Answer: Gopher, because it contains links to other Internet services, including FTP sites.

➤ What does the URL for every Gopher site start with?

Answer: gopher://

➤ Who rode Washington's white horse?

Answer: If you said "White," you lose.

➤ If Veronica and Jughead had a fight on the Internet, who would win and why?

Answer: Veronica, because she can search for resources stored outside the current server.

➤ You know about switches and Boolean operators; should you use them?

Answer: If you're lazy, like me, probably not. You're better off spending your time thinking of two or three specific words.

➤ To what family of animals does the gopher belong?

Answer: Geomyidae.

➤ Extra credit question: True or False—A gopher is also a type of land tortoise found in the southern United States.

Answer: True. And this tortoise is edible. Yummy.

Chapter 14

Telnetting with Navigator (and a Little Help)

By the End of This Chapter, You'll Be Able To...

➤ Find the helper application you need to telnet from Navigator (and set it up) or use the one that comes with Windows 95

➤ Poke around on another person's computer while sitting at your keyboard

➤ Rattle off a list of 10 UNIX commands (and know what they do)

➤ Connect to at least one remote computer... and act as if you know what you're doing

Occasionally, you'll hear a story on the news about some X-Generation computer hacker who broke into a supposedly secure network to steal some credit card numbers or launch a nuclear missile. Maybe, you have your own secret desires to sneak into remote networks, perhaps to steal plans for building a biological weapon or to change your Visa balance.

Well, I hate to break it to you, but this chapter won't teach you how to do any of the cool illegal stuff you hear about. However, I will teach you to log in to computer systems that provide public access and use those systems to take advantage of resources that are unavailable at Web sites. You'll even learn how to play some cool, interactive computer games against other people.

The Ins and Outs of Telnetting

Telnetting is short for "networking over the telephone." When you network without the "tel," you type at a *terminal*, which is connected by cable to a huge central computer, which does all the work. When you telnet, you're dialing (with your modem) into this central computer and using your computer as a terminal.

If you've ever used a computerized card catalog at your local library, you've used a network. You use the terminal to search for books by author or title, to find out which branch library has the book, and to determine the book's status (whether it's in, or somebody stole it).

Some libraries allow you to dial into their networks. With your computer, a modem, and a basic communications program, you can use your computer as a terminal. Without leaving your home or office, you can dial into the network at the public library and look for books, just as if you were sitting at a terminal in the library. This is telnetting.

Whoa! You Need a Telnet Program First

The concept of telnetting from Navigator brings up all sorts of grand delusions. You might picture Navigator's smooth graphical interface replacing the prompts and texty menus you see on most terminals. Not so.

What telnetting from Navigator really means is that when you click on a link for a telnet site (or enter its URL), Navigator runs a separate program (just like a helper application). You then use *that* program (not Navigator) to do your telnetting. In other words, you still get the crude prompts and texty menus. Sorry, them's the breaks.

Getting a Telnet Program for Cheap

If you already have a telnet program, skip to the next section to learn how to set it up so Navigator can run it. (If you have Windows 95, you already have a telnet program; it's called Telnet.exe, and it's in the main Windows folder). If you don't have a telnet program, you can download a shareware program from an FTP site. Following is a list of good telnet programs you can download. I bet you'd love it if I gave you the locations of these files. Sorry, but I taught you how to fish with Archie in Chapter 11, so use Archie to find a recent copy of the file you want:

WinQVT Net   A telnet program for Windows. Search for **WinQVT** or **qvtws**.

NCSA Telnet   The NCSA telnet program for Windows. Search for **wintelb**. Try either of the following FTP sites:

> ftp.ncsa.uiuc.edu
> ftp://gatekeeper.dec.com/pub/micro/msdos/win3/winsock/

Trumpet Telnet   Yet another telnet program for Windows. Search for **trmptel** or try the following FTP site:

ftp://gatekeeper.dec.com/pub/micro/msdos/win3/winsock/

Keep in mind that most of these programs are stored in a compressed format. You'll have to unzip or expand the files after you download them. Also, these are *share*ware programs, the key term being *share*. If you choose to keep the program past the trial period, send a registration fee to the programmer. This prevents them from turning into bitter socio-paths.

Setting Telnet as a Helper Application

Once you've unpacked (decompressed) the telnet program and performed any additional installation steps, you need to set up Navigator to run the program automatically. Open the **Options** menu and select **General Preferences**. Click the **Apps** tab. Click inside the **Telnet Application** field and type the path and file name of your telnet program (or click on the **Browse** button and use the dialog box to select the drive, folder, and name of the telnet program). If you're using Win QVT NET, the path might look like this:

c:\network\qvt\wnqvtwsk.exe

If you have Windows 95, you have a telnet program in the Windows folder. You can type **c:\Windows\Telnet.exe** in the **Telnet Application** text box or click the **Browse** button and use the dialog box to select this file.

Running a Telnet Session

Have you ever tried using someone else's computer? You never know what you're going to find. Maybe a menuing system, maybe some fancy graphical interface such as Norton Desktop. Maybe you even get... horror of horrors... a DOS prompt! That's sort of what telnetting is like. You connect to another computer, never sure what you're going to encounter—a texty menu system, a UNIX prompt, or a spiteful warning explaining what will happen to you if you go any further.

In the following sections, you'll get a preview of what you'll meet at many telnet sites, and you'll learn how to manage a telnet session.

How Do I Connect?

One sure way you can connect to any Internet site with Navigator is to type the site's URL in the **Location** text box and press **Enter**. If you don't know of any telnet sites, try the library at Washington University in St. Louis:

telnet://library.wustl.edu

Navigator runs your telnet program and connects to the specified telnet *host*, the central computer that will be serving you. (In case you're wondering how you fit in, you're the *client*.) If you connected to the server in the example, your screen should look like this.

Telnetting to a library system.

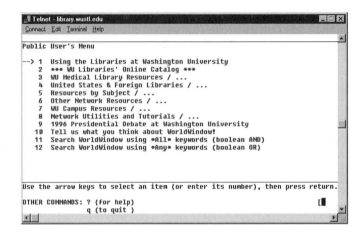

There are other ways to connect to telnet to sites through Navigator. You may, for example, stumble upon a link for a telnet site. When you click on the link, Navigator automatically runs your telnet program and connects with the telnet host. You may also encounter links to telnet sites when Gophering from Navigator (see Chapter 13).

Funky Hieroglyphics

If you connect to a site, and you get a bunch of characters that look as though they've been scrawled by a possessed Egyptian, you probably picked the wrong terminal type. Change the terminal setting in your telnet program. Most telnet programs have a Terminal or Options menu that lets you change the settings.

I'm Supposed To Know My Terminal Type?

The first thing most telnet sites will ask you is what type of terminal you're emulating (not you, personally, but your computer). If you don't know, just press **Enter** to accept the default setting. Then, if that doesn't work, try to change the setting in your telnet program. Common settings are VT100, VT102, and VT220. Some telnet hosts are very accommodating, as long as you can specify which terminal emulation you're using.

Emulating Terminals

Terminal emulation is a technique used to make one computer act like another so the two computers can carry on a conversation. Some mainframe computers will interact with only a specific type of terminal. If you want to connect to that mainframe computer using your personal computer, you must make your computer act like the required terminal.

Greeting Your Telnet Host

Very few telnet hosts just fling the door open and let you in. Most ask for some sort of identification: an e-mail address, a password, maybe a fake ID. Don't get rattled. Read the entire screen to see if the server allows for anonymous telnet sessions. You may be able to log in as **guest** or **visitor**.

No two hosts will greet you the same way. Some hosts are very formal. They require that you enter your name, address, and phone number and then type a user ID and provide a password. The next time you log in, the host prompts you to type your user ID and password. Other hosts will kick you out immediately, no questions asked, refusing the connection. And others will let you in, only to warn you that if you continue, you'll be in deep trouble. They never say what kind of trouble, or tell you who's coming to get you, but the vague threat is intended to make you disconnect.

What Do I Type?

When you've connected with your first telnet site, you have an overall feeling of accomplishment. You start to feel like the greatest computer wizard of the century. Once the glow passes, you go into mild shock as you realize that you've never met anything quite as ugly as the screen that you're staring at right now. What do you type? How do you proceed? And most importantly, how do you get out?

The best general rule I know for proceeding from this point is to read the screens. Most telnet hosts display messages and instructions that lead you through the login process and then tell you what to do to get help or exit. If you see no instructions, try the following keystrokes:

? The question-mark key usually displays a list of telnet commands. If this key doesn't work, try pressing **Ctrl+]** and then pressing the question-mark key.

Ctrl+] Interrupts the telnet session and usually returns you to the **telnet>** prompt. Use this command if your system locks up and prevents you from entering other telnet commands.

Ctrl+D Quits the current telnet session. This won't work on all telnet hosts.

q or **quit** If Ctrl+D doesn't quit the telnet session, press **Ctrl+]** to return to the **telnet>** prompt and then type **q**.

close Another way to close the telnet session. Press **Ctrl+]** to return to the **telnet>** prompt and then enter **close**.

Most public access telnet hosts offer additional command keystrokes, which are usually displayed with a caret (^). For example, the host may display ^Q to Quit. The caret stands for Ctrl (the Control key). To enter the command, you would hold down the **Ctrl** key while typing **Q**.

If you encounter a menu system, look for instructions on how to use it. Menu systems vary widely. In one, you might type the number that appears next to the desired option. In another menu, you might press the **Tab** key to move from option to option and then press **Enter** to select an option. In other menus, you must type the first few characters of the option's name and then press **Enter**. There's no consistency from one host to another. Just trust the experience you gained using other systems and think creatively.

Read the screen for important instructions when you first log on.

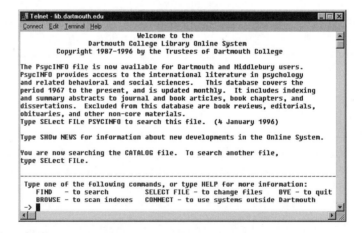

A Directory of Telnet Hosts

One way to tour various telnet hosts is to connect to HYTELNET, a directory of telnet hosts. This telnet host acts as a phone book for other telnet hosts. It contains addresses and login information for hundreds of online library catalogs, bulletin board systems

(BBSs), Free-nets (free online systems), and other information resources. To telnet to this site, enter the following URL (in Navigator, not in your Telnet program):

http://moondog.usask.ca/hytelnet/

This Web page contains links to information about Hytelnet. Click on the **Library Catalogs** link and then follow the trail of links to find the link to a specific Telnet site. For example, you might click on one link for libraries, another for a list of libraries arranged geographically, and another link for libraries in the Americas. Follow the links as you would on any Web site, till you find the link for the Telnet site you want to use. The last screen you get should contain the site's domain name and the username you must enter to telnet anonymously.

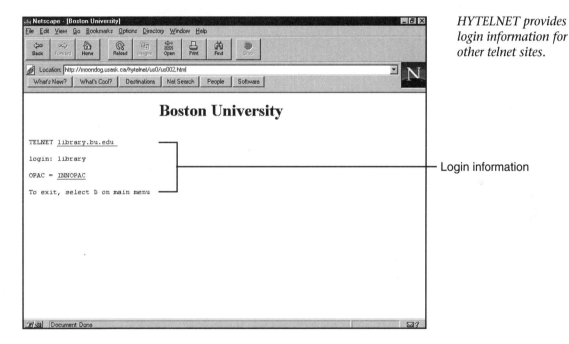

HYTELNET provides login information for other telnet sites.

— Login information

If you can't connect to **http://moondog.usask.ca/hytelnet/**, try one of the following URLs:

http://www.cam.ac.uk/Hytelnet/index.html

http://library.adelaide.edu.au/gen/net/telnet.html

http://www.nova.edu/Inter-Links/hytelnet.html

http://www.einet.net/hytelnet/HYTELNET.html

Playing Games with Telnet

MUDs (Multi-User Dungeons and Dragons), and their offshoots (MOOs, MUSes, MUSHes, or LPMUDs), are interactive role-playing games that involve many users from all over the world. To play a MUD, you have to telnet to a specific MUD site and enter your character's name and a password (many MUDs let you watch a game by logging in as a guest).

Because each MUD has its own list of commands for playing the game, you must familiarize yourself with these commands before you start playing. When you first connect to a MUD, enter the system's help command (usually by typing help at the prompt) to view a list of commands.

One of the best places to find out about MUDs and MOOs before you play them is at the Mud Connector Web site at **http://www.absi.com/mud**. Here, you'll find a list of over 300 MUDs and MOOs, complete with a description of each. For many MUDs, the Mud Connector has links for obtaining more information about playing the game. Another good place for links is at Spinal Tap's Gopher server:

gopher://spinaltap.micro.umn.edu:70/11/fun/Games/MUDs/Links

The Mud Connector provides links to over 300 of the best MUDs.

Click on a link for more information about the MUD.

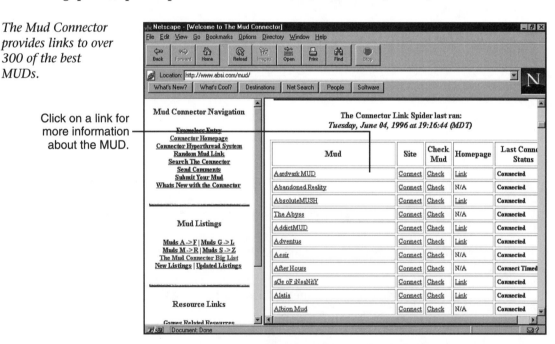

166

UNIX Primer

If you do much telnetting, chances are you'll wander into one or more sites that give you nothing but a UNIX prompt. If you have a Mac or use Windows exclusively, getting dumped at a UNIX prompt is like waking up surrounded by a tribe of aborigines. Although I'm not about to teach you how to speak UNIX (or "aboriginese," for that matter), I will teach you enough to survive your first encounter with UNIX.

Bare Bone Basics

The first lesson is that all UNIX directories are separated by forward slashes (files/files/Morefiles). Second, capitalization matters: **MYFILE.TXT** is not the same as **myfile.txt** or **MyFile.txt**. So when you're trying to get a file, make sure you type the directory and file names **eXactly** as they appear.

What's in This Directory, Anyway?

Now, you're at a UNIX prompt, and you want to see what's in the current directory. Type **ls** and press **Enter** to view a *list* of files and directories. Enter **ls -l** if you want more information, including file sizes and types. Enter **ls -m** to pause the file list at the end of each page; you can then view the next page by pressing the **Spacebar**.

Repeating a UNIX Command You can repeat the previous UNIX command by typing !! and pressing **Enter**.

Changing Directories

In most cases, you won't need any of the files or information stored in the root directory of the server. You'll want to change to one of the subdirectories. Type **cd** *dirname* (where *dirname* is the name of the directory you want to change to) and press **Enter**. To move back to the previous directory, type **cd ..** and press **Enter**. To find out which directory you're in, type **pwd** and press **Enter**.

Tracking Down Files

If you know the name of the file you're looking for, but you don't know which directory it's in, the UNIX **find** command can help. The **find** command searches the current directory and all its subdirectories for the specified file, so make sure you're in the correct directory, or in the root (topmost) directory, before entering this command.

Type the command as **find . -name** *filename* **-print** (where *filename* is the name of the file you're looking for). Make sure you type the command exactly as shown and use the proper capitalization in the file name. Press **Enter**. If the file is stored in the current directory, UNIX displays its location as *./filename*. If the file is in a different directory, UNIX shows the location as *./dirname/filename*.

Taking a Peek at a Text File

If you come across a text file you want to read, type **cat** *filename* and press **Enter**. If the text scrolls off the screen, try the **more** *filename* command. With the **more** command, UNIX displays the first page of the text file. Press the **Enter** key to scroll down line by line, or press the **Spacebar** to scroll page by page.

Grabbing a File

You're at a telnet site for one or two reasons: you want to use the programs and other resources at that site, or you want to grab some files. To get a file off a UNIX server, you use the **get** command. Change to the directory that contains the file, type **get** *filename*, and press **Enter**.

Running a Program

Most telnet sites greet you with a menu, which pretty much limits your options. However, on the rare occasion you get dumped at a UNIX prompt, you may be able to run a program on the UNIX server. If you type **ls -l**, you see a file list. To the left of the file names are attributes, such as **-rw** or **-rwx**. The **x** stands for executable. Type the name of the program file and press **Enter**. You're on your own when it comes to navigating the program.

Telnetting to an Archie Server

In Chapter 11, you learned how to use an Archie Request form to search for files. Hands down, this is the easiest way to search for files on the Internet. However, it may not be the fastest and most flexible of search tools. If you're daring, you may want to perform your Archie searches from a telnet site. Here's what you do:

1. Click inside the Location text box, type a URL for one of the following Archie servers, and press **Enter**:

   United States:
   telnet://archie.internic.net   New Jersey
   telnet://archie.unl.edu   Nebraska
   telnet://archie.ans.net   New York

| telnet://archie.rutgers.edu | New Jersey |
| telnet://archie.sura.net | Maryland |

Other Countries:

telnet://archie.au	Australia
telnet://archie.cs.mcgill.ca	Canada
telnet://archie.th-darmstadt.de	Germany
telnet://archie.wide.ad.jp	Japan
telnet://archie.switch.ch	Switzerland
telnet://archie.luth.se	Sweden
telnet://archie.doc.ic.ac.uk	United Kingdom

2. Enter **archie** when prompted to type your account name.

3. Enter **set pager** to make the display easier to read.

4. Enter one of the following commands to specify the type of search:

> **set search sub** searches inside file names for the search text and ignores capitalization. This command tells Archie to find all file names that contain the text you enter. So, if you search for wintelb, Archie will find files such as wintelb.zip, wintelb_3.zip, and so on.

> **set search exact** searches for only those file names that are identical to your search text. In other words, you have to know exactly what you want.

> **set search subcase** is like **set search sub**, but this command tells Archie to acknowledge capitalization. If you search for MYFILE.TXT, Archie won't look for myfile.txt.

5. Type **find** and follow it with a space and the name (or partial name) of the file you want to search for. Press **Enter**. If you're lucky, Archie displays your position in the search queue (line) and approximately how long the search will take. If you're less fortunate (which is more likely than not), Archie notifies you that it's too busy right now to search for your file. Try another server.

6. Wait. This could take awhile. When the search is complete, Archie displays a list of the files it found, including the location of the file and the date on which Archie last logged it in.

Check Out the Locals When choosing an Archie server, try the closest server listed first. That cuts down on Internet traffic, something every good Net citizen should be concerned with. Also, try accessing the servers during off hours.

169

7. Write down the domain of the server on which each copy of the file is stored, along with any other information you need to locate the file (for example, its complete name and the directory in which it is stored). If your telnet program has a Copy command, it can come in handy here. Copy the information to a text editor or word processor.

8. If there are additional files, press the **Spacebar** to view the next screenful of finds, and then repeat step 7.

9. When you reach the bottom of the list, type **q** to go back to the Archie prompt, then type **logoff** or **quit** and press **Enter**.

After you log off, you can use Navigator to connect to one of the FTP sites you found and then download the file.

Get Lots of Information

Copy the information for at least five sites. You may not be able to connect to some sites, or the file may no longer be stored at that site.

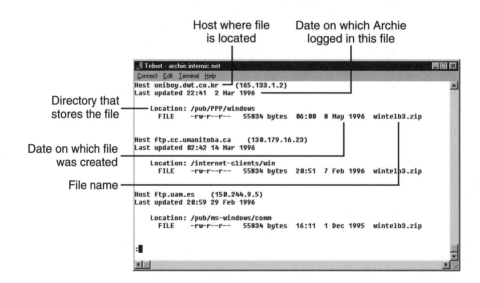

Host where file is located · Date on which Archie logged in this file · Directory that stores the file · Date on which file was created · File name

The Least You Need To Know

Okay, so you can't change the balance in your Visa account or launch nuclear warheads from your office, but you now have the power to connect to other computers all over the world. As you start your journey, keep the following in mind:

➤ To telnet from Navigator, you need to install a telnet program, which acts like a helper application.

➤ You can start a telnet session by clicking on the link of a telnet site or by entering its URL.

➤ The URL for all telnet sites starts with **telnet://**.

➤ When you connect to a telnet site, specify your terminal emulation and enter a login name.

➤ Most telnet sites display instructions on how to use the system. Read the screens thoroughly.

➤ When in doubt, type **?** to get help or **q** to quit.

NELSON? LARRY?

Chapter 15

Finding People on the Internet

By the End of This Chapter, You'll Be Able To...

➤ List three ways to search for people on the Internet

➤ Understand why it is so difficult to find someone on the Internet

➤ View a list of users at a given site

➤ Find a person's e-mail address by searching for his name

If you've ever used CompuServe, Prodigy, or America Online, you know how easy it is to find a member. You enter the command to look for a member, and then you enter the member's real name or screen name. Seconds after you give your okay, a list pops up, showing you the names of all the people who fit your description. With such power, it's easy to find friends and long lost relatives… assuming they're using the same online service.

Because the Internet consists of a loose collection of other computers, there's no master list of the millions of users who sign on. At best, each network within the Internet has a list of users at that site. In other words, you have to know where a person hangs out if you're going to have any chance of finding that person.

And that's not the only problem. Some sites don't allow you to view their lists of users. They consider such information confidential. Other sites allow their users to decide whether or not they want to make their e-mail addresses and other information publicly accessible. And even when this information is available, it may only provide a list of login names and e-mail addresses, names that may not exactly match the names as you would normally search for them. In short, as you work through this chapter, don't get your hopes up.

Fingering Your Friends

The best way to find people on the Internet is to search for them by e-mail address, using a program called *Finger*. Finger pokes around through the directory of users, and finds information about the person you're looking for. This info includes the person's e-mail address, and whether or not that person has read her mail recently (or even logged in).

If you've been paying attention, you're probably wondering, "What's the point? If you have to have a person's e-mail address to find the person, why not just send the person an e-mail message?" Admittedly, Finger isn't the best tool for tracking down lost contacts.

The most useful aspect of Finger is that it allows you to check on mail you may have sent to that person. If you finger the person and find out that they've never logged on or checked their mail, it's a good sign that you may need to call the person instead. In addition, Finger may dredge up the person's address or phone number, so you can contact the person if your e-mail isn't getting through.

To finger from Navigator, simply enter the URL of the finger gateway you want to use. (A *gateway* is a bridge between two incompatible computer networks.) Type one of the following URLs in the **Location** text box, and press **Enter**:

> **http://www.nova.edu/Inter-Links/cgi-bin/finger.pl**
>
> **http://www.cs.indiana.edu/finger/gateway**
>
> **http://www.rickman.com/finger.html**
>
> **http://www.middlebury.edu/~otisg/cgi/HyperFinger.cgi**

In moments, Navigator displays a page with a text box on it. Click inside the text box and type the e-mail address of the person you're looking for (for example, type jsmith@iquest.com). Press **Enter**.

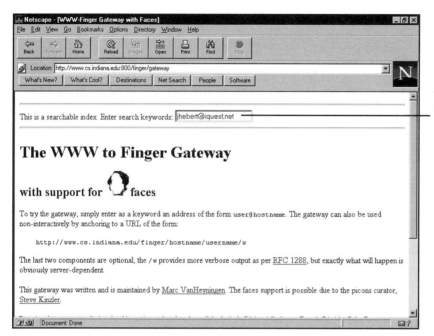

Indiana University can help you finger friends and relatives.

Type your search instruction here.

Assuming that Finger can find any information about the e-mail address you entered, Finger displays the information.

Other Things You Can Finger

Although Finger isn't the ideal tool for tracking down people, it does offer some interesting peripheral uses. For example, some users include something called a *plan* that appears when you finger that person. A plan is actually a hidden UNIX text file that can include additional information, including the person's address and phone number, job qualifications, interests, or anything else the user wants to include. When you

Draw Up Your Own .Plan For instructions on how to create and attach your own .plan files, buy *The Complete Idiot's Next Step with the Internet.*

finger someone, look at the bottom of the information screen. If the person has no plan, you'll see **No Plan**. If the person has a plan, you'll see **Plan:** followed by the plan text.

Whois This Person?

If you can't finger the person you want, you might be able to find the person using Whois. *Whois* is just another UNIX search command that is customarily used locally. Whois is particularly useful for finding a person's phone number and e-mail address if you know the person's last name. For example, if you know an employee at Bell Laboratories, you may be able to get that person's phone number by using Whois.

To use Whois from Navigator, you have to work through a Whois gateway. Click inside the **Location** text box, and enter the following URL:

> **gopher://sipb.mit.edu:70**

This connects you to the Gopher server at MIT. Now, click on **Internet Whois Servers**. This displays a list of publicly accessible sites that allow Whois searches. Click the desired site to display a search form. Then click inside the Search Index text box. You can also try the following sites:

> **gopher://rs.internic.net/7waissrc%3A/rs/whois.src**
>
> **http://www.nic.ad.jp/cgi-bin/whois_gate**
>
> **http://services.bunyip.com:8000/products/digger/digger-main.html**

Type the name or partial name of the person you're looking for. Use only one name; if you're looking for Bill Clinton, type **Bill** or **Clinton**, but not **Bill Clinton**. If you're searching for a name, and you can't remember how it's spelled, type a portion of the name followed by a period. For example, if you can't remember how to spell Olieskieviezc, type **Olie.** and press **Enter**. You should get a list of all the names that matched your entry.

You're not done yet. In some cases, a Whois search displays the person's *handle*, the user's computerized nickname. You can usually get more details about a person by searching again, this time using the person's handle.

Repeat the search using the person's handle.

Person's handle

Other Tools and Services for Finding Lost Souls

Finger and Whois are the standard Internet tools you use to search for people, but new tools are constantly being developed. To try some of the more experimental tools, connect to the following site, and click a link for one of these tools:

> **http://www.nova.edu/Inter-Links/phone.html**

This site also contains links to Finger and Whois, and telephone directories of several organizations. Also, try using Yahoo's electronic, national phone directory at

> **http://www.yahoo.com/search/people/**

If your husband just cleaned out your savings account and flew off to some exotic land with mistress in tow, Finger and Whois probably won't help you track him down. For that, you need a professional service… and the Internet has links for those services, as well:

> **http://www.cache.net/finders/find.html**
>
> **http://www.greatbasin.net/~windsong/pef.html**
>
> **http://pages.prodigy.com/mikep/search.htm**

When All Else Fails, Write the Postmaster

You've tried Finger. You've done Whois. No luck. Your only option at this point is to try the postmaster at the Internet site where you think your friend hangs out. Fire up your e-mail program, and send a message to *postmaster@hostname*, inquiring as to the whereabouts of your friend or colleague. (In place of *hostname*, type the domain name of the server that the person uses—for example, compuserve.com). Be sure to tell the postmaster why you are looking for this person. You might also include your e-mail address and phone number. The postmaster may have a policy of not releasing information about members, but will gladly pass along any information about how to contact you.

The Least You Need To Know

Now that you know how to search for people, you can look up all your old college buddies, at least the ones who decided to stick around for their graduate degrees. Here are some things to keep in mind as you search:

➤ To use Finger or Whois, you have to go through a gateway.

➤ The URL for one of the Finger gateways is **http://www.cs.indiana.edu/finger/gateway**.

➤ The URL for a Whois gateway is **gopher://sipb.mit.edu:70**.

➤ To do a Finger search, enter your search text in the form *person@hostname*.

➤ To do a Whois search, enter the person's first name or last name, or enter a partial name followed by a period.

➤ If you can't find someone with Whois or Finger, try writing the postmaster at *postmaster@hostname*.

➤ If you still can't find someone, hang the person's photo in the post office.

Part 4
More Netscape, More Navigator

Netscape's corporate plan is world domination. Short of that, Netscape wants to dominate the software industry, to tear the honor from Microsoft Corporation.

How? By adding so many features to its Web browser that you'll have to buy it on CD. By giving you a Web browser that can handle e-mail and newsgroups. By providing an Internet phone program. By allowing you to chat with other users all over the world. And by making it all so seamless that you forget the huge operating system (what's its name?) that's running behind it.

In this part, you'll learn how to use some of the fancy gadgets that come with Navigator, and others that you can add to it. You'll learn how to create and publish your own Web pages. And you'll get a glimpse of a couple hundred of the best pages on the Web. Enjoy!

Chapter 16

Chatting Online with Other Users

By the End of This Chapter, You'll Be Able To...

➤ Type messages back and forth with your friends

➤ Swap Web pages with acquaintances and colleagues

➤ Prowl cyberrooms when you can't sleep

➤ Pretend you're someone you're not

You've probably heard of it on the news. Two people wandering the Internet or some commercial online service bump into each other in a virtual talk room, realize they are soul mates, decide to get hitched, and live happily ever after.

A more likely story would have one member of the "happy couple" (not to be sexist, but usually the male) already married and pretending to be single. He woos the young computer mistress, convinces her to meet him in New York, has a one night stand, confesses that he's married, and flies back to Podunk, Illinois just in time for breakfast with the wife and kids.

But not all people try to score in chat rooms (yeah, right). Some people actually like to talk shop, discuss the weather, argue politics, or just hang out and watch other people make fools of themselves. Now, you'll get your chance.

Where To Get Netscape's Chat Program

You can't chat on the Internet with Netscape Navigator alone. You need another program, called Netscape Chat, which provides a window that displays the running dialogue.

To get Netscape Chat, fire up Netscape Navigator, type the URL for Netscape's FTP site (**ftp://ftp.netscape.com**) into the **Location** text box, and press **Enter**. Assuming that the FTP site lets you in (BIG assumption), you'll see a list of directories. Use the directory list to change to the pub/chat/Windows directory.

Mirror FTP Sites

If the Netscape FTP server is too busy, it shows you the courtesy of displaying a list of URLs for mirror sites (other FTP servers that have the same files). Drag over one of the URLs, and press **Ctrl+C** to copy it. Then, click inside the **Location** text box, press **Ctrl+V**, and press **Enter**.

Okay, ready to download? Right-click on the file called **nc3220p0.exe** (the 32-bit version for Windows 95) or **nc1620p0.exe** (the 16-bit version for Windows 3.1). (Remember, the file name might differ, if Netscape has come out with a new version of Chat since the writing of this book, but the name should still start with **nc**.) Click **Save Link as**, and use the dialog box that appears, to select the drive and folder in which you want the file stored (the TEMP directory on your hard drive is usually a good place).

Installing Netscape Chat

The file you just downloaded is a self-extracting, self-installing file. Simply run the Windows Explorer (or File Manager, if you're using Windows 3.1), change to the folder or directory that contains the file you just downloaded, and then double-click on the file. The file extracts itself, and then runs the Netscape Chat Installation program. Just follow the on-screen instructions to install the Chat program.

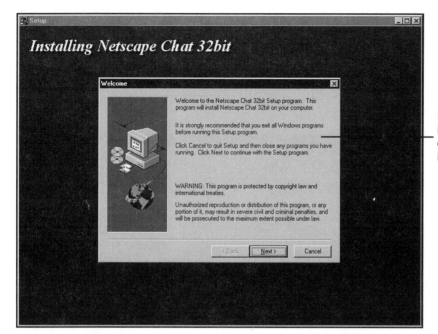

Installing Netscape Chat 32bit

The Netscape Chat Installation program installs Netscape Chat for you.

Follow the on-screen instructions to complete the installation.

When you're done, you should have a Netscape Chat 32bit icon on the Windows Start/ Programs menu (in Windows 95), or (if you're using Windows 3.1) in the Netscape program group. Don't run Netscape Chat just yet. If you try, you'll find yourself with no one to talk to. You first have to connect to an IRC (Internet Relay Chat) server, which you'll do next.

Finding a Chatty Cove

The hardest part about using Chat is finding a place to chat. Most Internet servers don't mind you flipping through Web pages and purloining an occasional file, but they don't like to devote their resources to a bunch of chatty slackers. Because of this, it's tough to find a chat room, and even when you do, it might be gone the next day.

If you're very lucky, your service provider has a chat server, which you can connect to and use. Find out the chat server's URL, and ask if you need to enter a special username and password for access.

When your service provider informs you that he offers no such server, you'll have to hunt for a public chat server. The first place to search is on your service provider's Web server. If your service provider has a technical support area on the Web, you might find a list of public chat servers on one of its Web pages. Because most service providers do not have dedicated chat servers, they try to provide links to servers, so you won't feel cheated.

If you still can't find anything, try grabbing a file called **servers.950301** (or a similar name) from the following FTP site:

> **ftp://cs-ftp.bu.edu:/irc/support/**

This file is a text file that contains a list of IRC servers throughout the world, along with each server's URL, as shown here.

You can acquire a list of chat servers.

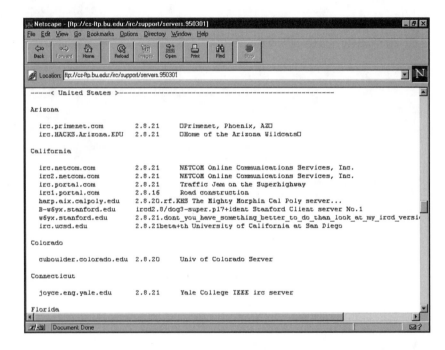

If you can't find that file, or the FTP server won't let you in, use your favorite Web search tool (Yahoo, AltaVista, WebCrawler) to search for IRC Servers. You should find several lists. If that doesn't turn up what you're looking for, try the newsgroup alt.irc (type **news:alt.irc** in Navigator's **Location** text box). A newsgroup is like an electronic bulletin board where you can read and post messages. This particular newsgroup (alt.irc) contains messages about Internet chat. Users commonly post lists of chat servers and their URLs. For details on how to read newsgroup messages, see Chapter 12.

Check This Out...

Find More Than One Chat Server
Chances are that you'll have to try several chat servers before you find one that actually exists and will let you in. Make sure you have a long list to start with.

Creating a New Identity

Before you start chatting, you should work on your online profile. Your profile consists of as much or as little information you want other chatters to have access to. It must contain a nickname, which distinguishes you from other chatters in the same room. You can also include your e-mail address, phone number, address, a description of yourself (usually phony), and other information that you don't mind people seeing and using to harass you and destroy your life.

Don't Be Stupid

The information you enter in your profile is accessible to anyone on the chat server you're connected to. Stupid people like to add as much information as they can. They might even include a list of passwords and credit card numbers, so deviant chatters can have all the tools they need. Be smart. Don't enter any information that can be used against you.

To create your on-screen profile, start Netscape Chat. If you're using Windows 95, click the **Start** button, rest the mouse pointer on **Programs**, point to **Netscape Chat 32bit**, and then click **Netscape Chat 32bit**. In Windows 3.1, open the Netscape program group window, and double-click the **Netscape Chat** icon. The Netscape Chat window appears, and the Server Connection dialog box is displayed. (It doesn't matter if you're connected to the Internet at this point.)

Navigator Runs Automatically

Whenever you run Netscape Chat, Navigator runs also. This allows you to trade Web pages with other users while you're chatting. For now, just realize that Navigator is supposed to run; you didn't do anything funky. Later, you'll learn how to use Navigator along with Chat.

Ignore the options at the top of the dialog box, and skip to the Your Information area. Type your name in the **Real Name** text box (you don't have to use your real name).

The **User Account Login** and **Password** text boxes may be optional. Some chat servers require that you enter a unique login name and password in order to gain access. In this chapter, we'll be connecting to chat servers that allow public access without this information, so you can leave these boxes blank. If you use a special chat server, the administrator will give you the login name and password you need to enter, and you can enter it here.

You can stop here, or you can click on the **My Profile** button and add the following information:

Nick Name: This is the same as the Nick Name you entered above. You can change it here, if desired.

Age: Most people lie about their age. Type the age you want people to think you are. Or, if you want to be original, type your real age.

Email: Type your e-mail address, if you don't mind people writing you letters and stalking you electronically.

Phone: I wouldn't type your phone number. If you want someone to know your phone number, e-mail it to the person later.

Home Page: If you have a personal Web page, you can type the URL here, so people can check it out.

Away Message: If you want a brief message to appear when people try to communicate with you when you're away from your keyboard, type it here.

Personal Description: Type a description of yourself. If you're a woman (or a man—doesn't matter), and you want a lot of action, type **Female, 5'6", 120 lbs, blonde, green eyes, hot** or something similar. If you want people to leave you alone, type **Male, 45, 5'4", 220 lbs, bald, MIS.**

When you're done entering a bunch of phony information, click on the **Update** button in the **Personal Profile** dialog box and the **OK** button in the **Server Connection** dialog box.

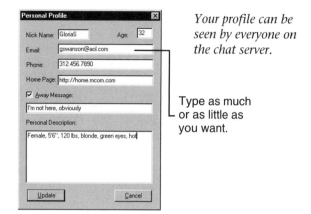

Your profile can be seen by everyone on the chat server.

Type as much or as little as you want.

Connecting to a Chat Server

Before you can chat, you must connect to a chat server and then enter a chat room (a place where people hang out and talk). The following steps show you how to connect to a chat server. Keep in mind, however, that you may have to try several servers to find one that will let you in:

1. Run your TCP/IP program (in Windows 3.1) or Dial-Up Networking (in Windows 95), and establish your Internet connection.

2. Start Netscape Chat. If you're using Windows 95, click the **Start** button, rest the mouse pointer on **Programs**, point to **Netscape Chat 32bit**, and then click **Netscape Chat 32bit**. In Windows 3.1, open the Netscape program group window, and double-click the **Netscape Chat** icon. The Netscape Chat window appears, and the Server Connection dialog box is displayed.

Type the URL of the chat server you want to use here.

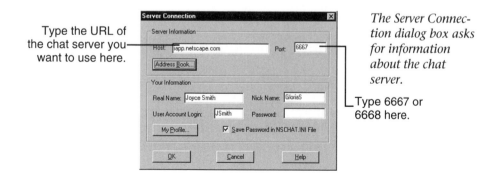

The Server Connection dialog box asks for information about the chat server.

Type 6667 or 6668 here.

187

3. Under Server Information, click inside the **Host** text box, and type the URL of the chat server you want to use (for example, irc.colorado.edu).

4. Click inside the **Port** text box, and type the server's port number (usually 6667). If 6667 doesn't connect you, try 6668 or 6669.

5. Click on the **Address Book** button, and in the dialog box that appears, click on the **Add** button. This adds the server name to a list, so you won't have to enter all this information again next time.

The Address Book lets you keep a list of IRC servers.

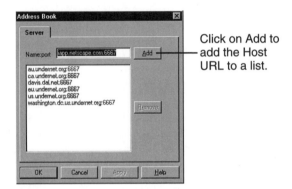

Click on Add to add the Host URL to a list.

6. Click **OK**. This returns you to the Server Connection dialog box.

7. Click **OK**. If all goes as planned, you are connected to the chat server (**Server Connected** should appear in the status bar). If you see a message saying that the chat server has no DNS entry or won't let you in, click **OK**, and repeat steps 3 to 10 to try connecting to the same or a different chat server. (You might have to click on the Connect button, the leftmost button in the toolbar, to display the Server Connection dialog box.)

Joining a Chat Room

Once you're connected the Quick Join dialog box appears, asking you to join a room. If you know the name of a room you want to enter, or if you want to create your own room, type its name in the Join Room text box. If the room requires a password, type the password in the Room Key text box. (You get a password only if someone sends you a personal invitation to a room.) Then, click **Join**. You're connected to the room, and you can start chatting; skip to the next section.

If you don't know the name of a room, click on the **List** button. This opens the Conversation Rooms dialog box, shown below. Click on the room you want to enter, and click on the **Join** button. This opens a chat window for the selected room, allowing you to start talking. Skip to the next section.

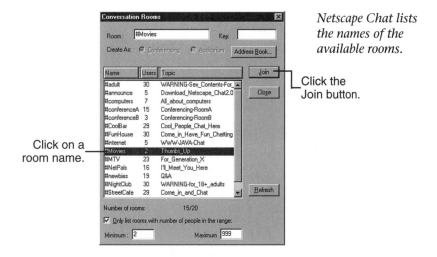

Netscape Chat lists the names of the available rooms.

Click the Join button.

Click on a room name.

Start Your Own Conversation

The steps here show how to enter an established chat room and start conversing. However, you can create your own chat room, and have people join *your* discussion. Instead of picking a room from the list, type a unique name for your room, and click **Join**. (Some servers don't let just anybody create rooms.) After creating the room, hang out for awhile and play host; otherwise, people won't stay long.

Start Talking

When you first enter a chat room, sit back and watch the conversation. Once you've picked up on the tone of the room, you can start typing your own messages. If this is your first attempt at chatting, be prepared for some teasing. You'll be a *newbie*, a novice, and seasoned Internet users will seize the opportunity to take an occasional jab at you. Don't let it rattle you; most chatters welcome a new face.

The conversation window consists of three panels: a list of users (on the left), a running transcript of the conversation (on the right), and a text box you can use to send your own messages (at the bottom). You can click the **Maximize** button to expand the window. You can also drag the pane borders to change the relative sizes of the panes; for example, you might want to increase the width of the column that lists people's names.

189

*Use the chat
window to converse.*

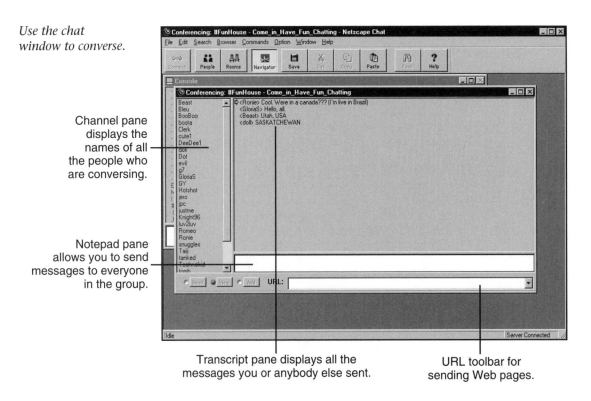

Channel pane
displays the
names of all
the people who
are conversing.

Notepad pane
allows you to send
messages to everyone
in the group.

Transcript pane displays all the
messages you or anybody else sent.

URL toolbar for
sending Web pages.

To add your own comments to the conversation, click inside the text box directly below the transcript pane, type your statement, and then press **Enter**.

Changing Chat Rooms

To leave the conversation, say your goodbyes, and then open the **Commands** menu and select **Leave Room**. You remain connected to the chat server. To join a different conversation, open the **File** menu, select **Show Rooms**, or open the **Commands** menu and select **Quick Join**.

If one discussion starts to lag, you can always leave it and join a different discussion. Or you can stay in that discussion and enter another room (in a separate chat window). You can enter up to ten separate rooms on the same server. Simply open the **File** menu, select **Show Rooms**, and then pick the conversation you want to join. You can then use the options on the Window menu to change windows or arrange them on your screen.

The Conversation Rooms dialog box (the one that appears when you select **File/Show Rooms**) has several helpful options. The **Address Book** button allows you to add a room name to a list of rooms so you don't have to search for or type the room name later. If you find a room you regularly hang out at, add it to the list.

Also, the bottom of the dialog box has text boxes that allow you to list rooms populated with a specific number of people. Because so many rooms have only one person in them, you might want to type 2 in the **Minimum** text box. This will prevent the names of less active rooms from appearing in the list. Make sure **Only list rooms with the number of people in the range** is selected.

Inviting People into a Chat Room

A chat server typically has hundreds of other users signed on, all chatting away in different rooms. You can check out a list of people on the server and invite people to join you in the room where you're currently chatting.

Open the **File** menu and select **Show People**. The Show People dialog box appears, as shown below. Click on the name of the person you want to invite to your room, and click on the **Invite** button. A dialog box appears, asking you to type a name for the room. Type the name of the room you're in and click **OK**. (You can't invite someone into a room that you're not in.) An invitation appears on the person's screen, allowing the person to accept or reject your invitation.

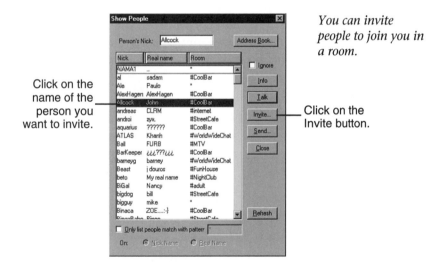

Click on the name of the person you want to invite.

Click on the Invite button.

You can invite people to join you in a room.

Meeting in Private

To have a private conversation with one or more people, first create a room. Be sure to assign it a room key (password). Then invite only those people who you want to join you. Don't forget to tell them the password.

The Show People dialog box allows you to do much more than simply invite people to a room. Try out the following options:

Ignore lets you stop a specific person (the one you've selected in the list) from sending messages to you. This is good for making obnoxious people go away.

Info displays the selected person's profile.

Talk lets you send messages that appear only on the selected person's screen. (This is just like entering the Commands/Talk command.)

Send opens a dialog box that lets you send the selected person a file. It's sort of like sending a file via e-mail.

Person-to-Person Conversations

If you're looking for privacy, you can talk to a person one-on-one. The person must agree to talk to you, of course, but once he or she does, the two of you will be in your own cozy window, typing clever quips back and forth.

For an informal chat with another person, you don't have to enter a private room. You can simply choose to talk to that person aside from the room you're in. To do this, click on the name of the person you want to talk to (in the names panel), and then open the **Commands** menu and select **Talk**. A window appears which you can use to type messages only to the selected person. Any messages that person types in response will appear in that window.

If someone else initiates a similar conversation with you, the separate talk window may not appear. Instead, you'll see a message in the room window that indicates the person is "whispering." This message and the person's comment appear only on your screen. To whisper back, click on the person's name, and then open the **Commands** menu and select **Talk**.

More You Should Know About Conversations

Now that you know how to enter group conversations (and leave them), you have all the information you need to chat in groups. However, there are some additional techniques you can try in group conversations:

➤ If you have text inside a document, and you want to send it, don't retype it. Simply highlight the text and copy it. Then return to the chat room, click inside the message area, open the **Edit** menu, and select **Paste & Send**.

➤ To ignore a person in the room, click on the person's name, open the **Commands** menu, and select **Ignore**. To stop ignoring the person, repeat the steps.

➤ To save a conversation transcript (the running dialog text that appears in the transcript pane), open the **Edit** menu and select **Save Transcript** (or press **Ctrl+S**). A dialog box appears, prompting you to name the file and select the drive and folder where you want the transcript stored. Enter your preferences, and then click the **Save** button.

➤ To clear the transcript from the window (and start fresh), open the **Edit** menu and select **Clear Transcript**.

➤ To find out about a particular person in the "room," double-click his or her name in the list on the left. The User Info dialog box appears, showing the person's real name, the names of the room that person is currently in, and (sometimes) the person's e-mail address and other information. You can click on the **Profile** tab for more information about the person. Click the **Cancel** button when you're done.

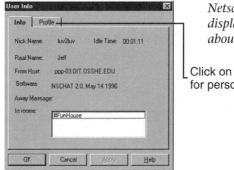

Netscape Chat can display information about each chatter.

Click on the Profile tab for personal information.

Joining an Auditorium Discussion

Group conversations are typically free and open. Anyone can join in at any time and say just about anything. However, you can join a more formal discussion group, called an *auditorium discussion*. These discussions feature a moderator and speakers, and may require permission to enter. Only the moderator and speakers talk. You can sit in and "listen" to the discussion, but if you want to talk, you must obtain permission from the moderator.

Auditorium discussions are usually scheduled ahead of time. You might hear about a particular discussion from a friend or colleague or from reading a newsgroup message. The moderator of the discussion may require that you fill out a form beforehand. The moderator will then send you (via e-mail) information about the discussion, including a list of featured speakers, the scheduled time and date, the channel on which the discussion will proceed, and the password you must enter to access the channel.

You follow the same procedure for joining an auditorium discussion as you follow for joining a group discussion. First, connect to the chat server on which the discussion is scheduled to take place. Then, open the **File** menu, and click **Show Rooms**. Use the dialog box that appears to specify the name of the auditorium discussion, click **Auditorium**, and then click **Join**.

Once you're "tuned in" to the auditorium discussion channel, you can watch the discussion, but you can't talk. If you want to speak, you can ask the moderator for the microphone. To ask permission, open the **Commands** menu, point to **Privilege**, and select **Request Microphone**. Type a request to one of the discussion moderators, and press **Enter**. Assuming your request is granted, you can now type messages to the entire group.

If you start an auditorium discussion yourself, or are picked to be a moderator for the discussion, you have the power to grant or refuse microphone requests. Click the name of the person to whom you would like to give the mike, and then open the **Commands** menu, point to **Privilege**, and select **Grant Speaker**. To take the microphone away, click the person's name, open the **Commands** menu, point to **Privilege**, and select **Revoke Speaker**. You can use the options at the bottom of the Commands menu to kick someone out of the room or ban them entirely.

You're the Moderator?

To start your own auditorium discussion, enter the **File/Show Rooms** command, type a unique name for your discussion, click **Auditorium**, and click **Join**. You can then use the options on the Commands menu to appoint and fire other moderators, and grant and revoke speaker requests. Hey, you're in charge. (However, not all servers will let you create your own rooms or channels.)

Sending and Receiving Web Pages

Here's where Netscape Navigator comes in. You may have noticed that whenever you enter a conversation, Netscape Chat attempts to run Navigator, which allows you to send and receive Web pages while you chat.

In Windows 95, you might have a little trouble with this feature, because Chat looks for Navigator in the Netscape folder (not in the Program Files\Netscape\Navigator\Program folder). If you receive an error message indicating that Chat can't find Navigator, open the **Option** menu, click **Preference**, and click on the **Navigator** tab. Click the **Browse** button, and, using the dialog box that appears, pick the drive and folder where Navigator is stored. Click the Netscape file and click **OK**.

If you don't want Netscape Navigator to start automatically whenever you join a discussion, click **Automatically start-up** to turn it off (remove the check mark). Click the **OK** button to save your changes. If you don't click **OK**, the next time you run Chat, you'll encounter the same problem.

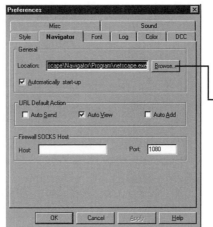

You must tell Chat where Navigator is stored.

Click the Browse button to display a dialog box that lets you specify where Navigator is stored.

Sending Web Pages to Discussion Participants

Once you have Navigator set up, you can use it in tandem with Chat to send Web pages to other people in the room and to receive and view pages they've sent to you. To send one or more Web pages to one or more people in the room group, here's what you do:

1. Change to Netscape Navigator, and display one of the Web pages you want to send. Whenever you display a Web page in Navigator, the page's URL is automatically inserted into the URL text box in Chat.

2. If you plan on sending more than one Web page, click the **Add** button. This adds the URL for the current Web page to a list of pages you want to send. You can repeat steps 1 and 2 to add URLs to the list.

   (You can have the URLs for any Web pages you view in Navigator automatically added to the list. Open the **Browser** menu, and click on **Auto Add**.)

3. In the panel that shows the nicknames of those involved in the discussion, click the name of the person to whom you want to send the Web page(s). To send the page to all the people in the list, make sure that *no* names are selected.

4. Click the **Send** button in the URL toolbar, or open the **Browser** menu and select **Send URL**. The specified Web pages are sent to the selected individual or to all the people in the room, who can then view the pages in their Web browser. You can then continue to use Chat to discuss the Web page(s) you sent.

You can also set up Chat to automatically send the URL of any page you open in Navigator. First, click on the name of the person to whom you want to send the URL (or make sure nobody is selected, to send the URL to everyone in the room). Open the **Browser** menu and click on **Auto Send**. Now, whenever you open a Web page in Navigator, its URL is sent to the selected person or to all people in the room.

If the URL list contains URLs that you no longer want on the list, you can clear the list to start over. Open the **Browser** menu, point to **URL List**, and click on **Clear**.

Check This Out...

Swapping GIFs and JPEGs

People love to swap pictures of themselves, so they can picture the person to whom they're talking. Consider creating your own Web page complete with a picture of yourself. You can then quickly send the Web page to anyone in the chat room who has Netscape Chat and Navigator. For details on how to create a Web page, see Chapter 20.

Receiving and Viewing Web Pages Sent by Others

You can now send Web pages, but what if someone sends a Web page to you? How do you view it? The best way to view incoming Web pages is to turn on the automatic viewing feature. Open the **Browser** menu, and make sure there is a check mark next to **Auto View**. (The Browser menu is available only if you are currently in a discussion on one or more channels.) If the checkmark is missing, click **Auto View** to turn it on.

With Auto View on, the View button in the URL toolbar has a green dot next to it. Now, whenever someone sends you a Web page, Chat opens the Web page in Netscape Navigator. The only trouble is that the Navigator window might be minimized. In Windows 95, use the taskbar to change to Navigator, and then maximize (or restore) the Navigator window. In Windows 3.1, use **Ctrl+Esc** to display the Task List, and then use the Task List to change to Navigator.

You can continue your discussion in Netscape Chat. Using Chat and Navigator together in this way is especially useful if you're creating a Web page with someone else's help. You can discuss and change the Web page you're creating and immediately see the results of a change.

If Auto View is off, you can still view the page. Simply wait until someone sends you the URL for the page, and the URL appears in the URL text box. Then, click the **View** button. This activates Navigator, which displays the associated Web page.

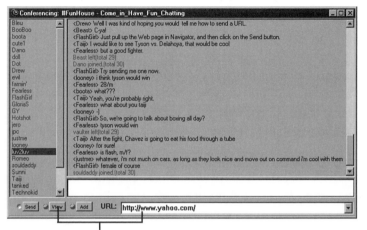

You can use the URL toolbar to view incoming Web pages.

When you see the Web page's
URL here, click the View button.

Saving a URL List

You can create a list of Web page URLs that you might want to send again to different people. You can then open that list later to quickly send it, without having to find and open all those Web pages again.

After creating the list of URLs you want to send, open the **Browser** menu, point to **URL List**, and click on **Save As**. Use the Save As dialog box to save the list to a folder or directory on your hard drive. To send the list later, open the **Browser** menu, point to **URL List**, and click on **Load**. Use the Open dialog box to select the file in which you saved the list, and click **Open**. You can now send the list.

Configuring Netscape Chat

You've probably configured Netscape Chat already. You had to in order to tell Chat where Netscape was located. Well, you can further customize Chat, to turn off the status bar or toolbar, choose the style of text displayed in conversations, or make sure that the Chat window always stays on top of the desktop.

Since you've already dealt with the Preferences dialog box, let's start there. Open the **Option** menu, and click **Preference**. The Preferences dialog box appears. I'm not going to bore you with the details of all the options. Instead, I'll give you a list of the tabs in this dialog box with a brief explanation of each:

Style lets you control the way the main toolbar, URL toolbar, and message areas are displayed. The Private Message display options control how messages sent only to you are handled: Active (displays private messages along with the other messages in the transcript pane), Global (displays *all* private messages in a separate window), and Separate (displays private messages from each person in a separate window).

Navigator gives you a bunch of options you can set more easily from the Browser menu.

Font lets you specify a different type size to use for incoming and outgoing messages. This can help you quickly tell the difference between your messages and the messages of other people in the chat room.

Log allows you to specify settings for saving transcripts of conversations. Most conversations are forgettable, so you can skip this one.

Color lets you pick the colors you want to use for special messages, such as private messages, messages from the room's creator, or URL text.

DCC stands for Direct Client Connection, which allows people to transfer files across the Internet while chatting. These options are fairly important. If someone sends you a 20MB file as a practical joke, it could damage your system or lock you up. Make sure **Prompt when receiving file size larger than** is checked. Leave the file size set to 0 (zero), so you'll be prompted before receiving any file. (You might want to check any program files you receive for viruses before running them.) Also, check to make sure the File Save directory is the one you want to use.

Misc contains several options you can safely ignore. If you're really interested in them, check the Help system.

Sound lets you turn sounds on or off for specific events, such as warnings and private messages.

When you're done setting your preferences, click the OK button to save your changes.

Advanced Tip 1

For all you hackers out there, here's an advanced tip: Chat still uses the old Windows INI file to configure itself. If you'd like to change something in the program, and you can't do it with the Option menu, open the **nschat.ini** file in Notepad, and enter your changes.

The Least You Need To Know

You don't need to know a whole lot about chatting. Once you find a chat server, and tune into a channel, you'll receive plenty of help from the other chatters. Feel free to ask questions and to try out unexplored features with other people. When you connect to a chat server, look for a room that has "welcome," "newbies," "new users," "FAQ," or "Q&A" in the title.

Also, you can find answers to most Chat questions by using Netscape Chat's Help menu. Although it's not the best Help system, it can steer you in the right direction. Happy chatting!

Chapter 17

Free Long-Distance with CoolTalk

By the End of This Chapter, You'll Be Able To...

➤ Use one of those Internet telephone programs you've heard so much about

➤ Save 100% on long-distance calls *without* switching to MCI

➤ Understand why the other person's voice sounds so fuzzy

➤ Pretend you're a high-powered business executive collaborating on a project using CoolTalk's White Board feature

You've no doubt heard all the buzz about Internet Phone, WebPhone, and other programs that let you bypass phone companies (and their sky-rocketing rates) by placing calls over the Internet. What you may not have heard is that the process is a little convoluted. Let's just say it's not the best way to have a casual conversation with mom on Mother's Day.

First, your computer has to have a few accessories in order to function as a phone. It needs a sound board, speakers, a microphone, and the CoolTalk program (which comes with Navigator 3.0). Second, you can't just dial up an ordinary telephone. The person on the other end must have a computer with a sound card, speakers, and a microphone, too. And this person must also have CoolTalk.

Now, when you call this person, she has to know you're calling and have her computer all set to answer. The computer on the other end must be actively connected to the Internet, and it must be running CoolTalk or CoolTalk Watchdog (we'll talk about the dog later).

Alright, with all the caveats out of the way, and assuming you have someone to call who fits the bill (or someone to call you), we can embark on this futuristic phone adventure.

No Sound Card?!

If you don't have a sound card, you can still use CoolTalk's Chat Tool and White Board, but you won't be able to make voice calls or use the voice mail feature. You really should have a sound card if you're doing the Web.

Is CoolTalk Already Installed?

When you installed Navigator, it displayed a dialog box asking if you wanted to install CoolTalk. If you installed Navigator the way I told you to, you clicked on all the Yes and OK buttons, so CoolTalk should be on your system.

To check, open the Netscape program group. If you're using Windows 3.1, you know what to do. In Windows 95, click **Start**, point to **Programs**, and click on **Netscape**. If you see a CoolTalk icon, you're in business. If you don't see the icon, run the Netscape installation again, but this time, be sure you click **Yes** when asked if you want to install CoolTalk.

CoolTalk Watchdog

Cooltalk Watchdog sounds like some powerful program that protects your computer. All it does is keep tabs on your Internet connection to see if there are incoming phone calls from another CoolTalk user. If it detects an incoming call, it starts CoolTalk automatically. We'll discuss Watchdog in greater detail later.

Using the CoolTalk Setup Wizard

To run CoolTalk, open the Netscape program group as you did earlier. Then, double-click on the **CoolTalk** icon. This starts CoolTalk and runs the Setup Wizard. This Wizard is a series of dialog boxes that lead you through the process of configuring CoolTalk to work with your sound card, speakers, microphone, and modem. This is a one-time deal, so don't fret. Just follow the on-screen instructions, and keep clicking on the **Next>** button.

After the Wizard performs a system test and tells you whether or not your computer is up to snuff, it displays the dialog box shown below, allowing you to create a business card. This card is used to help the person you're calling identify you. Type as much or as little information as you want the other person to know about you.

The only tricky part is if you want to add a photo of yourself, or a photo of the person you're impersonating. The photo will appear in the upper right corner of your business card. You can insert a photo in either of two ways:

➤ Scan in a picture of yourself, and save it as JPG, GIF, PCX, BMP, or TIFF file. Click on the little file icon next to Photo, and use the Open dialog box to select it.

➤ In your graphics program, display the image you want to appear on your business card, select it, and use the Copy command to place it on the Windows clipboard. Then, click on the little clipboard icon next to Photo, to insert the clipboard contents.

When the setup is complete, click on the **Finish** button. You're now ready to use CoolTalk.

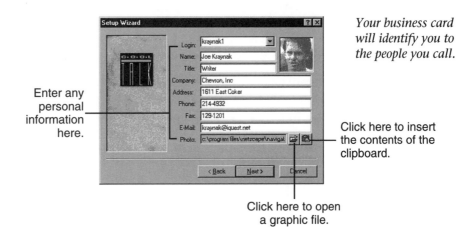

Enter any personal information here.

Click here to open a graphic file.

Click here to insert the contents of the clipboard.

Your business card will identify you to the people you call.

No Sound During Test?

If you don't hear any of the test sounds during the Wizard setup, something may have run amok with Windows or in one of your sound card programs.

Windows 95 has a gazillion ways to set your sound output and microphone input volume. The easiest way is to right-click on the speaker icon in the taskbar, and click on **Volume Controls**. Drag all the sliders to the top. If there is no slider for your microphone, open the **Options** menu, select **Properties**, and make sure all the check boxes at the bottom of the dialog box (except PC Speaker) are selected. This should display the sliders you need to set the volume.

If you have Windows 3.1, and you're using SoundBlaster, or one of the many SoundBlaster clones, look for a program group that contains the SoundBlaster program icons. Double-click on the Creative Mixer icon, and use its control panel to crank up the volume. For some strange reason, the Microphone slider likes to creep to the bottom.

Priceless Troubleshooting Tip 1

If you can't figure out what's wrong, try using some other audio program to record sounds. In Windows, you can use the Windows Sound Recorder. If you can record and play back sounds successfully with it, but not with CoolTalk, the problem is with CoolTalk, not Windows.

Placing a Call and Hanging Up

Okay, your friend in Atlanta is waiting for your call, and your wife's in bed. Time to try out this CoolTalk program. Connect to the Internet, and run CoolTalk.

Now, open the **Conference** menu, and click on **Start**. The Open Conference dialog box appears, prompting you to pick a person to talk with. Click on the **Address Book** tab, if it is not already up front. In the **Enter or select a conference participant** text box, type the e-mail address of the person you want to call. Click **OK**.

Assuming the person you're trying to contact is connected to the Internet, is running CoolTalk, and is not tied up in another call, CoolTalk displays an invitation on the person's screen. If the person accepts your invitation, and starts talking into her microphone, you'll be able to hear her voice. (At this point, the main CoolTalk window is displayed on both your screen and the other person's screen.)

You can start talking, and she'll be able to hear your voice. Of course, your wife will probably hear your voice, too, and then your little chat friend will hear your wife's voice. I can't help you with that.

Priceless Troubleshooting Tip 2

If you can't connect using the person's e-mail address, try the person's IP address. To get your address, click on the big **CoolTalk** button, and click on the **Host** tab. E-mail your IP address to your friend (using Netscape Mail), and tell her to use it to call you. Or, have your friend e-mail her IP address to you.

If you have trouble hearing the other person (or if the other person has trouble hearing you), you can crank up the volume. To adjust the microphone volume, click on the plus or minus button to the right of the microphone button. The speaker adjustment buttons are to the right of the speaker button.

Set the microphone volume.

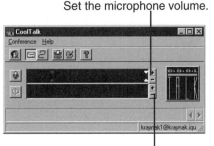

You can adjust the volume of incoming and outgoing sounds.

Set the speaker volume.

You can have a conference call by inviting other people to join your conversation. As long as these other people are not already engaged in another conference, they'll be able to see your invitation.

To view the business card of someone else who's involved in the conference, open the **Conference** menu, point to **Participant Info**, and click on the name of the participant.

Now, if you want to disconnect, open the **Conference** menu, and select **Leave**.

Speed Dial Buttons

You can create buttons for people you call frequently. In the Open Conference dialog box, on the Address tab, click on the e-mail address of the person. Click on the **Add to Speed Dial** button. Type the person's name in the **Label** text box, leave the entry in the **Address** text box alone, and click **Add**. The next time you want to call the person, start CoolTalk, and click on the button at the bottom of the CoolTalk window. To delete a button, right-click on it and select **Delete**.

Answering Incoming Calls

If you know someone is going to call you at a particular time, connect to the Internet and run CoolTalk. When the person calls, and invitation pops up on your screen, as shown below. Accept the invitation, and start talking. Once you accept the invitation, the main CoolTalk window appears on your screen.

Answer the phone!

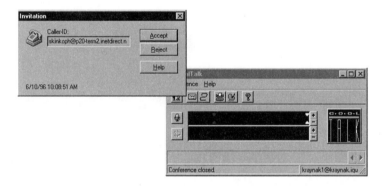

Typing Messages with the Chat Tool

If you don't have a sound card, or you're tired of talking into a microphone and interrupting each other, you can type messages back and forth using CoolTalk's Chat Tool.

In the CoolTalk window, click on the **Chat Tool** button (the one with the typewriter on it), and the Chat Tool window opens. Type a message in the area at the bottom of the window, and click on the **Send** button or press **Ctrl+Enter**. Your message pops up on the other person's screen. Any messages that the other person sends you pop up on your screen. (You can send an entire text file by clicking on the **Include** button.)

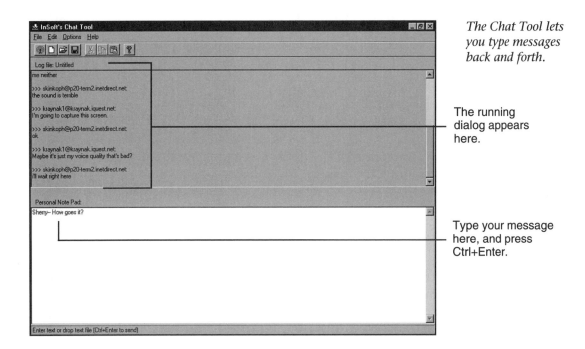

The Chat Tool lets you type messages back and forth.

The running dialog appears here.

Type your message here, and press Ctrl+Enter.

You can save a transcript of the conversation (in case you decide to sue the person later). Click on the **Save** button, or open the **File** menu and select **Save**.

When you're done chatting, and you want to return to your voice call, open the **File** menu and select **Close**.

Collaborating with White Board

CoolTalk's White Board is a tool that allows you to send pictures to the other person and annotate them. Such tools have become much more popular now that all the companies in corporate America are giving their employees the opportunity to become self-employed or sending them home as telecommuters. With White Board, you can collaborate on projects and doodle together during virtual corporate meetings.

With White Board, you can send graphics files across the Internet, just as if you were sending a typed message. If you don't have any graphics files, you can display what you want to send (a document, spreadsheet, whatever) and have CoolTalk capture and send the screen. This image then pops up on your colleague's screen, and you can start to mark it up.

To use White Board, click on the **White Board** button (the button with the paintbrush and palette on it) in the CoolTalk toolbar. You can then send an image from disk by opening the **File** menu and selecting **Open**. Use the dialog box to select the file you want to send, and click on **Open** or **OK**.

If you're using Windows 95, you can capture a screen and send it. Display the image you want to send, and then open the **Capture** menu and select **Desktop**. You can capture and send only the open window (instead of the entire desktop), by selecting **Window** from the **Capture** menu. Or, you can send a portion of the screen by selecting **Capture/Region**, and then dragging over the area you want to send. However you do it, the image is immediately sent to all the people in the conference (and it pops up on your screen).

Once the image is there, anyone in the conference can start drawing on the screen by using White Board's drawing tools, as shown below. Click on the button for the tool you want to use, and then drag the mouse to draw. It's just like drawing in Paintbrush.

The White Board work surface consists of two layers: an image layer and a drawing layer. If someone in the group drags the mouse all over the screen and turns the display into a primordial blob, you can clear the drawing layer and start over. Open the **Edit** menu and select **Clear Markups**. To scrap the entire work area, select **Edit/Clear White Board**.

White Board lets you mark on the image.

Click on a tool. ———

Drag to draw lines and shapes. ———

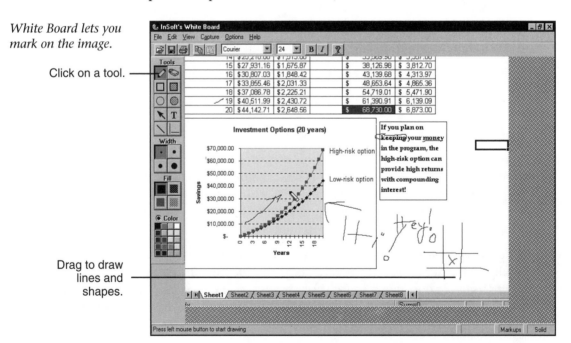

When using the White Board with the Chat Tool and voice, things can become a little confusing. Every time anyone in the conference sends a message, the message pops up in front of the White Board. When someone marks on the White Board, its window jumps in front of all the other windows. And, of course, all this data floating across the phone lines messes up the voice signals. It's a good idea when you're using the White Board to use only the White Board. When you're done with it, then go back to chatting.

Setting Up CoolTalk Watchdog

CoolTalk Watchdog is nothing more than a personal secretary who answers the phone and runs CoolTalk whenever someone invites you to a conference. If you have a network Internet connection and you're connected to the Internet all day, CoolTalk Watchdog is useful. It can catch incoming calls for you, so you don't have to sit by the phone all day. However, if you're not permanently wired, then CoolTalk Watchdog consumes memory for no real purpose.

You don't have to run CoolTalk Watchdog at startup to use it. If you plan on stepping away from your computer for a few minutes, and you want Watchdog to catch an incoming call, simply run Watchdog by selecting its icon from the Netscape Program group.

When someone calls, Watchdog starts CoolTalk and answers the incoming call.

If you didn't set up CoolTalk Watchdog to run on startup (and you want to), you can do so by adding it to the Start Up menu. In Windows 95, right-click on a blank area in the taskbar, and click on **Properties**. Click on the **Start Menu Programs** tab, and click on the **Add** button. Click on the **Browse** button, and use the dialog box to select CoolTalk Watchdog. The Watchdog icon should be on the Windows desktop; if it's not there, check **Program Files/Netscape/Navigator/CoolTalk** for a file called **Wdog.exe**. Save your changes.

In Windows 3.1, simply **Ctrl+drag** the CoolTalk Watchdog icon from your Netscape program group into the Start Up group.

Leashing Watchdog

When Watchdog is running, you can deactivate it so it doesn't watch for incoming calls. Double-click on its icon in the taskbar (the dog face all the way to the right, next to the time). Reactivate it by double-clicking on it again.

All This, and Voice Mail, Too?!

Yes, CoolTalk can take voice and text mail messages for you. Although it cannot answer your regular phone (even if it's connected to your modem), CoolTalk can answer any incoming CoolTalk calls, play your recorded greeting, and record a brief message. You can then play them back at your leisure. Yes, Internet phone screening!

Interested? Here's what you do to set it up:

1. Open the **Conference** menu, select **Options** and click the **Answering Machine** tab.

2. Get your microphone ready; you'll need it.

3. Click on the **Record Greeting** button, and say your greeting into the microphone. Click **Stop Recording**.

4. Click **OK** to close the dialog box.

5. Make sure your modem is on, you're connected to the Internet, and CoolTalk is running. (I know you didn't exit CoolTalk. Just do me a favor and check, okay?)

6. Click on the **Answering Machine** button. The button appears pushed in when CoolTalk is ready for voice mail.

When someone calls, they'll hear the "phone" ring a few times, and then the Answering machine will pick up and play your greeting. (On your computer, a dialog box appears, allowing you to answer the call. You can click on the Answer button and start talking to the person.) Unless the caller is stuck in the stone age and has something against voice mail, the person will leave a message.

After one or more people leave you messages, the Read Messages button in your toolbar will display a number, indicating how many messages you have. Click on this button to view a list of messages. Click on a message, and click on the **Play Message** button to listen to it. You can save the message by clicking on the **Save WAVE File** button, or delete the message by clicking on **Delete Message**. To return a call, click on the **Return Call** button. Chances are, you'll get that person's answering machine, where you can then leave a message.

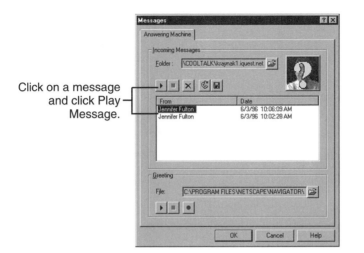

Click on a message
and click Play
Message.

*The Answering
Machine takes voice
mail messages while
you're away.*

The Least You Need To Know

CoolTalk is a fairly easy tool to use to place voice calls over the Internet. Before calling, make sure you get the person's e-mail address, and let them know when they'll be receiving a call.

When you're ready to call, simply open the **Conference** menu, select **Start**, and fill out the necessary forms. From there, everything else is a cake walk.

Chapter 18

Becoming a Java (and VRML) Junkie

By the End of This Chapter, You'll Be Able To...

➤ Understand why there are so many coffee metaphors on the Web

➤ Play interactive Java applets

➤ Explore virtual, three-dimensional worlds with Live3D

➤ Find other, better tools for exploring virtual worlds

In Chapters 6 and 7, you were busy downloading and playing video clips, audio recordings, pictures, and other types of multimedia files, as if you were channel surfing on your TV. You acted as some passive voyeur, hungry for more sensory stimulation than the Web could serve up. Aren't you ashamed of yourself? I didn't think so.

If your hard drive isn't full yet, you'll get a chance to interact with your downloads. Sounds warm and fuzzy, eh?

The Web is exploding with interactive programs, games, tutorials, and presentations that you should experience first-hand. In this chapter, you'll get your chance by playing Java applets and exploring three-dimensional, interactive worlds. I'll even tell you where to find the best interactive games.

What Is Java?

Java is the first and most popular programming language for the Web. Developed by Sun Microsystems, Java is a tool that allows programmers to create small applications (called *applets*) that you can download and run. These applets are similar to old DOS shareware programs. For example, with a loan calculator applet, you can type in the amount you borrowed, the interest rate, and the term, and the calculator will determine your monthly payment. Another applet might allow you to shoot missiles out of the sky. Most applets aren't very powerful.

To run a Java applet, you need a Java-enabled web browser, which you have (Netscape Navigator). There is no Java helper application; either your Web browser can handle Java or it can't.

When you encounter a link to a Java applet, all you have to do is click on the link. Netscape Navigator downloads the Java code, interpets it, and starts the applet. Once the applet is downloaded, it's on your computer, and you can use it just like any of your other applications (although you have to run these applets through Navigator).

Don't Wait for Me

In the next section, I'll tell you where to look for Java applets. But you can look for yourself. Connect to your favorite search page on the Web, and search for **Java applet**. You'll find scads of them.

Can These Applets Hurt Me?

Sun Microsystems, creator of Java, claims that Java has built-in safeguards that prevent programmers from inserting any viruses or destructive code into their applets. But saying that to a hacker is like poking Mike Tyson in the eye. As soon as you claim that your code is secure, every hacker who was busy chugging a Mountain Dew drops his drink and starts trying to figure out ways to crack it.

It's no different with Java. Although Java is relatively safe, there are ways to insert destructive code into Java applets. You can visit the Hostile Applets page at **http://www.math.gatech.edu/~mladue/HostileApplets.html**, to check out some of these codified vandals.

Does that mean you shouldn't play Java applets? Of course not! You just need to be a little careful, play Java applets that look legitimate, and if you hear of a destructive applet, avoid it.

However, if you're paranoid, you can disable Navigator's Java feature. Open the **Options** menu, click on **Network Preferences**, and click on the **Languages** tab. Click on **Enable Java** and **Enable JavaScript** to remove the checks from the boxes. Now, Navigator won't download or play Java Applets. Happy?

HotJava Required?

If you connect to a Java site, and you see a message saying that HotJava is required, you probably won't be able to play the applets at that site. HotJava is the other Java-enabled Web browser created by Sun Microsystems (yes, the creators of Java). HotJava is on the cutting edge of Java code, so it may be able to play Java applets that Navigator can't handle. You'll have to ditch Navigator if you want to play those applets.

Playing Java Applets

There's no trick to playing Java applets. You don't have to install a plug-in or set up a helper application. So, let the fun begin.

To play a cool similation of how airplanes land at a typical airport, go to **http://www.db.erau.edu/java/pattern/**. When the applet window appears on your screen, click the **Start Sim** button in the upper right corner of the window. The planes start circling the airport, landing, and pulling into the hangar.

Turn Off the Buttons

Java applets commonly use more screen than Navigator has to offer. When playing applets, consider turning off the toolbar and Directory bar at the top of the screen.

You've been cooped up in your office too long. You probably haven't seen the news, and you have no idea what the weather's doing. Do you care? If so, you can check out Blue Skies for an interactive Java weather report at **http://cirrus.sprl.umich.edu/javaweather/#Java**. Once you get there, click on the link for the type of weather information you want (for example, Precipitation or Surface Temperature). This displays a weather map with hot spots (no pun intended) that you can click on to get weather data for a specific city or area of the country.

Java landing simulation.

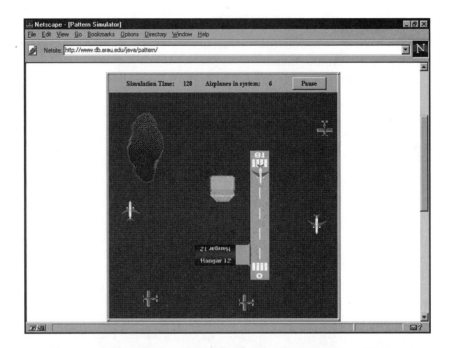

Blue Skies lets you check the weather around the country.

Current weather data appears here.

Point to a city.

Okay, I won't bore you anymore with this tour of Java applets. You get the idea. The applet runs, you stare at the controls on the screen and figure out what you need to click on to use it. Easy stuff. However, I will give you the URLs of a couple Java repositories on the Web, so you have some idea where to look for these little Java gems.

The first place is JARS (the Java Applet Rating Service). This place not only contains links to thousands of Java applets, but it also rates the applets, so you can screen out the losers. Connect to JARS at **http://www.jars.com/**.

At JARS, you'll find links to thousands of applets.

When you've exhausted the JARS Java applets, check out Café del Sol, where employees of Sun Microsystems display their Java creations: **http://www.xm.com/cafe/**. This is also a good place to find more information about Java, including information on how to start creating your own applets.

What Is VRML?

VRML (sounds like "vermal," stands for Virtual Reality Modeling Language) is another programming language that allows developers to create applications they can place on the Web. However, VRML lets these developers create interactive, three-dimensional worlds that you can walk through, fly over, and explore. For example, at the Ziff Davis Terminal Reality site, you can take a virtual elevator to various levels of its bookstore, board the ZD cruise liner to sail to Nubble's Treehouse, or fly the blimp to Paragraph International.

With VRML, you can explore three-dimensional worlds.

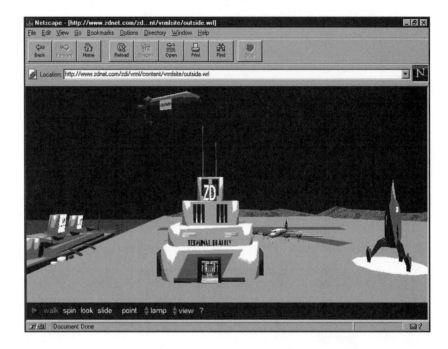

In the following sections, you'll learn how to use Netscape's Live3D VRML player and other VRML browsers to explore these virtual worlds and see for yourself what they have to offer.

VRML Hazards

Don't go too crazy downloading and installing a bunch of VRML browsers. Most browsers are four or more megabytes as compressed files, and can consume as much as ten megabytes when installed. VRML files are no lightweights either. Make sure you have enough disk space before proceeding.

Using Netscape's Live3D

Not to be outdone by Microsoft Corporation's focus on VRML (over Java), Netscape has created its own VRML browser called Live3D. You can look for Live3D using the following URL, although Netscape may have moved this page since the writing of this book:

> **http://home.netscape.com/comprod/products/navigator/live3d/download_live3d.html**

Once you've downloaded the file (its name looks something like 3dns32d.exe), run it. (By the way, the 32 in the file name stands for 32-bit; most VRML browsers require a 32-bit operating system, such as Windows 95, to operate.) This is a self-extracting ZIP file that places the setup files in the same directory or folder from which you run it. Now, look for a file called **setup.exe**, and run it. This runs the installation program. Simply follow the on-screen instructions.

Live3D is a plug-in for Navigator, so you don't have to set it up as a helper application. As soon as you click on a link for a VRML file (most end in .gz or .wrl), Navigator downloads the file and starts playing it.

GZ Files

GZ stands for GZip, a compression utility used to squish VRML files so they take up less hard disk space and travel faster through the phone lines. Most VRML browsers have a built-in decompression utility that automatically decompresses GZipped files, so you don't have to worry about it.

Navigating with Live3D

To see how this vermal thing works, connect to ZD3D Terminal Reality, the world you saw earlier in the chapter at **http://www.zdnet.com/zdi/vrml/content/vrmlsite/outside.wrl**. When you first connect, the world will look dark. Click on **lamp** at the bottom of the window to light the world.

Unlike most virtual worlds or 3D objects you'll encounter on the Web, Terminal Reality has hotlinks. If you move the mouse pointer over the cruise liner, building, plane, blimp, or rocket, a brief description of the link appears, telling you where the link will take you if you click on it.

Live3D supplies the controls you need to explore.

Live3D's virtual world controls

Click on lamp to light the world.

At the bottom of the window are Live3D's controls. You've already used the lamp button to light the world. Most of the other buttons control your movement through the world. For example, if you click on the walk button, you can drag the mouse in the viewing area to saunter through the streets and approach objects. Here's a list of all the buttons and what they do:

walk lets you walk through the scene. Drag the mouse pointer or use the arrow keys to walk.

spin pivots the world on an imaginary center point. Click on this option and then drag the mouse to spin the world or object in three-dimensional space. If this option is off, you can right-drag to spin.

look lets you move your point of view. You're standing still, moving your head to focus in on different areas of the world or on different objects, but you can't approach these objects, as you can with the walk option.

slide shifts the world up, down, left or right when you drag the mouse. If this option is off, you can Alt+drag to slide.

point takes you closer to an object. Point and click on an object, and you'll walk right up to it. If this option is off, you can Ctrl+click to point.

lamp illuminates the scene. Click on it again to turn off the lights.

view returns you to the original view of the world.

? displays information on how to navigate in the world. (After turning on help, click on the other buttons and watch the information change.)

For additional controls, try right-clicking inside the viewing area. This displays a shortcut menu with gobs of options. Some sites offer a bunch of rooms or viewpoints where you can go in a hurry. Right-click inside the viewing area, point to **View Points**, and click on the desired viewpoint.

VRML Control Panel

Unlike Java applets, each of which comes with its own set of controls, VRML worlds have no built-in controls. The VRML browser supplies the controls, so you'll be working with the same controls no matter which world you explore.

Exploring Some Worlds

Terminal Reality is one of the best worlds you'll find on the Web. Other places might just provide VRML objects, such as trees, spheres, and cones that you can spin around in three-dimensional space (oh boy!). So as you hunt for other worlds, don't get your hopes up.

I'll take you to a couple other worlds on the Web that offer some neat features that you won't find in other worlds. When you're done here, assuming you want to explore some more worlds on your own, pull up a Web search page and search for **VRML world**. The resulting list should give you plenty of links to explore.

First, let's drop by the VRML Mall at…. I have to warn you before you enter this URL. This Mall is huge. And when I say huge, I mean it's going to take you a good part of your adult life to download it. (Don't try downloading it with a 14.4 Kbps or slower modem.) I wrote most of this chapter while waiting for the Mall to open. However, it's worth the wait. The VRML mall is a virtual world that acts as sort of a mega-mall where you can shop for other VRML worlds. To shop at the mall go to **http://www.ocnus.com/models/mall.wrl**. When the world finally arrives, you can enter the mall and click on links to load other worlds.

When you enter the VRML Mall, you'll find links to other VRML worlds

Okay, now you've mastered all the controls, right? Right-click on a spot in the viewing area. A pop-up menu appears giving you about a hundred more navigational options. Point to **View Points**, and you'll get a list of rooms that group the worlds in categories, such as Animals or People. Click on the desired group.

For some fun, visit Grafman's VR World at **http://www.graphcomp.com/vrml/**. This site has a few off-beat characters from the world of animation that you can take control of and have a little fun. Don't leave without visiting the virtual-reality, randomly generated bunny or the virtual snowman. Grafman's virtual gallery is also a visual treat, although it takes awhile to download.

As you wander and explore, you might also want to check out some of the worlds at Planet Nine. These worlds are no match for ZD3D, but they do provide a DOS video game quality that can help you reminisce about the good ol' days. You can go to Planet Nine at page **http://www.planet9.com**. When you get there, use links to find the various worlds.

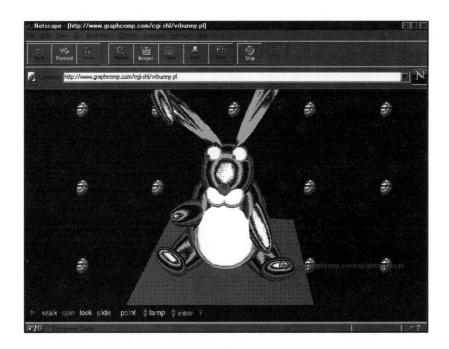

Grafman's VR World offers some high-quality models.

Other VRML Browsers

Live3D is no slouch in the VRML deparment. Its simple controls and the point option are enough to get my vote for top VRML browser of 1996. I've used about ten other browsers, and Live3D stacks up with the best of them. WIRL (covered in Chapter 7) and Pioneer are the other two VRML browsers I would recommend. Here's where you can get them if you're interested in taking them for a test drive:

WIRL: **http://www.vream.com/3wirl.html**

Pioneer: **http://www.caligari.com/**

Another browser that has gotten positive reviews is *VRealm*, although I find its controls infuriatingly frustrating. *VR Scout* isn't bad. It offers simple controls, like those used in Live3D, but when you drag the mouse pointer to move an object, it's likely to fly off your screen. *WebSpace* is another popular browser with lousy controls. And last, but not least, is *WorldView*, which has the best looking opening screen of all VRML browsers. When you start it, WorldView displays a spinning globe. WorldView looks more like a Web browser than a VRML browser, but it's positioning itself in the market for when the Web goes entirely 3D... sometime in the next century.

The Least You Need To Know

What's to know? Navigator is Java-enabled, so if you click on a link for a Java applet, Navigator will play it. And once you install Live3D, Navigator is VRML-enabled, so all you have to do is click on links. Other than that, this Java/VRML stuff is pretty easy.

Chapter 19

Digital Certificates, Cookies, and Other Security Topics

By the End of This Chapter, You'll Be Able To...

➤ Tell if you're on a page that complies with the latest security standards

➤ Enter security settings to protect your computer and the information you send and receive

➤ Understand what cookies are and how you get them

➤ Not worry so much about Internet security

If you listen to the news, or if you saw Sandra Bullock in *The Net*, you're probably at least a little concerned that while you're fooling around at Grafman's VRML world, someone might hack into your computer, grab all your personal information and credit card numbers, and run up an enormous Visa bill at Parisian.

I'm not saying that the scenario isn't possible; it's just not all that common. People who steal credit card numbers and personal information usually have more clever and easier ways to get that information. For instance, they might dig through your trash, pay off an underpaid employee at the Visa office, or break into your house and steal your whole computer.

The point here is that you shouldn't do on the Internet anything you wouldn't do in real life, including handing out your credit card number (or phone number, for that matter) to anyone you don't trust.

This chapter explains some additional security measures you can take in Navigator, and explains some of the security features over which you have no control (so why worry about them?).

Transferring Information Securely on the Net

The biggest security worry on the Internet is the result of one of the biggest improvements on the Web: forms. Forms, such as search forms used in Yahoo or other search programs, let you enter information and receive feedback. They also allow you to order products by entering your credit card number.

The problem with entering any personal information (including credit card numbers) on a form is that the information is not sent directly to the server where that information will be used. Instead, the information bounces around from one server to another till it finds its destination. At any point in this little adventure, someone with the proper know-how can read the information.

How often this happens, no one really knows, but it *can* happen, and that's the concern.

Complete Protection

To *completely* protect yourself, never enter any sensitive information on a form. If you want to order something from a mail-order company, get their phone number from the Web page, and call in your order. Because phone orders travel over private lines (owned by phone companies), there is less chance that someone can grab your credit card number in transit.

Setting Navigator's Security Options

Although the Internet is not completely safe, Navigator does have some built-in security options to help protect you. For one, Navigator displays a warning whenever you enter information on any form. If you never enter sensitive information, these warnings can become more annoying than useful. However, if you don't trust yourself, keep the warnings on.

The following sections explain how to turn Navigator's security warnings on and off, tell whether you are at a secure site (even if the warnings are off), and use other Navigator security features.

Turning Security Warnings On and Off

Navigator's security options provide a gentle reminder that you're entering information that could be read by the wrong person. When the dialog box pops up, all you have to do is confirm that you want to send the information, and Navigator sends it. If the dialog boxes don't bother you, there's no reason to turn them off.

However, most people don't need to be reminded that they're sending information. You typed the information. You clicked on the button to send it. Heck, yes, you want to send it! Once you've gained a little experience on the Web, the warnings become intrusive. So, turn them off.

The easiest way to turn off warnings is when you receive a warning. At the bottom of the warning dialog box is Show This Alert Next Time. If you click on this option, and remove the check box, this warning will never disturb you again.

Another way to turn security warnings on or off is via the Security Preferences dialog box. Open the **Options** menu, click on **Security Preferences**, and click on the **General** tab. You can then select any of the following options to turn them on or off:

Entering a Secure Document Space (Server): Displays a warning whenever you view a Web page that complies with the latest security standards. Why would you turn this on, I wonder?

Leaving a Secure Document Space (Server): This is another warning you can turn off. If you're leaving, why do you care if it's secure?

Viewing a Document with a Secure/Insecure Mix: If it's mixed, why do you care? Either you can send information securely or you can't. Leave this one off, too.

Submitting a Form Insecurely: This is the option that makes the security warning pop up on your screen all the time. If you don't trust yourself, leave it on.

Enable SSL v2: Turns on data encryption for Web pages protected with the Secure Sockets Layer (version 2) standard. Keep this on, so that when you do enter information on secure Web pages, that information will be encoded.

Enable SSL v3: Turns on data encryption for Web pages protected with the Secure Sockets Layer (version 3) standard. Keep this option on, too. This is the latest security standard from Netscape.

You can turn the security warnings on or off.

Security warning options

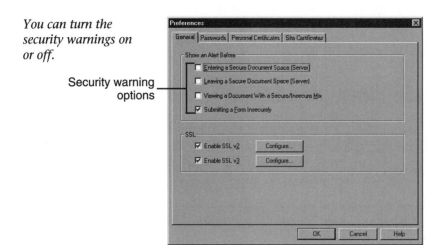

When you're done entering your settings, click on the **OK** button. Even if you turn the warnings off, Navigator has ways of showing you whether you're on a secure Web page. The following section explains.

Is This Site Secure?

If you turn the security warnings off, there are four main ways you can tell that a site is secure:

➤ The URL (in the Location text box) starts with https instead of http. The "s" indicates that the document is protected by Netscape's SSL (Secure Sockets Layer) protocol.

➤ The key icon in the lower left corner of the Navigator window is unbroken and on a blue background. If the key is broken and on a gray background, the document is *insecure*.

➤ A blue bar appears at the top of the page viewing area (just below the toolbar). If there is no blue bar, the site is insecure.

➤ The Document Info window shows that the document is secure. To display the Document Info window for the current page, open the **View** menu and select **Document Info**. Look at **Security** to find out if the document is secure or not.

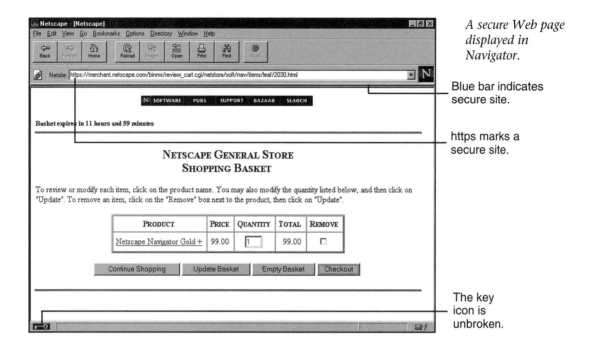

A secure Web page displayed in Navigator.

Blue bar indicates secure site.

https marks a secure site.

The key icon is unbroken.

Grabbing Some Cookies

Cookies are sort of like tokens that a Web page hands you when you connect to the page or enter information. These cookies stay with Navigator, so that the next time you visit the site, or visit another area at the site, the Web server can identify you. For example, whenever you visit a page, it might give you a cookie to mark how many times you visited. Each time you connect, the Web page will show you how many times you've been to the page.

Cookies are also used at shopping pages on the Web. As you add items to your "cart," the page gives you a cookie for each item. When you go to check out, the page knows (from the cookies) which items you have in your cart.

Because cookies allow Web servers to write information to your program (Navigator), there are some conceivable security risks. If you are concerned about this, you can have Navigator warn you whenever a server attempts to send you a cookie.

To turn on the warning, open the **Options** menu and select **Network Preferences**. Click on the **Protocols** tab. Click on **Accepting a Cookie** to place a check in the box. Click **OK**.

Using Digital Certificates

If you've wandered the Web much, you've encountered sites that request information from you and then give you a username and password, so you can access additional information at the site. Maybe you had to pay a one-time fee for the additional access, or you had to subscribe to the service.

Of course, you never want to enter the same username and password at each site. If anyone were to steal your password and username at one site, they could use it at all the other sites, and really foul up your life. However, keeping track of all your usernames and personal ID numbers can become difficult. To solve this problem, Internet developers came up with the concept of *digital certificates* or *digital passports*.

With a digital certificate, you enter information about yourself one time. The Web server sends you a certificate, which stays with Navigator. Whenever you connect to the site, Navigator identifies you to the site by sending your digital certificate, so you don't have to remember your username or password.

For a fee, you can also apply for a generic digital certificate that you can theoretically use to identify yourself at any site.

The following sections explain how to obtain, use, and protect your digital certificates.

Nontransferable

Each digital certificate works for only one application and on only one computer. If you set up a certificate on your computer at work, it won't work for your computer at home. You need to create a separate certificate for each copy of Navigator you run.

Obtaining and Using Digital Certificates

This digital certificate concept is fairly new, so you may not find many companies (Certifying Authorities) where you can pick up a certificate. One company that offers digital certificates is VeriSign, which you can visit at **http://digitalid.verisign.com/**.

Once here, you must specify the application for which you want a digital certificate (Navigator), and then enter personal and billing information. VeriSign then sends you a temporary digital certificate. (You will receive your permanent digital certificate via e-mail.)

Navigator displays a dialog box, asking if you want to protect your certificate with a password. If you are on a network, you should choose Yes, and then enter a unique password. If you're using a computer that no one else has access to, you can choose not to use a password. Navigator then asks you to enter a nickname for the certificate, which will be used in Navigator to identify this certificate.

When you're done, check to see if your certificate has been set up in Navigator. Open the **Options** menu, select **Security Preferences**, and click on the **Personal Certificates** tab. You should see the nickname you entered for the new certificate.

The nickname of
your personal
certificate

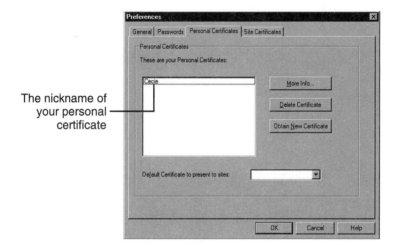

*Navigator lists all
your digital certifi-
cates.*

Protecting Your Certificates

If you're using a computer that others may have access to, or you're on a network, you should protect your certificates with a password. When you first obtain a certificate, Navigator asks if you want to give it a password. If you enter a password, Navigator will prompt you to enter it the first time you try to use the certificate during the current session.

You can change your password and password settings through the security Preferences dialog box. Open the **Option** menu, select **Security Preferences**, and click on the **Passwords** tab. To change your password (or remove password protection), click on the **Change Password** button. In the dialog box that appears, enter your old password, and click **Next**. You can then choose to use no password or change the password. Click **Next** again. If you chose to change your password, type the new password into the **Password** and **Retype Password** text boxes, and click on **Finished**.

You can also change the frequency at which Navigator asks for the password. By default, Navigator prompts you for the password only once each time you use Navigator. You can choose to be prompted each time you use a certificate or at a specified interval (such as 30 minutes).

You can change your password and password settings.

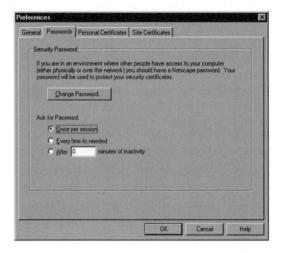

Using Site Certificates

Each secure Web site is certified by a licensed authority. If you open the security Preferences dialog box, and click on the Site Certificates tab, you can view a list of these authorities.

In most cases, you can ignore this list. However, if you hear that the sites certified by a particular authority have had security problems, you can prevent access to sites that this particular authority certified. Or, if you enter information at a site that has been certified by one of the authorities, and the site did something stupid like giving your name and e-mail address to other companies, you can prevent access to sites certified by that authority.

To delete a site certificate entirely (so any sites certified by that authority will appear as insecure), click on the name of the authority, and click on **Delete Certificate**. To display a warning whenever you attempt to send data to a site that has been certified by an authority, click on the name of the authority, and click on the **Edit Certificate** button. You can then block access to the site, or have a warning displayed.

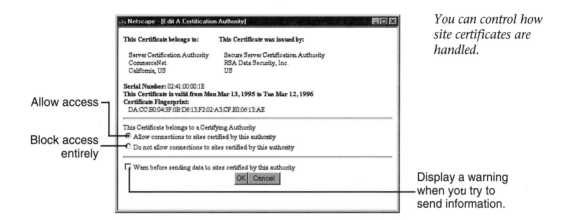

You can control how site certificates are handled.

Allow access

Block access entirely

Display a warning when you try to send information.

The Least You Need To Know

The Internet is no place for the paranoid. Wherever you go, whether in real or virtual life, there are some risks involved. To protect yourself on the Web, don't give your credit card number, phone number, passwords, address, or any other sensitive information to an unknown or untrusted person or company. Other than that little caution, don't worry so much. Have fun.

Chapter 20

Forging Your Own Hyperdocuments

By the End of This Chapter, You'll Be Able To...

➤ Create your very own hyperdocuments

➤ Give your home page a professional look

➤ Nab someone else's home page and use it as your own

➤ Add graphics and sounds to your home page

Now that you're a bona fide Web spider, you can snare just about any page that might fly into your web. You can track down any information you need and pull it up on your screen in a matter of seconds. But now you want more. You want to start giving back a little of what you've been taking... or you at least want to make your creative presence know on the Web. How do you create your own Web page? And how do you use it to your benefit?

In this chapter, you'll learn how to use the codes that transform a simple text document into a Web page. And, you'll learn how to use your Web page to save loads of time on the Web.

Crafting a Simple Home Page

To make hyperdocuments, you use a coding system called *HTML* (HyperText Markup Language). Don't worry, I'm not going to slap a bunch of codes at you in a vain attempt to impress you with the complexity of HTML. Instead, I'll teach you how to make a simple document using just five HTML codes. If I use any more, you can call me for a complete refund. My number is (555) NOT-HERE.

Check This Out...

Cheat a Little If you have bookmarks for all your favorite places, start with your Bookmark.htm file. Open Bookmark.htm in Notepad and use the **File/Save As** command to clone the file under another name (be sure to keep the htm extension). Then, edit the file to change the title of the page and enter any other changes.

First, run your favorite text editor or word processing program. You need a program that lets you save *plain* (ASCII) *text* files. Windows Notepad will do (turn on Word Wrap by opening the **Edit** menu and selecting **Word Wrap**). You don't want any fancy formatting codes that can confuse Navigator. Open an empty window for a text file. You'll type a series of lines in this text file to create your document.

The first line in your home page should be the document's title. Now, you'd think a title would appear at the top of your document. It doesn't. It appears only in the Navigator title bar when you open the document. Although this doesn't do you much good, you still need a title line, so model yours on the following sample:

<h3><title>Peeble's Home Page</title></h3>

Note that the title is sandwiched between two codes. The first code turns the title on, and the second one turns it off. Most (but not all) HTML codes are paired like this. Also, the codes can be uppercase or lowercase; it doesn't matter.

Techno Talk

Tagged Ya! HTML codes are often referred to as *tags*. Tags can control the look of text (as in titles and headings), insert anchors that link this document to other documents, and control character formatting (by making it bold or italic).

Since the title won't appear at the top of your page, you need something that *will* appear: a top-level heading. You can use the same text you used for the title, or you can use something more unique. Wedge this text between two heading codes: **<h1>** and **</h1>**. Here's a sample:

<h3><h1>Peeble's Points of Interest</h1></h3>

In case you're wondering, HTML lets you use up to six heading levels: h1 to h6. Think of h1 as a chapter title, h2 as major heading levels, and h3 as minor heading levels. If you get down to h6, your page is too long, you're too ambitious, and you probably need some counseling.

Now, divide the page into two or three sections with level 2 headings. For example, say you have a bunch of URLs you want to include on your home page. You can use level-2 headings to divide your links into logical groups. The following headings divide the page into four groups:

> **<h2>Hairy Tunes</h2>**
> **<h2>Fun Stuff</h2>**
> **<h2>News Centers</h2>**
> **<h2>Philosophical Rags</h2>**

Finally, add links for all your favorite URLs. This is the hard part. You use what are called *anchor codes* to insert two items in the document: a URL and link text. The URL remains invisible; it simply tells Navigator which document to load when you click the link. The *link text* is the actual word or phrase that appears in your document (link text is usually blue and underlined). Here's a sample anchor code to get you started:

> **<a href="http://www.yahoo.com">Yahoo's Starting Points</a>**

In this example, **<href=>** is the code that tells the link where the Web page is located. The URL is **http://www.yahoo.com** (it must be surrounded by quotation marks and be embedded inside the <href=> code). The link text (which will appear in the document) is **Yahoo's Starting Points**. And the <a/> represents the end of this command line. Add each link on a line of its own, and add a **<p>** (*paragraph*) code at the end of each line. The <p> code tells Navigator to insert a line break. You can type the codes in uppercase or lowercase, but when you type URLs, make sure the capitalization matches that of the URL.

Check This Out...

URL Extravaganza

Where you get the URLs for these links is your business. However, if you hate to type, consider copying and pasting these URLs. You can copy a URL wherever you see one: in a hotlist, in the URL text box, in a menu item edit box. Highlight the URL and then press **Ctrl+C**. You can then switch to your text editor and paste the URL where desired.

Save the document (be sure to give it the extension **.htm**), close your text editor, and you're done. You've created your first hyperdocument. In the next section, you'll get to take it for a test drive.

Keep it simple.

Title ———
Heading 1 ——
Heading 2 ——

Links to other
documents

Does It Work?

You can slap together HTML documents in any number of ways. The only thing that matters is whether or not the document works when you're done. To test your document, start Navigator (you don't have to be connected to the Internet). Open the **File** menu and select **Open File**. A dialog box appears, prompting you to specify the location and name of the file you want to open.

Select the drive and directory, or folder, that contains the HTML document you created. Select the name of the file, and then click **OK** or the **Open** button. Navigator loads the document from your hard disk and displays it on-screen. To have your home page load automatically, look back at Chapter 4 in the "Starting from Your Home (Page)" section.

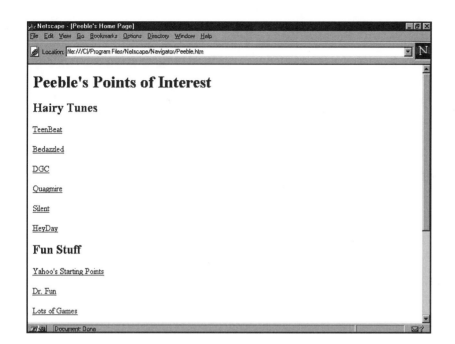

Your home page in Navigator.

More Stuff You Can Stick in a Home Page

If you show your five-code home page to an experienced Web-walker, they'll laugh you off the server. To give your home page a professional flair, you need to add some lines, include a couple of paragraphs and lists, add an inline image or two, and maybe use some bold and italic text.

Because the paragraph is the bread and butter of any document, let's start there. The rule is pretty simple. Wherever you want to end a paragraph, type a **<p>** code. Although pressing the Enter key in your text editor inserts a line break in your document, Navigator doesn't recognize that line break. Navigator breaks a line only when it sees a <p> code.

Another simple, commonly used code is <hr>, which stands for *horizontal rule*. Use this code at the end of a section, to separate it from the next section. To add space before the horizontal line, precede the **<hr>** code with a **<p>** code. To insert space after the line, add a **<p>** code after the **<hr>** code.

You want to emphasize a word or phrase by making it bold or italic, what do you do? To italicize text, bracket it with <i></i> codes. To make text bold, use <b></b> codes. Underlining? You guessed it; use <u></u>. For example, <i>increased spending</i> results in *increased spending*. You can also make text bold *and* italic, but if you plan on sharing your home page with people who use a browser other than Netscape Navigator, the text may not appear bold and italic on their screen. To add two text enhancements, simply embed one pair of codes in the other: <i><b>increased spending</i></b>.

Inserting Inline Images and Sounds

Now, for the more advanced codes. Say you have a graphic or sound file on disk, and you want to insert it into your document. You must create a link that tells the document where to look for the file. To add an inline image, insert a code like the following:

<IMG SRC="file:///C|/DIR/SUBDIR/FILE.GIF" ALIGN=middle>

Translation: IMG stands for *image*, which tells Navigator to insert the specified image. **SRC** stands for *source*, which indicates where the image is stored. Make sure you start with **file:///**, because your inline image is stored locally (that is, on your hard disk). Also be sure to use three forward slashes (NOT two), follow the drive letter with | (not a colon), and use forward slashes to separate directory names. **ALIGN** is an optional code that tells Navigator how to position the image in relation to the text that follows it: top, middle, or bottom.

Creating links for sound files is a little different; it's more like inserting a link for a URL. You use the anchor codes <a> and </a> to insert the link. Here's a sample:

<a href="file:///C|/WINDOWS/CHIMES.WAV">Click here for sound</a>

In the example, **Click here for sound** appears highlighted in the document. When you click on that text, Navigator opens the associated application you use for playing WAV files. You can then click the **Play** button to play the sound.

You might want to use a speaker icon to represent the sound link you inserted in your document. To use an icon in your document, store a small GIF file on your hard disk, and then replace *Click here for sound* with an image link that points to the .GIF. Your code might look like the following:

Check This Out...

Relative References
When you look at professional hyperdocuments, you may not see a lot of long directory paths. An anchor may specify only a file name. You can do this too by storing all your linked files in the same directory or folder in which you store your hyperdocument. The anchor then "knows" to search in the current directory for the file.

<A HREF="file:///C|/WINDOWS/CHIMES.WAV"><IMG SRC="file:///C|/DIR/ SOUND.GIF"></A>

The **<IMG SRC=>** code tells Navigator to insert the specified GIF image in the document. You can then click on this image to play the sound.

Listing Things

People love lists. I love lists. You can scan a list and skip right to the item that catches your eye. You may have already figured out that you can create rudimentary lists by writing short sentences and ending each one with a couple of **<p>** commands. Hey, if it works, why not? You'll find, however, that HTML offers some additional codes for creating fancy lists with bullets and numbers.

The most popular list is the *unordered list* (or bulleted list). You bracket the entire list with **<ul></ul>** codes, and then start each list item with an **<li>** code. Here's a sample of a 3-item list:

<ul>
<li>4 pork chops
<li>1 egg
<li>1 can Italian bread crumbs
</ul>

If you're giving step-by-step instructions, the *ordered list* (or numbered list) is better. With ordered lists, you bracket the entire list with **<ol></ol>** codes and start each list item with an **<li>** code (just as you did with the unordered list). When a Web browser displays the list, it inserts the numbers where required. Here's a sample of a three-step list:

<ol>
<li>Preheat the oven to 350 degrees.
<li>Bread the pork chops.
<li>Bake the pork chops for 45 minutes.
</ol>

One final list. If you want to create your own online glossary of terms, you can create a *definition list*. Bracket the entire list with **<dl></dl>** codes. Precede each term you want to define with a **<dt>** code; follow it with the definition, preceded by a **<dd>** code. Here's a sample list for two terms:

Embedding Codes Keep in mind that you can insert additional codes in a list. For example, you can insert links to your favorite URLs. You can also use the <b> and <i> codes to format text within a list.

241

```
<dl>
<dt>Clipper Chip
<dd>A hardware encryption device promoted by the government that's de-
signed to keep data communications private from anyone . . . except the
government.
<dt>Download
<dd>To snatch a file from another computer or online service and drag it to
your computer. You usually download using a modem.
</dl>
```

The Philosophy of Logical Codes

Earlier, I'm not sure when, you learned how to use the codes <b>, <i>, and <u> to make text bold, italic, and underlined. In HTML lingo, these codes are called *physical* codes, as opposed to *logical* codes. Personally, I try not to separate the physical from the logical. Whenever I do, I end up walking into a wall or driving through red lights.

Nevertheless, there *is* a difference. Physical codes are absolute. A <b> code tells Web browsers to make text bold, no questions asked. Logical codes, such as **<em>** (for *emphasis*), tell the browsers to emphasize the word; the method is up to the browser. One browser might underline the marked text, another might make it bold, and another might add italics. You can save time by using logical codes, because they're usually easier to remember. Here are a list of some of the more popular logical codes:

<em></em>	Adds emphasis.
<strong></strong>	Adds stronger emphasis.
<cite></cite>	Use this for a citation to another work or authority.

Proper Form (for the Culturally Elite)

If you're doing home pages for yourself and friends, you don't have to worry too much about following the proper HTML format. As long as the page works, you're in business. However, if you're doing this for money, or you get serious about it and start putting your pages on the Web (making them accessible to other users), you should follow some HTML conventions.

First, start each document with an **<html>** code and end with an **</html>** code. These codes tell whatever Web browser is being used that this document is, in fact, an HTML document. Currently, these <html> codes don't do much of anything, because HTML is the only game in town. However, sometime in the future, other hyperdocument languages may come into use, and when they do, the <html> codes will help Web browsers distinguish between document types.

Another currently useless code pair is the **<head></head>** pair. Not to be confused with the <h1></h1> head*ing* pair, the <head> codes indicate a head. In most current HTML documents, the <head> codes bracket the <title> codes, and do nothing. In some documents, the <head> codes bracket some advanced codes that are way beyond the scope of this book. For example, if your home page describes a database that you can search, you can insert the **<isindex>** code. This code inserts a Search Index text box at the bottom of the Navigator window into which a user can enter search instructions. But as I said, that's too complicated for this book.

Now that you have a head, you need a body, so after the </head> code, you need a <body> code that indicates the beginning of the rest of the document. At the very end of the document, but before the </html> code, you must insert a **</body>** code that indicates the end of the body.

Inserting JavaScript Applets

Once you've mastered the codes for inserting text, graphics, sounds, and other media on a Web page, you might want to spice up your pages with Java applets. You don't have to be a Java programming wizard to do this. Many creators of JavaScript applets place their scripts on the Web, so users like you can copy them and adapt them for your own use.

To use an existing script (text), first display the script. There may be a link you can click on to display the script, or you can use the **View/Document Source** command. Drag over the JavaScript portion (there's usually a <script> code to mark the beginning of the script, and a </script> code that marks the end). Use the **Edit/Copy** command to copy the script to the clipboard. Then, change to your Web page (in your text editor), and use the **Edit/Paste** command to insert the script where desired.

Once you have pasted the script into your Web page, you can adapt it. Sample scripts commonly include a list of *parameters*, codes you can change to modify the applet. For example, if an applet shows a spinning top, you can replace the graphic of the top with a different graphic (for instance, a globe or your head). Or, you can use the applet as is (if you get permission), and add a credit to the creator. Changing these parameters is much easier than writing a Java applet from scratch.

You can adapt the Java script for your own use.

Parameters you can change

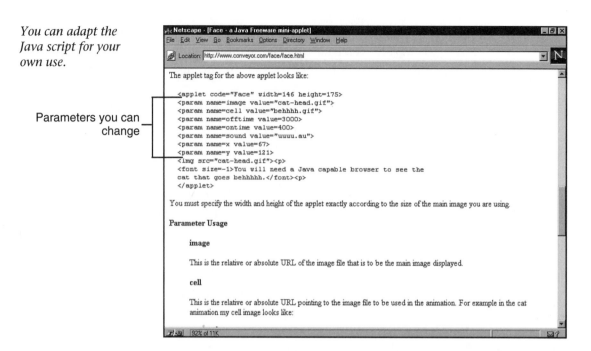

As you see what other Java creators have made, you might want to start developing your own applets. There's no better place to learn how to do this than on the Web. Check out the following sites for more information:

Brewing Java: A Tutorial   http://sunsite.unc.edu/javafaq/javatutorial.html

Gamelan   http://www.gamelan.com

Candle Web's Live Java   http://www.vaxxine.com/candleweb/java/java.html

Applet Library   http://www.applets.com/cgi-bin-applets/

JavaSoft   http://www.javasoft.com

Java World   http://www.javaworld.com/

The Web Development Cyberbase   http://www.hamline.edu/personal/matjohns/webdev/java/

JARS   http://www.jars.com

Cheating Your Way to HTML

The best way to learn proper HTML coding—and to get ideas for how to create your own home pages—is to nab a few home pages and look at their codes. Find a willing victim, download it, and then open it up in your text editor to take a peek. Think of it as a biology lesson without the stench of formaldehyde. Here's the URL of a great place to pick up some home pages… and share your own:

http://web.city.ac.uk/citylive/pages.html

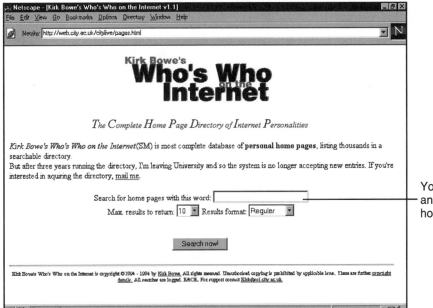

The CityLive! Complete Home Page Directory.

You can search for and download home pages.

Making Pages with Navigator Gold

You've done the manual coding. You created your first HTML document in a text editor. Now I'll tell you: There are a couple of HTML editors that act as desktop publishing programs for the Web. If you downloaded Netscape Navigator Gold (instead of Netscape Navigator), you already have an HTML editor. Navigator Gold offers all the Web browsing features of the standard version of Netscape Navigator, but Gold doubles as an HTML editor. (You can download Navigator Gold from Netscape's Web site. When you install it, Navigator Gold replaces your current version of Netscape Navigator.)

When you start Navigator Gold, one difference between it and the standard edition will immediately catch your eye. Navigator Gold's toolbar contains an extra button labeled **Edit**. To quickly modify an existing page, open the page in Navigator Gold, and then click on the **Edit** button. If you opened a page on a remote Web server (instead of one that's on your disk), a dialog box appears, asking if you want to save the page to your disk. Click on the **Save** button and answer the series of dialog boxes. Navigator Gold then displays the page, along with a bunch of tools for editing the page (cutting, pasting, changing font sizes and colors, and so on).

Besides the obvious addition of the Edit button, Navigator Gold's menu system offers other, less obvious accessories:

➤ The **File/New Document** submenu offers options for creating a new Web page from scratch (**Blank Document**), **From Template**, or **From Wizard**. (The **From Wizard** option is explained in the next section.)

➤ The **File/Publish** command lets you send your Web page to a Web server to place it on the Web. (Of course, you must first obtain permission from the Web server's administrator, and probably pay a fee, before you can do this.)

➤ The **Edit** menu lists additional commands for selecting and deleting tables.

➤ The **View** menu offers an option for displaying paragraph marks (codes).

➤ An additional **Insert** menu offers options for inserting links, tables, lines, line breaks, non-breaking spaces, and more.

➤ An additional **Properties** menu lists commands for formatting elements on your Web page. For example, you can transform a paragraph into a heading, change the font size, or give your table a unique look.

➤ The **Options** menu contains many more options for turning the various editing toolbars on or off. In addition, the **Editor Preferences** option lets you change the overall settings for the HTML editor part of Navigator Gold.

➤ The **Help** menu offers a **Web Page Starter** option that takes you to a Netscape site that has tools to help you create Web pages.

Making It Easy with the Web Page Wizard

Navigator Gold's HTML editor also includes a link to a page starter site that offers a bunch of Web page templates, design help, and a page wizard that can help you start creating and publishing pages right away.

To start creating a page with Navigator Gold's wizard, connect to the Internet, and run Navigator. Open the **File** menu, point to **New Document**, and click on **From Wizard**. This connects you to the Netscape Page Wizard site, where you'll find instructions on how to proceed. The wizard leads you through the process of inserting a title, links, graphics, and sounds, and gives you access to sample media files you can include on your pages. As you construct your page, the preview shows you how it looks.

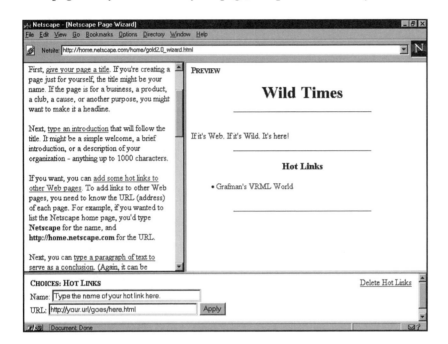

With Netscape's Page Wizard, creating Web pages is easy.

Other HTML Editors

Another popular HTML editor for Windows is HotDog, which you can download from the following Web site:

>   **http://www.sausage.com/**

Or, if you like working with products from Microsoft Corporation, try Microsoft's FrontPage Web editor. Go to Microsoft's home page at **http://www.microsoft.com** and look for the link to FrontPage. If you have Microsoft Word, Excel, or PowerPoint, you can also use Microsoft's Internet Assistants to transform your existing documents into Web pages.

Learning More About HTML

If you find HTML exciting and you want to make a career of it, you can get additional information, codes, and instructions from a number of sources. The best source is a book by Paul McFedries, called *The Complete Idiot's Guide to Creating an HTML Web Page*. (Okay, it was a cheap plug, but McFedries is an HTML wiz, who writes in a very entertaining and informative style, so I don't feel too guilty.)

You can also find HTML information on the Web. Here are a couple of sites to check out. The first site provides some simple instructions on how to start with HTML. The second site provides a quick overview of many of the HTML commands:

> **http://www.ncsa.uiuc.edu/General/Internet/WWW/HTMLPrimer.html**

> **http://kuhttp.cc.ukans.edu/lynx_help/HTML_quick.html**

The Least You Need To Know

You can spend days wandering the Web to learn the intricacies of HTML. The following list will teach you the basics in less than 30 seconds:

➤ Create hyperdocuments in a text editor or in a word processing application that lets you save plain text files.

➤ Every home page needs a title line bracketed with **<title>** and **</title>** codes.

➤ Use **<h1></h1>** codes to mark the text that you want to appear as the title at the top of your home page.

➤ Use **<h2></h2>** codes to mark any headings under the <h1> heading.

➤ Use anchor codes to insert links to your favorite URL. The proper form for an anchor code is:

> **<a href="URL">Link Text</a>**

More Internet Sites Than You'll Have Time To Visit

Quick Guide to Web Sites

Fasten your seat belt, and squeeze your mouse tight. You're about to take a joy ride on the Web. This chapter provides you with a list of the best Web sites organized by category (in alphabetical order, of course). You get the name of each site, its URL, and a brief description of the best site in each category (in my humble opinion). Enjoy!

Check This Out...

Mark It! As you drive along, don't forget to make bookmarks for your favorite sites. Some of these URLs are pretty long.

CMA Legal Disclaimer: Because of the dynamic nature of the Web, some of the URLs in this chapter may not work for you. People are constantly moving their home pages, and making life miserable for us computer book authors. However, usually when a page moves, the mover (or shaker) inserts a link at the old location which kicks you out to the new location, so you won't even notice the move. Another problem is that the pages shown in this chapter might not look the same as the pages you see when you connect. Okay, now that you're aware of all this nonsense, get on with your life.

The Arts, Fine and Otherwise

World Wide Arts Resources

http://wwar.com/index.html

Although this page doesn't have any artworks of its own, it contains links to over 250 art museums, 560 galleries and exhibitions, 50 publications, 40 art institutes, and much much more. Use this site as your starting point, and fly to any of the museums listed, without even boarding a plane. This page can also help you contact art dealers and other people who may share your aesthetic tastes.

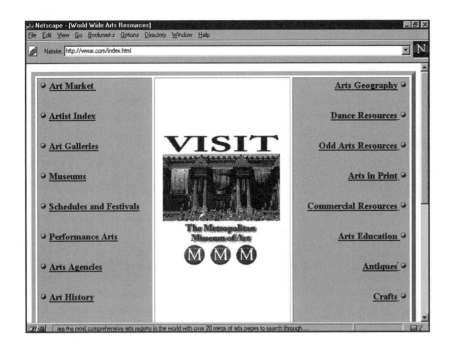

If you're interested in art, there's no better starting point than this.

The Web Museum

http://sunsite.unc.edu/louvre/

Art on the Net

http://www.art.net

Norton Museum of Art

http://www.norton.org/

Arts Gopher

gopher://marvel.loc.gov/11/global/arts

Arts and Images

gopher://gopher.cs.ttu.edu/

Michael C. Carlos Museum

http://www.cc.emory.edu/CARLOS/carlos.html

FineArt Forum Online

http://www.msstate.edu/Fineart_Online/index.html

Krannert Art Museum

http://www.art.uiuc.edu/kam/

New York Art Online

gopher://gopher.panix.com/11/nyart

dEPARTURE fROM nORMAL Art Magazine

http://www.xwinds.com/dfn/dfn.html

Techno-Impressionist Gallery

http://www.tlc-systems.com/techno/index.html

Specific Artists

Salvador Dali Museum in St. Petersburg

http://www.webcoast.com/Dali/

Francisco Goya, "Father of Modern Art"

http://www.imageone.com/goya/goya.html

Frida Kahlo's Home Page

http://cascade.net/kahlo.html

Kandinsky Page

http://www.oir.ucf.edu/wm/paint/auth/kandinsky/

M. C. Escher Collection

http://surf.tstc.edu/~qsmitr/escher.html

The Georges Seurat Homepage

http://www.pride.net/~dbirnbau/seurat.html

Leonardo da Vinci Museum

http://www.leonardo.net/museum/main.html

Vincent Van Gogh

http://hops.cs.jhu.edu/~baker/van_gogh.html

Books, Magazines, and Other Rags

The Gutenberg Project

http://www.promo.net/pg/

The Gutenberg Project is an attempt to transform the great (and not so great) works of literature into electronic form (text files). When you connect to this site, you'll get a glimpse of how extensive this project is. You can find everything from the complete works of William Shakespeare to Ed Krol's *Hitchhiker's Guide to the Internet*. If you like to read books on a computer screen, or if you like to count the number of times the word "see" appears in *King Lear*, you'll love this list.

For electronic books, visit the Gutenberg list.

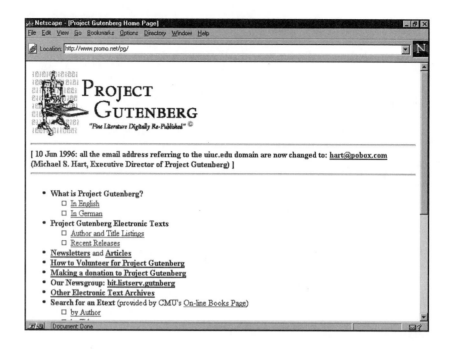

On-Line Books

http://www.cs.cmu.edu/Web/books.html

Internet Book Information Center

http://sunsite.unc.edu/ibic/IBIC-homepage.html

The Web's Best Bookstore

http://intertain.com/store/ibic.html

The English Server at Carnegie-Mellon University

http://english-server.hss.cmu.edu/

Electronic Text Center at the University of Virginia

http://www.lib.virginia.edu/etext/ETC.html

Macmillan Computer Publishing

http://www.mcp.com

The Electronic Newsstand

http://www.enews.com/

Future Fantasy Bookstore

http://futfan.com/home.html

Shadow Dance (Speculative Fiction)

http://www.leba.net/lebnews/shadow/

The Freethought Web

http://freethought.tamu.edu/freethought/

The E-Zine List

http://www.meer.net/~johnl/e-zine-list/index.html

Your Favorite Magazines

HotWired: Wired Magazine Online

http://www.hotwired.com/

Mother Jones

http://www.mojones.com/

The New Republic

http://www.enews.com/magazines/tnr/

Prison Life Magazine

http://prisonlife.com/

Playboy

http://www.playboy.com

(Sorry, ladies, *Playgirl* hasn't made the Net...yet.)

PC Computing

http://www.zdnet.com/~pccomp/

Esquire

http://www.esquireb2b.com/

A Woman's Perspective

http://www.uvol.com/woman/

(Sorry, guys, men don't have a perspective yet.)

Sports Illustrated

http://pathfinder.com/

More Cool Magazine Sites...

MIT's Oldest Newspaper: *The Tech*

http://the-tech.mit.edu/The-Tech

Some Weird Stuff

http://www.cybercom.net/~fnord/eic/index.html

Famous Authors

Shakespeare's Complete Works

http://ipl.sils.umich.edu/reading/shakespeare/shakespeare.html

http://the-tech.mit.edu/Shakespeare/

Beat Generation Authors

http://www.charm.net/~brooklyn/LitKicks.html

Edward Abbey

http://www.abalon.se/beach/aw/abbey.html

Jane Austen

http://uts.cc.utexas.edu/~churchh/janeinfo.html

Lewis Carroll

http://www.literature.org/Works/Lewis-Carroll/

Tom Clancy (Newsgroup)

news:alt.books.tom-clancy

Mark Twain

http://www.literature.org/Works/Mark-Twain/

William Faulkner

http://www.mcsr.olemiss.edu/~egjbp/faulkner/faulkner.html

Winston Groom (*Forrest Gump*)

http://gump.sgi.com/

Herman Melville

http://www.melville.org/

Ayn Rand

http://www.aynrand.org/

Salman Rushdie

http://www.nyu.edu/pages/wsn/subir/rushdie.html

J.R.R. Tolkien

http://www.math.uni-hamburg.de/.relippert/tolkien/rootpage.html

Walt Whitman

http://www.cc.columbia.edu/acis/bartleby/whitman/index.html

Business, Not Pleasure

Small & Home-Based Business Links

http://www.ro.com/small_business/homebased.html

If you feel compelled (either internally or from outside sources, like your boss) to start working at home or to build your own business, this site contains scads of links to Web pages that can help. At this site, you can learn how to draft a successful business plan, get money from reluctant customers, market your products and services, manage vendors, and even find a franchise.

At Small & Home-Based Business Links, you can learn how to start and manage a business.

Wall Street Journal

http://info.wsj.com/

SoHo Central (Home Office Center)

http://www.hoaa.com/

Internal Revenue Service

http://www.irs.ustreas.gov/

Tax Tips and Facts

http://www.rak-1.com/

Business Opportunities Handbook

http://www.w2.com/businop.html

Entrepreneurial Edge Online

http://www.edgeonline.com/

Entrepreneurs on the Web

http://www.eotw.com//EOTW.html

Interesting Internet Business Sites

http://www.owi.com/netvalue/

Commerce Business Daily

gopher://usic.savvy.com/

Curious About GATT and NAFTA?

http://itl.irv.uit.no/trade_law/

http://the-tech.mit.edu/Bulletins/nafta.html

Asian Pacific Chamber of Commerce

http://oneworld.wa.com/apcc/apcc1.html

Computers, Hard and Soft

Microsoft Corporation

http://www.microsoft.com/

If you're having trouble with Windows 95, you own Microsoft stock, or you're just curious about Microsoft's new products, connect to Microsoft's Web site for answers. Like most Microsoft projects, this site is carefully constructed, and easy to navigate. Although it may be a bit busy at times, when you do gain access, you'll find lots of cool computer information here.

Of course Microsoft has a Web site!

IBM

http://www.ibm.com/

Compaq Computer Corporation

http://www.compaq.com/

Dell Computer

http://www.dell.com/

Gateway 2000

http://www.gw2k.com/

Midwest Micro

http://www.mwmicro.com/

Packard Bell

http://www.packardbell.com/

Windows Magazine

http://www.winmag.com/

C Net

http://www.cnet.com/

Windows Sources Magazine

http://www.zdnet.com

Ed Tiley's Windows 95 Home Page

http://www.supernet.net/~edtiley/win95/win95unl.html

Micromedia CD Kiosk

http://micromedia.com/

Novell's Tech Support Site

http://www.novell.com

The Boston Computer Society

http://www.bcs.org/

Hewlett-Packard

http://www.hp.com/

Sun Microsystems

http://www.sun.com/

Kestrel Institute

http://kestrel.edu/

More Computer Companies

http://www.hal.com/pages/hops.html

Education for Students and Teachers

Cyberspace Middle School

http://www.scri.fsu.edu/~dennisl/CMS.html

The Cyberspace Middle School is directed toward students from sixth to ninth grades who are interested in using the Web to further their education. The site also has a link for teacher resources. If you have kids, and you'd like to introduce them to the Internet, you can't find a better Web page than this. (Well, maybe *you* can, but I sure couldn't.)

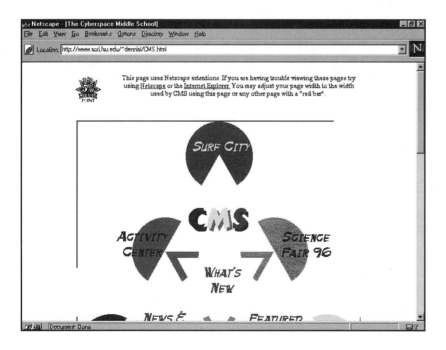

Cyberspace Middle School focuses on using the Web to educate.

Kids On Campus Internet Tour

http://www.tc.cornell.edu/cgi-bin/Kids.on.Campus/top.pl

The Teacher Education Internet Server

http://curry.edschool.Virginia.EDU/insite/

SchoolNet

gopher://gopher.nstn.ca/11/info_kiosks/SchoolNet

Franklin Institute Virtual Science Museum

http://sln.fi.edu/

DeweyWeb

http://ics.soe.umich.edu

Quest! NASA's K-12 Internet Initiative

http://quest.arc.nasa.gov/

Map Reading 101

http://info.er.usgs.gov/education/teacher/what-do-maps-show/index.html

U. S. Geological Survey

http://info.er.usgs.gov/

The Vatican Exhibit

http://sunsite.unc.edu/expo/vatican.exhibit/Vatican.exhibit.html

The Dead Sea Scrolls

http://sunsite.unc.edu/expo/deadsea.scrolls.exhibit/intro.html

Dinosaurs in Hawaii!

http://www.hcc.hawaii.edu/dinos/dinos.1.html

Homespun Web of Home Educational Resources

http://www.ICtheWeb.com/hs-web/

Introductory Accounting Course

http://www.people.memphis.edu/~fdeng/acct/2010.html

Financial Aid Information

http://www.cs.cmu.edu/afs/cs/user/mkant/Public/FinAid/finaid.html

Grantseeker's Resource Center

http://oeonline.com/~ricknot2/grant_seekers.html

Educational Online Sources

http://netspace.students.brown.edu/eos/main_image.html

KIDLINK

http://www.kidlink.org/

National Teachers Enhancement Network

http://www.montana.edu/~wwwxs/

On-Line English Grammar

http://www.edunet.com/english/grammar/index.html

TeeNet

http://www.dnai.com/~aaronv/teenet/

The Village Learning Center

http://www.snowcrest.net/villcen/vlchp.html

Fun, Games, and Entertainment

Yahoo's Entertainment Page

http://www.yahoo.com/Entertainment/

Yahoo provides links to thousands of other Internet sites, including sites for business, education, and law. Their fun and games links are so incredible, however, that I had to place Yahoo in the games section. Here, you'll find links to comics, food recipes, drink recipes, pranks, hobbies, toys, virtual reality, and anything else you might find entertaining.

Check out the best in entertainment at Yahoo.

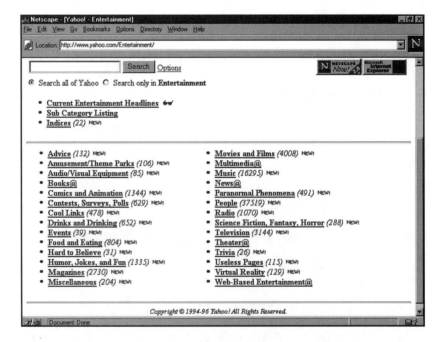

MUDs and MOOs

gopher://spinaltap.micro.umn.edu/11/fun/Games/MUDs/Links

MUDs, MOOs, and MUSHes

These hip games all started with MUDs, Multi-User Dimensions (or Dungeons or Dialogues). The term was derived from the game Dungeons and Dragons. MOO stands for MUD Object-Oriented, which makes use of a more dynamic programming language. There are several other types of games available, as well, including MUSHes, MUSEs, and LPMUDs.

Doctor Fun and Other Comic Strips

http://sunsite.unc.edu/Dave/drfun.html

Comic Books in Print and Not

http://www.eden.com/comics/comics.html

Barney's Home Page

http://asylum.cid.com/barney/

The Captain James T. Kirk Sing-a-long Page

http://www.ama.caltech.edu/users/mrm/kirk.html

Fortune Cookie (Without the Cookie)

http://www.twentymule.com/Fortune.acgi

Calvin and Hobbes Gallery

http://eos.kub.nl:2080/calvin_hobbes/

Bloom County Page

http://www.math.fsu.edu/~pbismu/BLOOMCOUNTY/bc.html

Dilbert (A Daily Cartoon Strip)

http://www.unitedmedia.com/comics/dilbert/

The Far Side

http://www.cad.uni-sb.de/elzer/farside.html

The BOG (Internet Graffiti)

http://www.technet.sg/BOG/

Cool Site of the Day

http://cool.infi.net/

t@p online

http://www.taponline.com/

Alien On Line

http://www.crs4.it/~mameli/Alien.html

Web-Tender: Online Bartender

http://www.pvv.unit.no/~pallo/webtender/

Cook's Corner

http://wchat.on.ca/merlene/cook.htm

Sin City (Penn & Teller Home Page)

http://www.sincity.com/

Letterman's Top Ten List

http://www.cbs.com/lateshow/ttlist.html

Health and Fitness

The Weightlifting Page

http://www.cs.unc.edu/~wilsonk/weights.html

The Weightlifting Page is for hard core weightlifters. Here, you'll find links to hundreds of sites that deal with weightlifting techniques, stretching, diets, gyms, videos, training equipment, newsgroups, and anything else that's even remotely helpful to weightlifters. In addition, the page contains pictures of pumped up bodies, so be prepared to feel grossly inadequate.

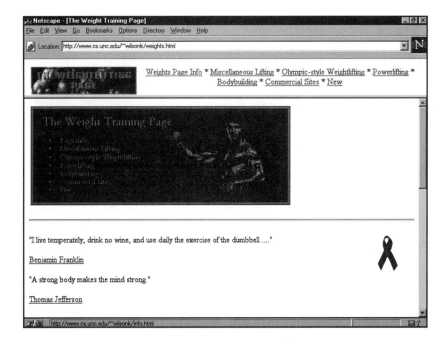

This page will pump you up.

Global Health Network

http://www.pitt.edu/HOME/GHNet/GHNet.html

Aerobics and Fitness Association of America

http://www.cybercise.com/affa.html

MetroSports (Magazine)

http://virtumall.com/newsstand/metrosports/

HealthNet

http://debra.dgbt.doc.ca/~mike/healthnet/

USF Health Sciences News

http://www.med.usf.edu/PUBAFF/news1.html

Welch Medical Library

gopher://welchlink.welch.jhu.edu/

Cancer Research with OncoLink

gopher://gan.ncc.go.jp/

AIDS Foundation in Houston

http://www.powersource.com/afh/

On-Line Allergy Center

http://www.sig.net/~allergy/welcome.html

Lyme Disease Resource

http://www.sky.net/~dporter/lyme1.html

Arthritis Foundation

http://www.arthritis.org/

Center for Food Safety and Applied Nutrition

http://vm.cfsan.fda.gov/list.html

Yahoo's Health Page

http://www.yahoo.com/Health/

Naturopathic Physicians

http://infinity.dorsai.org/Naturopathic.Physician/

Hobbies and Recreation

Antiques and Other Collectibles

http://www.ic.mankato.mn.us/antiques/Antiques.html

If you're interested in becoming an antique collector, this should be your first stop. The mission of the Antiques & Collectibles site is to bring beginners up to speed so they won't get ripped off at antique shows. In addition to texty explanations of what to look for, this site offers graphics that can help you tell an original from a fake and help you judge the value of a particular item.

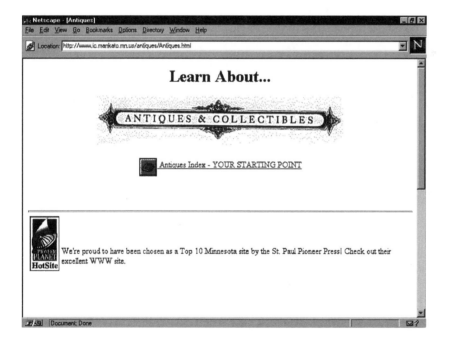

Learn about antiques and collectibles here.

Spencer's Beer Page

http://realbeer.com/spencer/

Callahan's Cookbook

http://www.ruhr-uni-bochum.de/callahans/cookbook.html

The Garden Gate (Gardening)

http://www.prairienet.org/ag/garden/homepage.htm

Juggling

http://www.hal.com/services/juggle/

Woodworking Ideas and Techniques

http://access.digex.com/~mds/woodwork.html

Dogs and Cats

http://snapple.cs.washington.edu:600/canine/canine.html

http://www.fanciers.com/

Snakes and Other Reptiles

http://www.mtcnet.com/repcat.htm

Guide to Lock Picking

http://www.lysator.liu.se:7500/mit-guide/mit-guide.html

KiteParadise

http://www.hermes.de/KITE/

Andreas Wistuba's Carnivorous Plant Page

http://www.rhein-neckar.de/~carnivor/index.html

The Potter's Page (Pottery)

http://www.aztec.co.za/users/theo/

Cigar Smoker's Page

http://www.law.vill.edu/~kmortens/humidor/

HobbyWorld

http://www.hobbyworld.com/

Internet News and Information

Lycos Internet Catalog

http://www.lycos.com/

Lycos is the "catalogue of the Internet." Each day, Lycos searches the Internet for new and interesting sites, and then catalogues these sites. You can then use the Lycos search form to look for sites that pertain to a specific topic.

Lycos can help you navigate the Internet.

Internet World Magazine

http://www.iworld.com/

The Internet Society

http://info.isoc.org/home.html

Internet Services Directory

http://www.directory.net/

Internet Search Form

http://www.cmpcmm.com/cc/

Zen and the Art of the Internet

http://sundance.cso.uiuc.edu/Publications/Other/Zen/zen-1.0_toc.html

Easy Internet

http://www.futurenet.co.uk/netmag/Issue1/Easy/index.html

Investing Your Money

100% No Load Mutual Fund Council

http://networth.galt.com/www/home/mutual/100/100guide.htm

Don't invest in mutual funds until you've visited this site. It offers an online book about investing in mutual funds. You'll learn how to choose funds, put together a portfolio that's right for you, and invest once you've made your decision.

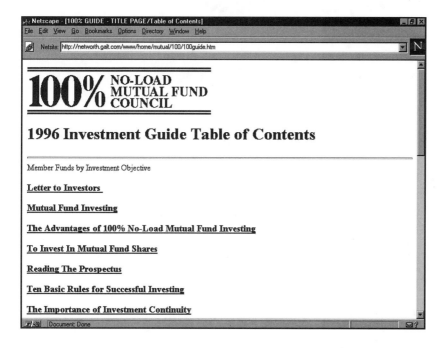

Before you invest in mutual funds, stop here.

The Morningstar Spotlight

http://pawws.secapl.com/How_phtml/mstar.shtml

StreetLink Corporate Financial Reports

http://www.streetlink.com/

Quote.com Investment Service

http://www.quote.com/

Stock Broker Information

http://www.cs.cmu.edu/afs/cs.cmu.edu/user/jdg/www/invest_brokers/
index.html

DTN Wall Street

http://www.secapl.com/dtn/info/top.html

The New York University EDGAR Project

http://edgar.stern.nyu.edu

Experimental Stock Market Information Sites

gopher://una.hh.lib.umich.edu/00/ebb/monetary/tenfx.frb

http://www.secapl.com/secapl/quoteserver/sp500.html

The Chicago Mercantile Exchange

http://www.cme.com/

The Economic Bulletin Board

gopher://una.hh.lib.umich.edu/11/ebb/

Irnetserve, Inc. (Public Companies on the Web)

http://199.170.0.96/index.html

NASDAQ Financial Executive Journal

http://www.law.cornell.edu/nasdaq/nasdtoc.html

Global Village News for Investors

http://info.globalvillag.com/i_relations.html

Job Hunting

E-Span Interactive Employment

http://www.espan.com

Start your career planning and job searches here. The E-Span service provides advice on writing resumés, networking, and interviewing. Have you ever mulled over the thought of salary requirements? At E-Span, you can view lists of national averages for various positions in different parts of the country. The online job database lets you perform a WAIS search of job openings by state, city, job title, or anything else you want to search for. You can even post your own resume. For additional job search advice, check out the Dunn & Bradstreet site described earlier:

http://www.dbisna.com/

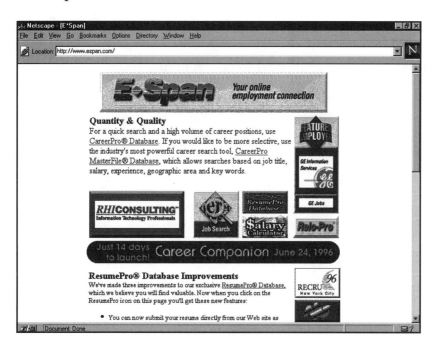

Your first stop for job-hunting hints.

JobHunt

http://rescomp.stanford.edu/jobs.html

The Monster Board

http://www.monster.com/home.html

Career Magazine

http://www.careermag.com/careermag/

Resume Bank

http://www.careermag.com/careermag/resumes/index.html

College Grad Job Hunter

http://www.collegegrad.com/

Job Hunting on the Internet

http://copper.ucs.indiana.edu/~dvasilef/jobsearch.html

JobCenter

http://www.jobcenter.com/

More Job Leads (and Links)

http://www.yahoo.com/Business_and_Economy/Employment/Jobs/

Laws and Other Legal Stuff

The Seamless WEBsite

http://seamless.com

If you're a lawyer or student of law, you'll find all the resources (and links to other resources) you'll need. From this Web page, you can advertise, find legal documents, acquire lists of expert witnesses, chat with other lawyers, and even look for a job.

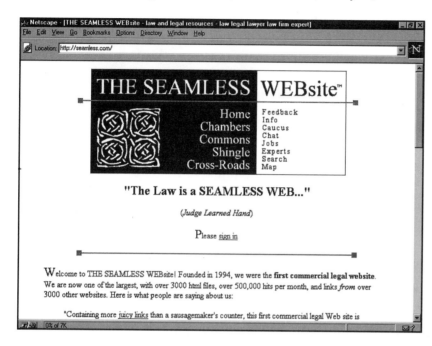

The Seamless WEBsite is a hangout for lawyers.

Nolo Press Self-Help Law Center

http://www.nolo.com

LawTalk—Business Law and Personal Finance

http://www.law.indiana.edu/law/bizlaw.html

Supreme Court Decisions

http://www.law.cornell.edu/supct/

Labor Law

http://www.webcom.com/~garnet/labor/labor.html

Case Western Reserve University Law Library

http://lawwww.cwru.edu/cwrulaw/library/libinfo.html

Emory University School of Law

http://www.law.emory.edu/

Index of Law Schools and Libraries

http://www.law.indiana.edu/law/lawschools.html

Federal Tax Code

http://www.tns.lcs.mit.edu/uscode/

American Civil Liberties Union

http://www.aclu.org/

Lisa's Green Page

http://www.echonyc.com/~kamml/enviro.html

Lawyer Jokes

http://www.scroom.com/humor/lawyer.html

O.J. Simpson Joke Page

http://www.webpub.com/oj/

More Legal Sites

http://www.yahoo.com/Government/Law/

Musical Notes

Adam Curry's The Vibe

http://metaverse.com/vibe/index.html

Adam Curry, former MTV video jock, has his own Internet site. Here you can read Curry's newsletter (the *Cyber-Sleaze Report*) for musical reviews, musician interviews, and even Adam Curry's quote of the day. You can listen to sound clips, view music videos, get concert information, and check out the charts.

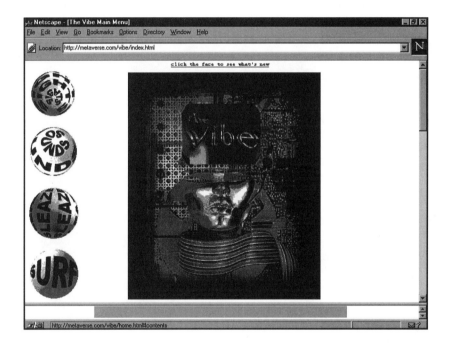

Adam Curry's The Vibe.

Eden Matrix Music Online

http://www.eden.com/music/

American Recordings

http://american.recordings.com/

The Internet Underground Music Archive

http://www.iuma.com/

CDworld The Internet Music Store

http://cdworld.com/

Tom Waits Digest

http://www.nwu.edu/waits/

Paula Cole Page

http://cpcug.org/user/titusb/pcole/

The Cranberries Information Page

http://www.wolsi.com/~cranberry/

Counting Crows Page

http://www.monmouth.com/~jkochel/crows.html

Hans Zimmer Worship Page

http://www.ugcs.caltech.edu/~btman/hanszimmer/

Links to Other Artists

http://www.yahoo.com/Entertainment/Music/Artists/

The Internet Music Review Service

http://www.monsterbit.com/IMRS/

WZLX Classic Rock Trivia

http://www.wzlx.com/scripts/fishtriv.cgi?prezoom=31,0&postzoom=0,0

Global Music Outlet

http://www.iuma.com/GMO/

Jerry Garcia's Haight Street Shrine

http://www.sirius.com/~jmelloy/jerry.html

And Still More Music Areas

http://www.yahoo.com/Business_and_Economy/Companies/Music/Labels/

Movies and Videos

The Internet Movie Database

http://us.imdb.com/

To search for movies by title, actor, or director, visit The Internet Movie Database (formerly known as Cardiff's Movie Database). This place also offers a ballot that allows you to cast a vote for your favorite movie, and a movie quiz to test your expertise.

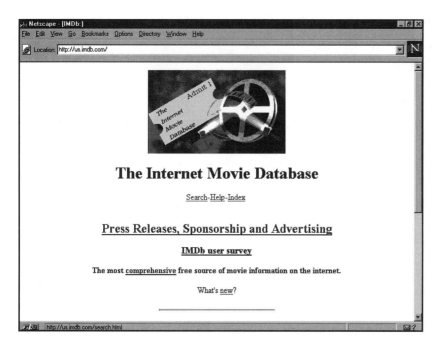

The Internet Movie Database is a great place for film buffs.

MPEG Movie Archive

http://www.eeb.ele.tue.nl/mpeg/index.html

Movies Directory

http://www.cs.cmu.edu/afs/cs.cmu.edu/user/mleone/web/movies.html

The Woody Allen Page

http://www.idt.unit.no/~torp/woody/

Batman Forever

http://www.batmanforever.com/

Blade Runner Page

http://kzsu.stanford.edu/uwi/br/off-world.html

Disney Home Page

http://www.disney.com/

Sandra Bullock Page

http://weber.u.washington.edu:80/~louie/sandra.html

Cannes International Film Festival

http://www.interactive8.com:80/cannes/welcome/welcome.html

Cinema Muerto (Really Bad Movies)

http://users.aol.com/Cinemam/muerto.htm

The Envelope, Please (Academy Awards)

http://guide.oscars.org/

Hollywood Online

http://www.hollywood.com/

The Stanley Kubrick Page

http://www.lehigh.edu/~pjl2/kubrick.html

The Rocky Horror Picture Show

http://www.cs.wvu.edu/~paulr/rhps/rhps.html

Ed Wood, Jr. Home Page

http://garnet.acns.fsu.edu:80/~lflynn/edwood.html

Guide to Film and Video Resources on the Internet

http://http2.sils.umich.edu/Public/fvl/film.html

News, Real News

Time Magazine

http://www.pathfinder.com

This online version of the *Time Magazine* offers articles from the latest issue, and you don't even have to run out to the newstand! Of course, the articles are teasers, but if all you want is the cover story and a few other tidbits, this will satisfy your thirst for weekly news. You can also use this site to send letters to the editor.

Pathfinder seems to have a monopoly on digitized versions of magazines. Here, you'll find links to *People*, *Money*, *Fortune*, *Sports Illustrated*, and a host of other rags.

Time Magazine in its digitized form.

CNN Interactive

http://www.cnn.com/

New York Times Electronic Edition

http://nytimesfax.com/

USA Today

http://www.usatoday.com/

Chicago Tribune

http://www.chicago.tribune.com/

Indianapolis Star and News

http://www.starnews.com/

Philadelphia Online

http://www.phillynews.com/

Washington Weekly

http://dolphin.gulf.net/

The Detroit Free Press

http://gopher.det-freepress.com:9002/

The Seattle Times

http://www.seatimes.com/

The Nando Times

http://www.nando.net/

Today.com

http://today.com/

Vocal Point (A Student Newspaper for K-12)

http://bvsd.k12.co.us/cent/Newspaper/Newspaper.html

The Classifieds

gopher://merlin.nando.net/11/nando/classads

The Guardian

http://www.guardian.co.uk/

Philosophy and Religion

Sean's One-Stop Philosophy Shop

http://www.rpi.edu/~cearls/phil.html

Why do you exist? Why should you care? And who is this Kierkegaard fellow? On this Web page, you'll find answers to all your existential and metaphysical questions... or at least, you'll have a place to start looking. This page, rated in the top 5% of all Web sites, is more of a starting point in your future intellectual, Internet travels. In addition, you'll find links to humorous philosophical sites, and links to all your favorite philosophers—from Aristotle to Zeno.

Sean's One-Stop Philosophy Shop combines humor and thought.

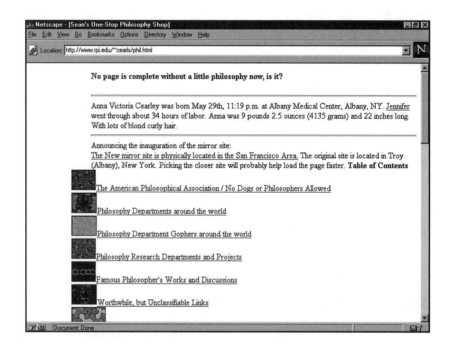

Philosophy Around the Web

http://users.ox.ac.uk/~worc0337/index.html

Su Tzu's Chinese Philosophy Page

http://mars.superlink.net/user/fsu/philo.html

Hyper-Philosophy

http://www.physics.wisc.edu/~shalizi/hyper-weird/philosophy.html

American Philosophical Association

gopher://apa.oxy.edu/

The Kierkegaard Gopher

gopher://info.utas.edu.au/11/Publications/Kierkegaard

Online Journal of Analytical Philosophy

http://www.phil.indiana.edu/ejap/ejap.html

Christian Coalition

http://cc.org/

Our Daily Bread

http://unicks.calvin.edu/rbc/odb/

Jewish Web World Online

http://www.nauticom.net/users/rafie/judaica-world.html

Unofficial Pope John Paul II Page

http://www.zpub.com/un/pope/

Guide to Christian Literature

http://www.calvin.edu/Christian/pw.html

1-800-JUDAISM Online

gopher://israel.nysernet.org/11/800judaism

Confession Booth

http://anther.learning.cs.cmu.edu/priest.html

Politics and Government

The White House

http://www.whitehouse.gov/

Visit the White House without leaving your home! Here you can find out about the First Family, take an online tour of the White House (with a personal greeting from Mr. Clinton), sign the guest book, hear Al Gore welcome you, and select from a list of government publications. You can even visit the New and Improved Hillary Rodham Clinton Home Page (I'm not sure whether "New and Improved" modifies "Hillary" or "Home Page.")

Take an online tour of the White House.

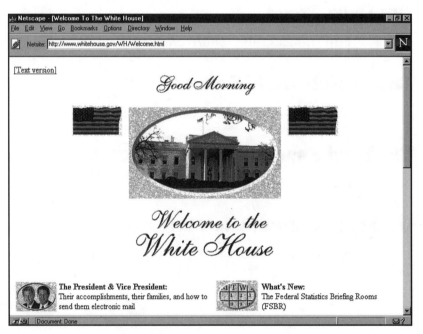

The Jefferson Project

http://www.voxpop.org/jefferson/

United States Information Center

http://www.usia.gov/usis.html

Congressional E-Mail Addresses

http://www.webcom.com/~leavitt/cong.html

The Deficit Page

http://www.texas.net/users/andyn/deficit.html

The CIA Page

http://www.odci.gov/cia/

FBI's Ten "Most Wanted Fugitives"

http://www.fbi.gov/toplist.htm

Food and Drug Administration

http://www.fda.gov/

The United Nations Development Program

http://www.undp.org/

Bad Subjects: Political Education for Everyday Life

http://english-www.hss.cmu.edu/bs/

Abortion & Reproductive Rights Resources

http://www.matisse.net/politics/caral/abortion.html

All Things Political

http://dolphin.gulf.net/Political.html

The Black Panther Coloring Book

http://www.cybergate.com:80/~jonco/thebpcb.html

Countdown '96

http://www.comeback.com/countdown/

Institute for Policy Innovation

http://www.ipi.org/

The Unofficial Rush Limbaugh Page

http://www.rtis.com/nat/pol/rush/

Punch Rush Limbaugh Page

http://www.indirect.com/www/beetle87/rush/index.html

NewtWatch

http://www.cais.com/newtwatch/

PC (Politically Correct) Primer

http://www.umd.umich.edu/~nhughes/htmldocs/pc.html

Propaganda Analysis Home Page

http://carmen.artsci.washington.edu/propaganda/home.htm

Shopping Networks

The Branch Mall

http://branch.com/

The Branch Mall is the Mall America of mail order. In the Branch Mall, you can shop for everything from bonsai trees to exercise equipment, from flowers and candy to computers and vacuum cleaners. You can even find a divorce lawyer! Of course, you don't get the same feel as a real mall. You won't see people with blank looks on their faces talking into cellular phones, but the storefronts might look familiar.

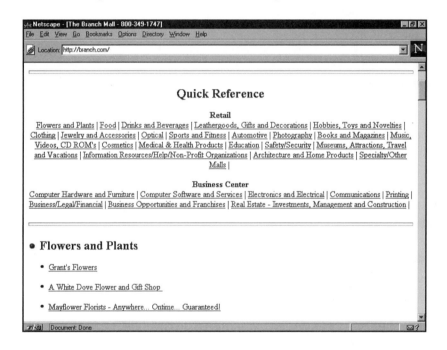

The Branch Mall dwarfs Mall America.

The CyberMall

http://www.nstn.ns.ca/cybermall/first.html

Above and Beyond Mall

http://www.abmall.com/

Brookstone

http://www.netplaza.com/plaza/strfrnts/1015/storepg1.html

Internet Shopping Network

http://www0.internet.net/cgi-bin/
getNode?node=1&source=DYHO&session=2208644

Tuppertime (Online Tupperware)

http://www.he.net/~tupper/index.html

AutoRow

http://www.autorow.com/

Sea Ray Boats

http://www.searay.com/boats/

The Smoke Shop

http://www.thesmokeshop.com/smoke/

The WorldWide Marketplace

http://www.cygnus.nb.ca/mall/mall.html

Sports Scores and Schedules

Nando X Sports Server

http://www.nando.net/SportServer/

This sports service is for serious sports nuts who want the latest scores and stats. When you first sign on, you'll have to fill out a form and subscribe to the service. This sports service is so slick, I suspect it will soon become a pay service.

The Nando X Sports Server is for mondo sports nuts.

The NFL Football Server

http://sports.yahoo.com/nfl/

Southern Utah Golf Courses

http://sci.dixie.edu/StGeorge/Golf/golf.html

Dirt Rag (Mountain Biking Magazine)

http://cyclery.com/dirt_rag/text-index.html

1996 Summer Olympics

http://www.intadv.com/olympic.html

College Basketball Page

http://www.cs.cmu.edu/afs/cs.cmu.edu/user/wsr/Web/bball/bball.html

ESPN Sports Page

http://espnet.sportszone.com/

PGA News

http://sports.yahoo.com/pga/lgns/

NASCAR Online

http://www.nascar.com/

WWW Women's Sports Page

http://fiat.gslis.utexas.edu/~lewisa/womsprt.html

Jerry Yang's Sumo Information Page

http://akebono.stanford.edu/users/jerry/sumo/

Travel

Epicurious Travel

http://travel.epicurious.com/travel/a_homepage/home.html

If you're planning a vacation (a real getaway), and you're not sure where you want to go, then start here. Epicurious Travel (formerly Conde Nast Traveler) is the online version of the printed version of this jet-set vacation guide. However, this online version is more than just an electronic magazine. It includes digitized photos, online games, and interactive maps that will keep you clicking for hours.

Visit the Conde Nast Traveler for exotic getaways.

Costa Rica Tourism

http://merica.cool.co.cr/cgi-bin/turismo

Village Voice (New York Hot Spots)

http://www.villagevoice.com/

Foreign Languages for Travelers

http://insti.physics.sunysb.edu/~mmartin/languages/languages.html

The Grand (Canyon) Tour

http://www.gorp.com/gcjunkies/canyon.htm

Healthy Flying with Diana Fairechild

http://www.maui.net/~diana/

Internet Guide to Bed & Breakfast Inns

http://paradiso.com:80/inns/

The Las Vegas Leisure Guide

http://www.pcap.com/lasvegas.htm

U.S. National Park Service

http://www.nps.gov/

PC Travel (Airline Ticketing)

http://www.pctravel.com/

Travel Weekly Web Page

http://www.traveler.net/

Foreign Exchange Rates

gopher://una.hh.lib.umich.edu/00/ebb/monetary/tenfx.frb

Travel Services

http://www.cygnus.nb.ca/mall/travel.html

Weather Reports and Maps

National Climatic Data Center

http://www.ncdc.noaa.gov/ncdc.html

National Climatic Data Center is a site where you can view the latest satellite images from around the world. Simply click a link, and you're flying above the earth, watching the clouds spin.

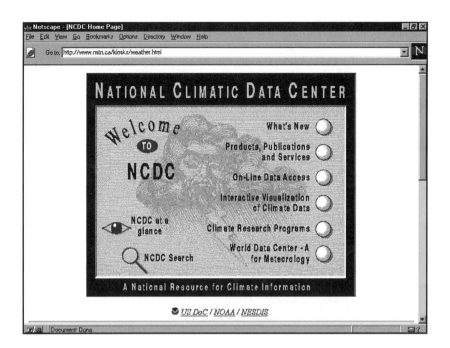

At National Climatic Data Center, you get a seat above the clouds.

Weather Information Service

http://www.nstn.ca/kiosks/weather.html

WebWeather

http://www.princeton.edu/Webweather/ww.html

Fox Weather Services

http://www.foxweather.com/

Weather Information (Links to Other Sites)

http://atmos.es.mq.edu.au/weather/

World Meteorological Association

http://www.wmo.ch:80/

Intellicast

http://www.intellicast.com/

The Uncategorical Category

Top 5% Web Sites

http://www.pointcom.com/

As you bounce around to the various Web pages that my URLs point to, you'll notice that some have a tiny badge that says "Top 5% of All Web Sites." Well, these special sites were awarded their badges from this site. You'll find links to the top 5% of all Web pages here... at least the top 5% in some people's eyes.

The best of the Web.

Internet Pizza Server

http://www.ecst.csuchico.edu/~pizza/

News of the Weird

http://www.cs.su.oz.au/~giovanni/humour/weird.html

Peeping Tom Home Page (It's Not What You Think)

http://www.ts.umu.se/~spaceman/camera.html

The Joe Boxer WWW Playground

http://www.joeboxer.com/

Virtual Voyager—In Search of Elvis

http://www1.chron.com/voyager/elvis/

Visit the Faherty Family

http://www.ultranet.com/~faherty/

The Heart: An Online Exploration

http://sln2.fi.edu/biosci/heart.html

Speak Like a Geek: The Complete Archive

absolute reference   In a Web document, a link that refers to a specific document regardless of the current document's address. Think of it like this: If you give a person an absolute reference, it's sort of like telling them to go to a specific address. A relative reference would be like saying, "It's two blocks west of the Village Pantry."

anchor   The part of a link that causes the mouse pointer to turn into a pointing finger. See also *link*.

anonymous login   The process of connecting to a system incognito. Many FTP sites (places where you can get files) allow users to connect anonymously and access public areas. Anonymous login privileges usually do not allow you to place files on the server or change anything.

Archie   An Internet search tool that helps you find files. In most cases, you need to know the exact name of the file or a partial file name. See also *Veronica* and *Jughead*.

associate   To establish a connection between a given file type and the helper application needed to view or play that file type. In Navigator, you must create file associations so Navigator will "know" which application to run when you choose to view, watch, or listen to a file. For example, you might associate movie files that end in .mpg with an MPEG movie player.

Auto Load Images   A setting on Navigator's Options menu. When on, Navigator automatically loads and displays pictures on a Web page. You can turn this option off to prevent pictures from appearing, and speed up Navigator.

BBS   Short for *bulletin board system*, a BBS is a computer that's set up to automatically answer the phone and allow callers to exchange messages, files, and information. Special interest groups, professional organizations, and software companies commonly set up BBSs.

bookmark   A Navigator tool that lets you mark your favorite Web pages so you can quickly return to them later.

Boolean operators   Conjunctions, including "and" and "or," used to separate search terms. For example, if you search for "Clinton and Whitewater," you get a list of all resources that relate to both "Clinton" and "Whitewater." If you use "or" the search is much broader, finding anything that relates to either "Clinton" or "Whitewater."

bps   Short for *bits per second*, this is a unit used to measure the speed of data transfer between two computers. As far as the Web is concerned, anything slower than 14,400 bps is a snail's pace.

browser   See *Web browser*.

cache   A temporary storage area that Navigator creates both in RAM and on your hard disk. Navigator stores Web pages in the cache, so it can quickly load these pages if you decide to return to them. In other words, Navigator doesn't have to yank the pages back through the phone lines.

channel   The equivalent of a conference room. When you chat on the Internet, you first connect to a chat server, and then you tune in to a channel. Each channel is supposed to deal with a different topic, but people mostly talk about the weather and where they're from, or they simply flirt with one another. See also *chat*.

chat   To "talk" to another person by typing at your computer. What you type appears on the other person's screen, and what the other person types appears on your screen. You can't chat with Navigator; you need another program such as Netscape Chat if you want to get chatty.

client   Of two computers, the computer that's being served. Whenever you connect to a Web site, the computer at that site is the *server*, and you are the *client*. Think of yourself as the *customer*.

compressed file   A file that's been squished so it takes up less disk space and travels faster through network and modem connections. Before you can use the file, you must *decompress* (or expand) it using a special program. Popular decompression programs include PKZip (for DOS) and WinZip (for Windows).

cookie   A piece of information that a server can attach to Navigator, so the server can recognize you if you come back later. Cookies are commonly used to help a server keep track of what's in your shopping cart when you're shopping at a virtual mall.

CoolTalk   A program (bundled with Netscape Navigator) that allows you to carry on a phone conversation over Internet connections rather than by using phone company lines. CoolTalk allows you to avoid long-distance charges. CoolTalk also has a Chat Tool that lets you type messages back and forth, and a White Board that lets you transmit and mark up graphic images.

cyberspace   The universe created by the connection of thousands of computers. Computer users can use modems to enter cyberspace and converse with other users. This term was first used by William Gibson in his novel *Neuromancer*. In the novel, people plugged their brains into cyberspace. If you've ever seen the glazed look people get when they're wired to the Web, you know that Gibson's notion is not too far from the truth.

decompress   To unsquish a squished file and make it usable.

Dial-Up Networking   A program that comes with Windows 95 that establishes the Internet connection you need in order to run Navigator and access the World Wide Web.

digital certificate   An electronic ID badge that you can use in Navigator to identify yourself on the Internet. This badge passes your username, password, and personal information to a certified server, so you can gain access to the server without manually entering a password.

document   On the Web, this could be anything: an index of topics, several screenfuls of text, or even a page full of pictures.

document source   The coded document that controls the way Web pages appear. These are like the proverbial ugly twin.

domain name   A unique identification for an Internet site. Each computer on the Internet has a domain name that distinguishes it from other computers on the Internet. Domain names usually provide some vague indication of the establishment that runs the server. For example, here's the domain name of the Whitehouse server: www.whitehouse.gov.

domain name server (DNS)   A computer that matches a site's name to a number that identifies that site. All servers on the Internet have a domain name, for example ncsa.uiuc.edu. Each server also has a unique IP (Internet Protocol) number, such as 128.252.135.4. Your Internet service provider has an electronic database, called a *DNS (Domain Name Server)* that matches the domain to the IP number to find the server that has the requested data. As you innocently click links, the DNS is matching domain names and IP numbers to make sure you get where you're supposed to be.

download   To copy a file from another computer (usually an FTP server) to your computer.

e-mail   Mail that requires no postage and usually gets there on time. E-mail is a system in which people can send and receive messages through their computers, on a network or using modems. Each person has a designated mail box that stores messages sent by other users. He can then retrieve and read messages from the mail box.

e-zine   Pronounced "ee-zeen," this is an electronic rendition of a *zine*, a noncommercial magazine that leans toward the bizarre, twisted, or edgy side. One person or a small group of people typically put together zines, which rarely contain advertisements.

FAQ Pronounced "fack," short for *frequently asked questions*, this is a list of answers to the most-often-asked questions at a particular Internet site. Good Internet etiquette demands that you read the FAQ at a site before you post any questions. That way, you won't risk getting flamed. See *flame*.

finger A special UNIX command that pokes around through the directory of users and finds information about that person, including the person's e-mail address, and whether or not that person has read her mail recently or even logged in.

flame To verbally abuse another user during an online discussion, via e-mail, or in a newsgroup. Common flaming techniques include name-calling, abusive innuendos about one's parents, and other puerile gems of wit.

form A fill-in-the-blank Web document. Sites commonly use forms to take credit card orders, ask for your password, or let you enter search instructions.

frame A new Navigator feature that allows two parts of the same Web document to appear in the same window. One frame might contain an outline of the document. When you click on a heading in the outline, the other frame shows the contents of that heading.

FTP Short for *File Transfer Protocol*, a set of rules that govern the transfer of files between computers. True geeks use this acronym as a verb. For example, "I FTP'd to ftp-dot-netscape-dot-com to nab the latest Navigator beta."

geek 1. An overly obsessive computer user who will sacrifice food, sleep, sex, and other pleasantries of life to spend more time at the keyboard. 2. A carnival performer whose act usually includes biting off the head of a live snake or chicken.

GIF file Pronounced "giff file" or "jiff file," a picture file, commonly a photograph or painting. GIF is short for *Graphic Interchange Format*, a format developed by CompuServe for transferring graphic files. The format stores lots of graphic information in little space.

Gopher An indexing system that allows you to access various Internet services by selecting menu options. Whenever you connect to a Gopher site, it presents you with an opening menu. When you select a menu item, the server presents you with another submenu containing additional options and/or files. These options may kick you out to another Gopher server, an FTP server, a newsgroup, or other Internet servers. You proceed through the menus until you find the information you want... or reach a dead end.

handle A user's computerized nickname or ID number. When you look for a person using Whois, you might find the person's handle. You can often find out more about a person by performing the search again using the person's handle.

helper application   A program that performs a specialized job that Navigator is unfit to manage. Whenever you click a link that Navigator can't play, Navigator loads the file to disk and then summons (spawns) the helper application associated with that file. The helper application loads the file and plays it.

history list   A directory of all the Web sites you visited since you connected. You can view the history list in Navigator by opening the **Window** menu and clicking **History**.

hits   In a WAIS search, the number of times a search word was found in an article. The higher the number, the more likely it is that the article contains the information you're looking for. See also *score*.

home page   The page that greets you when you first start Navigator or first connect to a Web site. No relation to "home boy."

host   In biology, the being that is leeched on by a parasite. On the Internet, it pretty much means the same thing. The host is the computer that has the information. Your computer is the client, sucking the lifeblood out of the host.

HTML   Short for *HyperText Markup Language*, the code used to create Web documents. These codes tell the Navigator how to display the text (titles, headings, lists, and so on), insert anchors that link this document to other documents, and control character formatting (by making it bold or italic).

HTML editor   A program designed to make it easier to create Web pages. Instead of typing codes, you format the document as if you were using a desktop publishing program. The HTML editor inserts the codes for you.

HTTP   Short for *HyperText Transfer Protocol*, a set of rules that govern the exchange of data between a Web host and a client (your computer). The address for every Web server starts with **http**. If you see an address that starts with different letters (for example, **ftp** or **gopher**) the address is for a different type of server: Gopher (**gopher**), FTP (**ftp**), WAIS (**wais**), Usenet (**news**), or Telnet (**telnet**).

hyperdocument   A Web page that contains links connecting it to other pages. On the Web, a hyperdocument might contain links to other text, graphics, sounds, or movies.

hyperlinks   Icons, pictures, or highlighted chunks of text that connect two documents. For example, a document about pork might contain a link for sausage. If you click the link, Navigator displays a document about how to make sausage. Sausage is the link, although it's not actually a sausage link.

hypermedia   A dynamic computerized soup that contains movie clips, graphics, sound files, text, and anything else that can be stored in a digitized form. That's the "media" part, anyway. The "hyper" part deals with the fact that these ingredients are interlinked, so you can jump quickly from one to another.

HYTELNET   A phone book for other telnet hosts. It contains addresses and login information for hundreds of online library catalogs, bulletin board systems (BBSs), Free-nets (free online systems), and other information resources. See also *Telnet*.

inline image   A graphic that appears inside a Web document. You can tell Navigator not to display these images... if you can't stand waiting for them to load.

interactive   A user-controlled program, document, or game. Interactive programs commonly display on-screen *prompts* asking the user for input so he can decide how to carry out a particular task. These programs are popular in education, allowing children to follow their natural curiosity to solve problems and gather information.

Internet   The world's largest system of interconnected networks. The Internet was originally named ARPAnet after the Advanced Research Projects Agency in the Defense department. The agency developed the ARPAnet in the mid-1970s as an experimental project to allow various university and military sources to continue to communicate in a state of national emergency. Nowadays, the Internet is used mostly by private citizens for connecting to databases, exchanging electronic mail, and wasting loads of productive time.

Internet Phone   A program that lets you place voice phone calls over the Internet using a sound card and speakers rather than your phone. Because the voice signals travel over the Internet rather than over phone company lines, you can avoid long-distance charges.

IP address   A unique number assigned to each computer on the Internet. Most of the time, you work with domain names, such as nasa.uiuc.edu. Behind the scenes, whenever you enter a domain name, your service provider matches that name to the site's IP number (for example 128.252.135.4), and then calls that site. The idea here is that it's easier for you to remember names and easier for computers to remember numbers. The domain name/IP number link makes everyone happy.

IRC   Short for Internet Relay Chat, this is a technology that allows users to type messages back and forth using their keyboards. It's sort of like talking on the phone but less expensive and much slower.

Java   Coffee. Also, a relatively new technology that allows you (or at least someone who knows how to use Java) to create animations and other moving video clips and embed them in Web pages. All you need to know about Java is that if you click a link for a Java applet (application), Navigator will play it.

JPG   Short for *Joint Photograph Group*, a file-compression format used for storing graphic files. If you come across a file that ends in .JPG, you can view it in Netscape Navigator, or you can have one of your helper applications display it.

Jughead   An Internet search tool used to find resources at a specific site. Archie, Veronica, and Jughead (all Internet search tools) are related. Archie searches for FTP servers that contain the files you want to download. Veronica searches all Gopher sites to find the ones that store various resources. Jughead searches only the current Gopher site to find the specified resources.

links   Aka *hyperlinks*, these are icons, pictures, or highlighted chunks of text that connect the current page to other pages, Internet sites, graphics, movies, or sounds.

logical codes   In a Web document, codes that provide general directions on how to display text. For example, <em> stands for emphasis, which might mean bold or italic. Physical codes give more precise instructions. For example, <b> means bold.

log in   To connect to another computer on a network or on the Internet so you can use that computer's resources. The login procedure usually requires you to enter your username (or user ID) and a password.

log out   To disconnect from another computer on a network or on the Internet.

lurk   When you read newsgroup messages posted by other people but don't respond to them or post any messages of your own. This is sort of like being a peeping Tom, but you rarely see anything to get excited about.

map   A graphical navigational tool used on many Web pages. Think of it as one of those mall maps with the **YOU ARE HERE** arrow on it, but with a Web map, you can actually go places by clicking on different areas of the map.

MIME   Short for *Multi-purpose Internet Mail Extensions*, a protocol that controls all file transfers on the Web. Navigator uses MIME to recognize different file types. If an HTML document arrives, Navigator "knows" to play that file itself. If an .MPG file arrives, Navigator calls the associated helper application. MIME was originally developed to attach different types of files (usually multimedia files) to e-mail messages.

mirror site   A server that contains the same files as the original site. Why the redundancy? Because some sites are so busy that users might have trouble connecting during peak hours. The mirror sites offer an alternate location that helps users avoid Internet traffic jams.

MOO   Acronym for *MUD Object-Oriented*, another type of hip interactive computer game that involves several players. MOOs are written in a more dynamic programming language than the one used for MUDs.

MPEG   Short for *Moving Pictures Expert Group*, a video-compression and movie presentation standard used for most video clips stored on the Web. The only thing that matters is that if you encounter a file that ends in .MPG, you need an MPG or MPEG player to watch it.

MUD   Short for *Multi-User Dimensions* (or *Dungeons* or *Dialogues*), hip interactive computer games that usually involve several players. The term was derived from the game Dungeons and Dragons.

Navigator   A navigational program for the World Wide Web. Navigator transforms Web documents (which consist of boring codes) into exciting multimedia documents, complete with sounds, pictures, and movies.

newbie   Derogatory term for a new user on the Internet. Newbies are often the target of obnoxious Internet junkies who are bitter because their little secret is not so little nor so secret as it once was.

newsgroup   An Internet bulletin board for users who share common interests. There are thousands of newsgroups ranging from body arts to pets (to body art with pets). Newsgroups let you post messages and read messages from other users.

pane   A portion of a window. Netscape Mail uses panes to divide its window into logical areas.

physical codes   In a Web document, codes that provide specific directions on how to display text. For example, <bold> stands for bold. *Logical codes* give less precise instructions. For example, <em> means emphasis, which might mean bold or italic.

plan   A file that a user might attach to her finger file that includes more information. A plan might include the person's address, phone number, job interests, and anything else that person wants to make publicly accessible.

plug-in   A program that becomes a part of Navigator and increases its capabilites. Compare it to a helper application, which is an independent program that works with Navigator. You can get plug-ins for displaying graphics, playing audio and video clips, and for exploring virtual worlds.

port   A sweet, robust wine that has a rich taste and aroma. Also, the hardware connection through which a computer sends and/or receives data. And one more thing; a port can be an application that's set up on a server. When you specify the server's port, you're actually telling it to run one of its applications.

post   To tack up a message in a bulletin board or newsgroup for all to see.

postmaster   The person at a given site who is in charge of assigning users their e-mail addresses. You can usually send a message to the postmaster by addressing it to *postmaster@sitename*.

PPP   Short for *Point-to-Point Protocol*, which probably means as little to me as it does to you. What's important is that when you choose an Internet service provider, you get the right connection: SLIP or PPP; otherwise, you won't be able to use Navigator.

protocol   A set of rules that governs the transfer of data between two computers.

proxy   A special connection that allows two incompatible networks to communicate. For example, say you're on the Web with Navigator and you decide to use WAIS to search for a list of articles. You can't use WAIS directly from Navigator, so you have to work through a Web/WAIS proxy. The proxy acts as a middleman, ensuring that the data transfer goes smoothly.

relative reference   In a Web document, a link that refers to the location of another page or file in relation to the address of the current page. For example, if the page is in the /PUB directory, and a linked page is in /PUB/HOME, a relative reference might specify /HOME. An absolute reference would have to give the complete path: /PUB/HOME.

score   In WAIS searches, a number that indicates the relative likelihood that an article will contain the information you need. The topmost article gets a score of 1000. Subsequent scores are relative to 1000, so 500 would mean that the article had half as many occurrences of the search term than the top article.

server   In the politically incorrect world of the Internet, the computer that serves up all the data. The other computer, the client, acts as a customer, demanding specific information.

service provider   The company that you pay in order to connect to their computer and get on the Internet.

shareware   Computer programs you can use for free and then pay for if you decide to continue using them. Many programmers use the Internet to distribute their programs, relying on the honesty and goodwill of Internet users for their income. That's why most of these programmers have day jobs.

Shockwave   A multimedia player that can play Macromedia Director, Freehand, and Authorware files. These files are cool, interactive, multimedia presentations, tutorials, or games.

SLIP   Short for *Serial Line Internet Protocol*, a type of Internet connection that allows you to connect directly to the Internet without having to run programs off your Internet service provider's computer.

spam   To post the same announcement to multiple newsgroups, usually for the purpose of advertising a product or service. Think of it as newsgroup junk mail. Spamming is considered bad form in most newsgroups.

SSL   Short for *Secure Sockets Layer*, this is Netscape's new security technology. Web pages protected with SSL prevent misanthropic hackers from nabbing personal information that you might enter on the page (including your credit card number).

status bar   The area at the bottom of the Navigator window that shows you what's going on as you work. The little key in the status bar indicates whether a document is or is not secure; if the key looks broken, the document is not secure.

stop word   In a search, any word that is excluded from the search. For example, if you are searching a computer database, the database may refuse to look for common words, such as "and" and "computer."

tags   HTML codes that work behind the scenes to tell Navigator how to display a document and how to open other linked documents. Tags can control the look of text (as in titles and headings), insert anchors that link this document to other documents, and control character formatting (by making it bold or italic).

TCP/IP   Acronym for *Transmission Control Protocol/Internet Protocol*, the preferred method of data transfer over the Internet. With TCP/IP, the sending computer stuffs data into packets and sends it. The receiving computer unstuffs the packets and assembles them into some meaningful and useful form. The most famous TCP/IP program is Winsock.

telnet   The process of connecting to a server and using it to run programs, just as if you were sitting at its keyboard (or sitting at the keyboard of a terminal that's connected to the server). Think of it as using the computerized card catalog at the local library.

terminal connection   The type of connection you don't want to have if you're using Navigator. A terminal connection makes your computer act like one of your service provider's workstations. You run programs on the service provider's computer, and connect to the Internet indirectly through that computer. With a SLIP or PPP connection, you connect through the service provider's computer, but you use software on your computer to do all your work.

terminal emulation   A technique used to make one computer act like another so the two computers can carry on a conversation. Some mainframe computers will interact with only a specific type of terminal. If you want to connect to that mainframe computer using your personal computer, you must make your computer act like the required terminal.

thread   In newsgroups and e-mail, a way of grouping messages, so that you can quickly tell that they belong to the same topic of conversation.

UNIX shell   The equivalent of a DOS prompt for computers that are running the UNIX operating system. You type commands at the prompt, just as if you were using a PC.

upload   To copy a file from your computer to another computer. You usually upload files to share them with other users.

URL   Short for *Uniform Resource Locator* (or *Unreliable Resource Location*, depending on the URL), an address for an Internet site. The Web uses URLs to specify the addresses of the various servers on the Internet and the documents on each server. For example, the URL for the White House server is **http://www.whitehouse.gov**. The **http** stands for HyperText Transfer Protocol, which means this is a Web document. **www** stands for World Wide Web.

whitehouse stands for White House. And **gov** stands for Government.

USENET   Short for *user's network*, USENET sets the standards by which the various newsgroups swap information. See also *newsgroup*.

Veronica   One of many Internet search tools, this one finds Gopher sites that have what you're looking for. For a comparison of popular search tools, see *Jughead*.

viewer   A program that Navigator uses to play movie clips, sound clips, PostScript files, graphics, and any other file Navigator itself cannot handle. See also *helper application*.

virtual memory   Disk storage that is treated as RAM. Why am I including it in this glossary? Because Navigator uses so much memory that you'll need some virtual memory just to use it.

VRML   Pronounced "vermal," VRML stands for Virtual Modeling Language, a programming language used to place interactive, three-dimensional worlds on the Web. With a VRML player, such as Netscape's Live3D, you can explore these worlds.

W3   Another name for the World Wide Web.

WAIS   Pronounced "ways," short for Wide Area Information Server, a system that allows you to search various databases on the Internet for specific articles and other resources.

Web browser   Any of several programs you can use to navigate the World Wide Web. The Web browser controls the look of the Web documents and provides additional tools for jumping from one Web document to another. Navigator is a Web browser.

Web page   A specially coded file that acts as an electronic page on the World Wide Web. Most Web pages contain links that connect the page to other Web pages. They also commonly contain pictures, sounds, video clips, and other multimedia files that you can play.

Web robot   A search tool that regularly searches the Internet for Web sites and indexes the Web documents it finds. The robot then allows you to search its indexes for Web sites that contain the resources you need.

Webmaster   The person who created and maintains a Web document. If you find an error in a Web document, you should notify the Webmaster (in a nice way).

Web server   A specialized computer on the Internet devoted to storing and serving up Web documents.

Whois   Just another UNIX command that you can use to find out a person's e-mail address, mailing address, phone number, or other information, if you know the person's last name and the location of the server that person logs in to.

World Wide Web   A collection of interconnected documents stored on computers all over the world. These documents can contain text, pictures, movie clips, sounds, and links to other documents. You move from one document to another by clicking links.

zine   A noncommercial magazine that leans toward the bizarre, twisted, or edgy side. Zines started on paper but soon moved to the Internet in the form of e-zines. See also *e-zine*.

zip   The process of compressing a file so that it takes up less space and transfers more quickly. If you have a zipped file, you must unzip it before you can use it.

Index

319

Check out Que® Books
on the World Wide Web
http://www.mcp.com/que

As the biggest software release in computer history, Windows 95 continues to redefine the computer industry. Click here for the latest info on our Windows 95 books

Make computing quick and easy with these products designed exclusively for new and casual users

Examine the latest releases in word processing, spreadsheets, operating systems, and suites

The Internet, The World Wide Web, CompuServe®, America Online®, Prodigy® —it's a world of ever-changing information. Don't get left behind!

Find out about new additions to our site, new bestsellers and hot topics

In-depth information on high-end topics: find the best reference books for databases, programming, networking, and client/server technologies

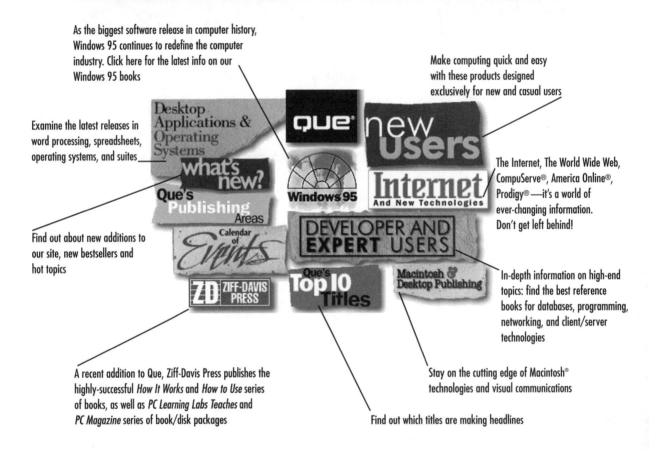

A recent addition to Que, Ziff-Davis Press publishes the highly-successful *How It Works* and *How to Use* series of books, as well as *PC Learning Labs Teaches* and *PC Magazine* series of book/disk packages

Stay on the cutting edge of Macintosh® technologies and visual communications

Find out which titles are making headlines

With 6 separate publishing groups, Que develops products for many specific market segments and areas of computer technology. Explore our Web Site and you'll find information on best-selling titles, newly published titles, upcoming products, authors, and much more.

- Stay informed on the latest industry trends and products available
- Visit our online bookstore for the latest information and editions
- Download software from Que's library of the best shareware and freeware

Complete and Return this Card
for a *FREE* Computer Book Catalog

Thank you for purchasing this book! You have purchased a superior computer book written expressly for your needs. To continue to provide the kind of up-to-date, pertinent coverage you've come to expect from us, we need to hear from you. Please take a minute to complete and return this self-addressed, postage-paid form. In return, we'll send you a free catalog of all our computer books on topics ranging from word processing to programming and the internet.

Mr. ☐   Mrs. ☐   Ms. ☐   Dr. ☐

Name (first) [ ][ ][ ][ ][ ][ ][ ][ ][ ]   (M.I.) [ ]   (last) [ ][ ][ ][ ][ ][ ][ ][ ][ ][ ][ ][ ]

Address [ ]

[ ]

City [ ][ ][ ][ ][ ][ ][ ][ ][ ][ ][ ]   State [ ][ ]   Zip [ ][ ][ ][ ][ ] [ ][ ][ ][ ]

Phone [ ][ ][ ] [ ][ ][ ] [ ][ ][ ][ ]   Fax [ ][ ][ ] [ ][ ][ ] [ ][ ][ ][ ]

Company Name [ ]

E-mail address [ ]

1. Please check at least (3) influencing factors for purchasing this book.

Front or back cover information on book .... ☐
Special approach to the content .... ☐
Completeness of content .... ☐
Author's reputation .... ☐
Publisher's reputation .... ☐
Book cover design or layout .... ☐
Index or table of contents of book .... ☐
Price of book .... ☐
Special effects, graphics, illustrations .... ☐
Other (Please specify): _____ ☐

2. How did you first learn about this book?

Saw in Macmillan Computer Publishing catalog .... ☐
Recommended by store personnel .... ☐
Saw the book on bookshelf at store .... ☐
Recommended by a friend .... ☐
Received advertisement in the mail .... ☐
Saw an advertisement in: _____ ☐
Read book review in: _____ ☐
Other (Please specify): _____ ☐

3. How many computer books have you purchased in the last six months?

This book only .... ☐   3 to 5 books .... ☐
2 books .... ☐   More than 5 .... ☐

4. Where did you purchase this book?

Bookstore .... ☐
Computer Store .... ☐
Consumer Electronics Store .... ☐
Department Store .... ☐
Office Club .... ☐
Warehouse Club .... ☐
Mail Order .... ☐
Direct from Publisher .... ☐
Internet site .... ☐
Other (Please specify): _____ ☐

5. How long have you been using a computer?

☐ Less than 6 months   ☐ 6 months to a year
☐ 1 to 3 years   ☐ More than 3 years

6. What is your level of experience with personal computers and with the subject of this book?

	With PCs	With subject of book
New	☐	☐
Casual	☐	☐
Accomplished	☐	☐
Expert	☐	☐

Source Code ISBN: 0-7897-0958-9

7. Which of the following best describes your job title?

Administrative Assistant .... ☐
Coordinator .... ☐
Manager/Supervisor .... ☐
Director .... ☐
Vice President .... ☐
President/CEO/COO .... ☐
Lawyer/Doctor/Medical Professional ...... ☐
Teacher/Educator/Trainer .... ☐
Engineer/Technician .... ☐
Consultant .... ☐
Not employed/Student/Retired .... ☐
Other (Please specify): _____ ☐

8. Which of the following best describes the area of the company your job title falls under?

Accounting .... ☐
Engineering .... ☐
Manufacturing .... ☐
Operations .... ☐
Marketing .... ☐
Sales .... ☐
Other (Please specify): _____ ☐

9. What is your age?

Under 20 .... ☐
21-29 .... ☐
30-39 .... ☐
40-49 .... ☐
50-59 .... ☐
60-over .... ☐

10. Are you:

Male .... ☐
Female .... ☐

11. Which computer publications do you read regularly? (Please list)

_____
_____
_____
_____
_____
_____
_____
_____
_____
_____

Comments: _____
_____

Fold here and scotch-tape to mail.

FIRST-CLASS MAIL PERMIT NO. 9918 INDIANAPOLIS IN

POSTAGE WILL BE PAID BY THE ADDRESSEE

ATTN MARKETING
MACMILLAN COMPUTER PUBLISHING
MACMILLAN PUBLISHING USA
201 W 103RD ST
INDIANAPOLIS IN 46290-9042

NO POSTAGE
NECESSARY
IF MAILED
IN THE
UNITED STATES